UNDER COVER OF DARKNESS

UNDER COVER OF DARKNESS

MURDERS IN BLACKOUT LONDON

AMY HELEN BELL

YALE UNIVERSITY PRESS
NEW HAVEN AND LONDON

For information about this and other Yale University Press publications, please contact:
U.S. Office: sales.press@yale.edu   yalebooks.com
Europe Office: sales@yaleup.co.uk   yalebooks.co.uk

Set in Adobe Garamond Pro by IDSUK (DataConnection) Ltd
Printed in Great Britain by TJ Books, Padstow, Cornwall

Library of Congress Control Number: 2024941357

ISBN 978-0-300-27005-1

A catalogue record for this book is available from the British Library.

10 9 8 7 6 5 4 3 2 1

To Steve Bland, a lighthouse on dark seas

CONTENTS

ILLUSTRATIONS

ACKNOWLEDGEMENTS

Sincere thanks to my editor Joanna Godfrey for her steadfast guidance and support, and to Katie Urquhart, Rachael Lonsdale and the publishing team at Yale University Press for their thoroughness and attention to detail.

I am endlessly grateful to the librarians and archivists who helped with the research, in particular the hardworking and helpful staff at The National Archives, Kew and the Imperial War Museum, Lambeth. Thanks also to the many authors and historians whose works have enriched this book.

Thanks to my wonderful colleagues at Huron University College for their encouragement and kindness during the writing process. Thanks also to my family, especially my children, Annabel and George Heath and Evie and Abby Bland. I'm grateful to my friend Erin Lemon for her generous comments on early drafts, and to Steve Fielding for letting me use his crime scene photographs. Thanks especially to those who shared their stories with me, including David Lewin, Ari Delevie and especially Roger Prevot, who told me about his mother's family and showed me photographs of little Marion Allalemdjian.

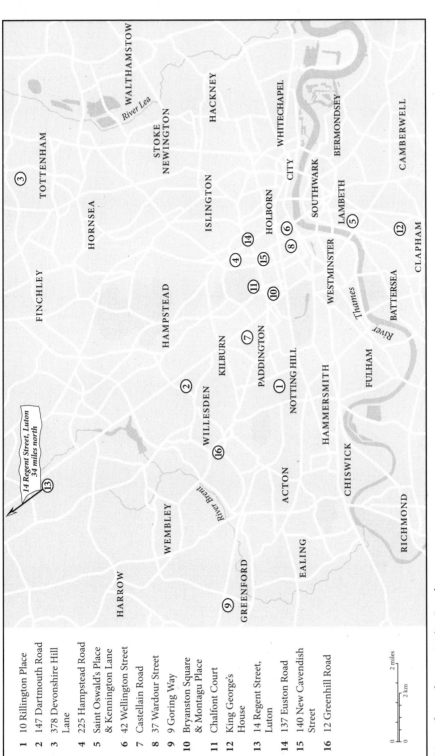

1 10 Rillington Place
2 147 Dartmouth Road
3 378 Devonshire Hill
Lane
4 225 Hampstead Road
5 Saint Oswald's Place
& Kennington Lane
6 42 Wellington Street
7 Castellain Road
8 37 Wardour Street
9 Goring Way
10 Bryanston Square
& Montagu Place
11 Chalfont Court
12 King George's
House
13 14 Regent Street,
Luton
14 137 Euston Road
15 140 New Cavendish
Street
16 12 Greenhill Road

14 Regent Street, Luton
34 miles north

Map of murders in 1940s London.

INTRODUCTION

One of the iconic images of blitzed London is of a house with a wall torn off on one side, opening up the rooms inside. Photographs sit on mantels, towels dry on washing lines, chairs and tables teeter on floors which lean out into open space, exposing the private lives disrupted by the calamities of war. What was hidden is suddenly open to public view, and passers-by must have craned their necks to see inside and imagine what the family was like and what happened to them after their world literally came tumbling down.

Murder is like that too. A violent attack destroys one life and exposes the lives around it. Once the crime is discovered, everyone wants to know the details. The scene of destruction is preserved for the police, who capture it forever on camera. Newspapers and other media report on the investigation and the trial to an eager audience, encouraging them to speculate about the people involved. Murder, like a bomb, blows open the closed rooms of private homes and personal relationships and exposes their bric-a-brac to the air. Murder reveals what we try to hide and displays all our complex human emotions and vulnerability.

This book is an exploration of murder in London during the Second World War. The bombing raids and effects of total war blew the city apart, with consequences that lasted for decades. The war created a new

1. *Bomb damage in South London, 1940.*

character of murder, one that was desperate and brutal, and often random. The social dislocation and the emotional toll of war increased deadly violence in the family and among strangers, while the bomb-scarred landscape helped to hide the victims.

In the early years of war, most murders were committed in a domestic setting by people who knew each other. The bombing raids and fears of invasion led to a rash of murder-suicides and 'mercy' killings within families, as well as unscrupulous spouses seeking to get rid of their part-ners. In the second half of the war, with the end of the Blitz and an influx of American soldiers, violence moved into the streets. Killings were more random and opportunistic, with casual encounters fuelled by drink, lust, race-hatred or desperation leading to deadly fights and robberies. Two serial killers stalked wartime London: Royal Air Force (RAF) aircraftsman Gordon Cummins and John 'Reg' Christie both took advantage of the unsettled atmosphere to kill vulnerable women.

In his history of the English and violence, Clive Emsley asked, 'Murder is rarely as public as . . . suicide [by jumping in front of a train], so what makes a private, generally personal act symptomatic of a national malaise?'[1] This book will try to answer that question. Murder is a private, and a sporadic, act, and the changes in one city over six or even twenty years are not statistically significant. But murder has a deeper meaning. In the case of Second World War London, murders show the fault lines of vulnerability in British civilian society and how war exposed people to violence from enemy attack and from those around them.

During the war, Britain projected an image of a resolved and resil-ient 'home front', in which a common purpose to defeat the enemy broke down class and cultural barriers and created a new sense of social solidarity.[2] But maintaining the discipline required for total war for six years was incredibly difficult. In recent years, historians have explored some of the cracks in this wartime unity: panic, defeatism, xenophobia, strikes, looting, black marketeering and crime, especially violent crime.[3]

One of the most important aspects of showing good civilian morale for Britons at home was controlling their negative feelings of fear, anxiety, grief or anger. Historian Lucy Noakes argues that Britain's wartime 'emotional economy' emphasised stoicism and restraint as the key to ultimate victory. When people's emotional self-control slipped, they were letting down the war effort. She also points to a difference between wartime deaths: civilian sacrifices had a political value to the war effort, but other types of death did not. We can see, then, how wartime murders were deeply troubling, both as evidence of poor self-control and as a waste of civilian lives, calling into question the popular commitment to the war effort.[4] Government posters may have told civilians to keep a stiff upper lip – 'Your Courage, Your Cheerfulness, Your Resolution Will Bring Us Victory' – but the cases in this book reveal dramatic examples of people who could not.

We can sense the profound anxiety which surrounded wartime murders in the discussions of trials and inquests. For example, American journalist Quentin Reynolds was a well-known foreign correspondent writing for *Collier's Weekly* between September and December 1940. In *A London Diary* (1941), he describes the trial of Florence Ransom, on trial for murder at the Old Bailey Court:

November 13th, 1940. I went to the Old Bailey today to see Mrs. Florence Ouida Ransom sentenced to death for the killing of her lover's wife. Her trial . . . was one of the most sensational in recent years. That is, in ordinary times it would have been sensational. But today the courtroom was empty.

It was a colourful scene of pageantry. There was an air raid on at the time. The judge and the court attendants ignored it although the court has a huge glass roof. The judge in his wig and red robes was the central figure in this drama. The lawyers sat stiffly in their wigs, their black robes and their white starched collars. All of the props for drama were there and yet the whole performance was a flop. There weren't more than a dozen spectators in court . . . Even the defendant herself looked bored. The sentence was passed; she was led away.

I walked out into the streets. The guns were roaring. We hadn't had a good daylight raid in some time, but judging from the noise this was a fairly big one. I felt a strong sense of anti-climax leaving that courtroom. The whole procedure had seemed trivial and unimportant. I bought an *Evening Standard* from a boy. I looked at page one. A line caught my eye, 'Blitz casualties to date: 16,000'. That was it, of course. Sixteen thousand decent neighbours of mine have been killed since September 7th. Naturally it was hard to feel any sympathy or feel that it was important that a half-balanced degenerate woman had just been sentenced to die. The dignity which surrounded her sentencing seemed ridiculous. My only reaction was: 'What of It?'[5]

Reynolds clearly felt disgusted by the judicial trappings surrounding murders and death sentences compared to the nobility of the civilian sacrifices in London. But for those involved in the criminal justice system, investigating and punishing crimes was even more important in wartime. Britons were fighting for their national traditions and values, including the commitment to upholding the rule of law. The thick police files of wartime murders are testimonies to the dedication of an under-strength police force. Even crimes that seemed impossible to solve were investigated as thoroughly as possible. As we'll see in Chapter 2, the young and vivacious meter-clerk Maple Church was found strangled in a derelict bombed-out house in Hampstead in 1941, with the contents of her handbag strewn around. There were no clues or witnesses. London Coroner Bentley Purchase called fourteen witnesses to her inquest, and Chief Inspector William Parker took over two hundred witness statements. According to Purchase's biographer, Robert Jackson, 'The police hunt for the murderers of Maple Church . . . was conducted as vigorously and skillfully as it would have been in peacetime, but in absence of clues and motive all inquiries came to nothing.'[6] Yet the thoroughness of the investigation itself showed the importance of justice to a beleaguered London.

A HISTORY OF MURDER

You picked up this book because you find crimes and murder interesting, just as Londoners have for hundreds of years. Since the seventeenth century, London's publishing industry has entertained the public with descriptions of sensational murders and murder trials. London's poorest citizens could buy ballads or broadsheets for a penny or two, and for a little more, Londoners could read trial reports in *The Old Bailey Proceedings* and biographies of famous criminals in the *Ordinary of Newgate's Accounts* or *The Newgate Calendar*.

By the twentieth century, most people learned about London's murders through the newspapers. Courtroom Number One at the Old Bailey was rebuilt in 1907 with dedicated seats for the press for the first time.[7] Murder trials made dramatic stories, as murder was the only crime other than treason which was punishable by death. Trials often featured impassioned speeches by defence and prosecution counsel and celebrity expert witnesses such as forensic pathologist Bernard Spilsbury and ballistics expert Robert Churchill.[8] These colourful characters provided rich material for the new style of crime reporting in the populist *Daily Mail* and the tabloid-style *Daily Mirror*, with their front-page photographs, thick black type and bold headlines.[9]

By 1939, Londoners had several national daily newspapers to choose from, such as *The Times* and the *Daily Mirror*, and over thirty local newspapers.[10] A sensational trial would also attract huge crowds, who would mill around in the street outside the courtroom, hoping for a glimpse of an important witness or an acquitted defendant.

Between 1898 and 1939, the number of murders in England and Wales averaged between 250 and 300 a year, but only a few of those became notorious.[11] Many of these took place in London. People were especially fascinated by stories of outwardly respectable domestic situations gone horribly wrong. First there was Hawley Harvey Crippen, the mild-mannered and bespectacled homeopathic doctor accused in 1910 of poisoning his vivacious wife Cora and burying part of her body in the basement of their suburban home in Camden Town.[12] Then there was George Smith, who bigamously married and abandoned four wives before he came up with a plan to drown his victims in the bath instead. He murdered Bessie Mundy in Dorset in 1912, Alice Smith in Blackpool in 1913 and Margaret Lloyd in a Highgate lodging house in 1914, collecting their savings and life insurance money.[13]

Londoners were also transfixed by stories of glamorous women who killed: Madame Fahmy, who shot her Egyptian playboy husband Ali Bey Fahmy in the back as he leaned down to pet his dog in the corridor at the Savoy Hotel in 1922, Edith Thompson, hanged in 1923 for conspiring with her lover Freddy Bywaters to kill her husband in suburban Ilford, and spoiled socialite Elvira Barney, who shot and killed her lover Michael Stephen in her Knightsbridge mews home in 1932. These cases all involved those basic elements of a good murder story: illicit love, extramarital sex, greed and violence, all set against a familiar London backdrop.

WARTIME MURDERS

But wartime London was a different setting entirely: darker both literally and metaphorically. The blackout, the acres of dusty rubble and the shabbiness and monotony of strict rationing stripped most of the glamour from the West End and the comfort from the suburbs. In her private diary, nurse Mary Morris described the nightmarish landscape of London in 1941: 'We went for a walk round the West End after lunch, and it was a renewed shock for me to see London as it is now. After twenty months of war there is a smell of death and destruction everywhere – blasted windows – clocks without hands – great mounds of yellow rubble. There is a poisonous tang of damp plaster and coal gas, a reminder that eighteen thousand Londoners have died here.'[14]

At night, London was a city of unrelieved blackness, with echoing streets and terrifying nighttime air raids. The opened doors of cinemas, pubs and dance halls only briefly illuminated the darkness, with short glimpses of chatter and laughter before the doors were quickly shut. By day, London maintained a 'carry-on' spirit, with people cleaning up the broken glass and rubble, queuing for food and getting on with their daily work, but in an atmosphere of tension and strain.

It's hard now to imagine wartime London as it was then, because so few uncensored images survive. Security restrictions on photography meant that most images presented the city in its best light, and newsreels and films aimed to bolster civilian morale by focusing on London's resilience. Newspapers, letters and published accounts were also heavily censored. To recall wartime London's atmosphere, we have to turn to the written descriptions in diaries and memoirs, as I did in my first book, *London was Ours* (2009). We can also recapture a sense of wartime London in the stories and descriptions of witnesses in criminal files. These documents evoke a London under constant threat, experienced by senses heightened by fear and excitement.

What did people see when they stepped out of their doors? London was transformed from the first moments of war. It began on the surface. All outside lights were blacked out and windows covered and reinforced to protect against bomb blast. Street signs were taken down to confuse spies and potential invaders. Propaganda placards were plastered on virtually every public wall, telling Londoners to 'Back up the Fighting Forces', 'Watch your Step in the Blackout', 'Grow More Food', and so on.

After the bombs began to fall in 1940, the changes went deeper. London's very fabric was ripped apart. Whole streets disappeared, and huge bomb craters gouged every neighbourhood. Londoners were surrounded by ruined buildings, walls leaning into nothingness and mounds of rubble overgrown by weeds. Peter Thorley, a child returning from evacuation in 1943, described his Kensington neighbourhood as looking 'like the face of the moon'.[15] Year after year, as the war dragged on, the destruction spread, and the surviving streets, buildings and people got greyer and shabbier.

The smell of these years was mostly unpleasant. Homes smelt of stale cigarette smoke, old damp wool, the ghosts of boiled root vegetables and unwashed bodies. Households were encouraged to use only five inches of bathwater per week, shared among family members, but with fuel shortages, broken gas mains and broken bathtubs, even fewer baths were to be had. Inside air-raid shelters, most of which used buckets for toilets, the smells were much worse. Whenever there was a raid, the acrid scent of human fear hung in the air. Outside, the combination of coal smoke and the dank plaster and debris of bombed houses had a distinctive caustic smell, which Elizabeth Bowen described as 'singed dust'.[16]

Sensory feelings and tastes were more subjective and depended more on social class. For the majority working class, the diet under wartime rationing was more nourishing but also blander, with less savoury meat and less sugar. Even beer was watered down, and pubs often ran out. Clothing was rough, made mostly of knitted or woven wool, and wardrobes were small. For those higher up on the social scale who could pay for restaurants and better-quality clothing, rationing and shortages did not bite as hard. The wealthy could keep the luxury of softness on the skin and variety on the tongue, up to a point. By 1943, even Audrey Withers, the editor of British *Vogue*, only owned three suits and an evening dress.[17]

The sounds of wartime were the most polarised. At one end were the uplifting songs played and sung to keep people's spirits up. Everyone listened to the wireless, and its one station. The BBC filled the airwaves with classical music, swing music, light instrumental, big band, radio plays and comedy sketches, along with the more somber nightly news bulletins. They ran up-tempo 'music while you work' programs in the day, and factories organised live concerts and dances in the lunch breaks. Myra Hess's piano concerts in the empty National Gallery became famous. Music helped to temper emotions in wartime, encouraging and uplifting people and binding them together. Vera Lynn's 1939 sentimental song 'We'll Meet Again', sung in her rich, deep voice, was one of the most popular of the war. Its lyrics were sung in concerts, shelters, pubs and workplaces and brought comfort to people facing war's uncertainties.

At the other end of the spectrum was the chilling, undulating wail of the air-raid siren, warning of approaching planes. It was the most feared sound of the war, and one that people remembered for decades afterwards. Hearing it made Londoners' scalps prickle and stomachs drop as they hurried to take cover. Londoners also recognised the sound of the German dive-bomber planes, the Junkers Ju 87, by the distinctive drone of their engines. Small sirens attached to the front of the landing gear made a wailing sound, known as the 'Stuka Scream', as the planes sped towards their targets.[18] Combined with the terrifying whistle of dropping bombs, the deafening explosions of direct hits and the heavy *ack-ack* sound of anti-aircraft guns on the ground, air raids were cacophonous and terrifying. Diarist Viola Bawtree wrote on 10 November 1940: 'I've not *heard* a warning for weeks, but today I heard almost every one and each time it gave me that horrible heave inside. I don't know how to describe it, like you might get if you heard a sudden wail of someone in distress, or a shriek of pain.'[19] The tension was only relieved with the sweet, smooth tone of the all-clear siren, which signalled that another raid was over.

Like London's soundscape, the emotional life of its people during wartime was a riot of extremes. Londoners were bored and annoyed by the long hours of queuing and waiting in shelters, and terrified and anxious during raids. Typist Vivienne Hall described the stress of a 'harassing, wearying week, of rushing to work to avoid the morning raids and hurrying through work in between raids and scurrying home before the night raids'.[20] They missed their evacuated children and conscripted loved ones and often felt lonely. While older people struggled with their disturbed sleep, extra household duties, harder daily travel and worry for the family, young people reveled in their freedoms and in meeting new people. The war filled many with a sense of purpose and adventure, and London's pubs and dance halls, especially after the Americans came in 1942, were exciting and fun. People in London were living on the edge of life and death, and they knew it. Whether they rejoiced in it or feared it depended on who they were.

RUTH FUERST

Ruth Fuerst was one young woman who lived on the edge during the war. Ruth was striking; she was pretty, tall (5 feet 9 inches), had a cloud of dark hair and wore a dramatic leopard-skin coat. Drawn to the light in the blackout, she was sociable, adventurous and restless. A Jewish refugee from Austria, separated from her family, she came to London to start a new life. She drifted from one address and set of friends to another, was interned, had a baby out of wedlock, and worked as a servant, a waitress and in a factory. She had fourteen addresses in the first four years of war.

Ruth was born on 29 March 1922 in Voslau, a small spa town near Vienna. She was the daughter of a Jewish painter, Ludwig Fuerst, and

2. Ruth Margaret Christine Fuerst, undated.

his wife, Frederike, the second of three children. In March 1938, Nazi Germany annexed Austria, and Jewish property was confiscated. The Fuersts knew they were in danger. They fled to Vienna and made their plans to escape. Their best chances lay in separation. Ruth's eldest brother, Gottfried, stayed in Austria, while her parents made plans to immigrate to New York with their youngest son Gabriel, eventually landing in June 1940. Ruth, with the help of the Swedish Mission, immigrated to England in 1939.

It was very difficult for Jewish refugees to gain entry to Britain if they, like Ruth, had no money and no private contacts. Britain was still recovering from the effects of the Great Depression and did not want any immigrants who might take jobs from the British workforce.[21] The only job that would almost always allow entry into Britain was the one that nobody wanted: domestic service. Servants were in demand because the work conditions were so bad: long hours, low pay, hard physical labour and lack of freedom. But desperate Jewish women took advantage: 20,000 of the 78,000 German and Austrian refugees who came to Britain before the war came as domestic servants.[22]

Ruth arrived in England on 8 June 1939 and registered as an alien under serial number 356710.[23] She was sponsored first by Edith Willis of Golders Green, London, who described her as 'very difficult to manage and very keen on the company of men'.[24] She did not last long there; by September 1939, she was working as a servant in St Gabriel's Children's Convalescent Home in Westgate-on-Sea, Margate, Kent.[25] But the beautiful seaside setting was not enough to make the hard work palatable, and soon she moved north. She went to work for the Reverend and Mrs Le Bas in Elswick, Lancashire. They found her to be 'morose and sullen', unhappy and uninterested in domestic work. Missing her family, lonely and isolated, she moved back to the sociability of London.

After the outbreak of war in September, all enemy aliens had to appear before special tribunals, which would determine the risk they posed to national security. In December 1939, Ruth appeared before Tribunal Number 2 and pleaded her case. The committee decided she was a genuine refugee from Nazi oppression, and she was exempted from internment. Ruth was still free, for now.

All this would change five months later. The Nazis swept through Europe in May 1940 and set their sights on Britain. Anxious about a potential German invasion and the influx of 55,000 new refugees from Belgium and Holland, the new Churchill government ordered the police to 'Collar the Lot!'[26] On 16 May 1940, 2,000 German nationals in London were rounded up under Defence Regulation 18(b), and ten days later 1,500 German women were rounded up.[27] In a series of early-morning raids, police constables, aided by members of the Women's Voluntary Service, went to addresses throughout London. They woke up the women, told them they were being taken to the internment camps, and gave them just enough time to pack one suitcase and warm clothing before taking them into custody.[28] Ruth was one of these women.

The German internees were headed to the Isle of Man, home of several internment camps. The men's camps were run by the military, but Ruth most likely went to the all-women's Rushen Camp, run by the Home Office for civilian internees. Rushen was not a typical camp: instead of building dormitories, the government fenced off the entire village of Port Erin, paying householders with spare bedrooms and boarding-house owners to take in thousands of women. Villagers and internees lived together behind the barbed wire surrounding the village and coastline.

In the camp, interned women had daily chores, but still time for leisure. They had enough food, a safe place to stay and some freedom: the barbed wire included a beach. It was a beautiful summer, and some internees later remembered the time as almost a holiday, and a respite from the stresses of blitzed London. Ruth may have enjoyed the rest, but as a social person who apparently liked male company, she must have found it dull. As fears of a German invasion faded that fall, internees campaigned to go back to their homes and help the war effort.

Two days before Christmas 1940, Ruth was released from the Isle of Man and returned to London. With no family and nowhere to go, she was sent to a home for unmarried mothers in Highgate.[29] The 'House of Mercy', established in 1854, was about to close but took in female internees over the holidays. Ruth was back where she started, looking for a way to survive.

It's not clear what happened to Ruth in the next year. She found work and places to stay, survived the intense nighttime raids of the London Blitz and made new friends. She must have been doing well for herself – in December 1941 she was working at the chic Mayfair Hotel on Stratton Street. Around that time, she met Anastasio Isiedoran, a Cypriot waiter working in a nearby Soho restaurant. They had a passionate affair, and she fell pregnant. But they did not stay together. And when Ruth's belly started to show, she was fired.

Ruth was now a single, pregnant refugee, homeless and with no job. She drifted from room to room, often so quickly she did not have time to register her new address with the local police station. In April 1942, the police verbally cautioned her for not notifying them that she had changed address and occupation. In May 1942, at Marylebone Police Court, she was bound over for again failing to notify a change of address.[30] Police and magistrates must have been sympathetic to her plight, as she was not arrested or fined.

On 9 October 1942, Ruth gave birth to a daughter, Christina Sonya, at the West End Lane Home for Unmarried Mothers in Hampstead. With no family and no money, Ruth decided to give her baby up. Christina was taken to St Christopher's Residential School in Tunbridge Wells and later adopted.[31]

The next year, Ruth moved away from service and into better-paid factory work. She worked the night shift from 30 March to 29 June 1943 at John Bolding and Sons, Grosvenor Works, Britannia Street, W1 as a capstan operator. Then she left, for reasons that are unclear. One colleague thought she was leaving to get married, others thought she was pregnant. She never collected her last week of wages.[32] She was living in a four-storey rooming house at 41 Oxford Gardens, a ten-minute walk from Rillington Place.

One day, Ruth was sitting in David Griffin's Refreshment Room, a cheap café that overlooked the busy intersection of Lancaster Road and Ladbroke Grove. Surrounded by the noise of clattering dishes and conversation and the smell of grease and cigarette smoke, Ruth was drawn into conversation with the man who would ultimately murder her: John Reginald 'Reg' Christie. Christie, who would go on to become one of the most notorious serial killers of the twentieth century, was working as a War Reserve policeman and had come into the snack bar to find a man who was wanted for theft. But it was more likely he really came to chat up women. He specialised in targeting women who seemed vulnerable, offering them friendship to gain their trust and entice them back to his house at 10 Rillington Place.

In 1953, as he was awaiting execution for the murder of his wife, Christie gave his version of his relationship with Ruth, which painted him as an admirable wartime figure. In an article in the *Sunday Mirror* titled 'My First Victim', he claimed that he met Ruth on his beat and that she was fascinated by his uniform. She accompanied him on his rounds and spent time with him whenever she could. He also claimed he once lent her 10 shillings for her rent, a generous gesture if it is true.

According to Christie's recollections, Ruth had visited his house twice when his wife, Ethel, was away. On 12 August 1943, Ethel was again away visiting her family in Sheffield when Ruth turned up on his doorstep at Rillington Place. Christie invited her in – 'Having a cup of tea seems as much a part of my murder career as whiskey does with other murderers' – and they talked.[33] Christie claimed that Ruth told him she was madly in love with him and asked him to go away with her and take care of her. But Christie was not keen. Although he didn't mention it to the reporter, in 1943 Christie was also having an extra-marital affair with Gladys Jones, a married woman who lived in 196 Ladbroke Grove, and was not anxious to leave his wife.[34]

Christie had sex with Ruth in his marital bed and, during the act, strangled her with a piece of rope. Knowing his wife was due to return, Christie put Ruth's clothes back on her, wrapped her in her leopard-skin coat and hid her under the floorboards in the back room. Ethel and her brother arrived home that night, unsuspecting.[35] The next day, while his wife was out, Christie put Ruth's body in the wash house in the yard and dug a hole in the small back garden: 'Neighbours watched me digging. They said, "Cheerio!" to me.' When it got dark, he buried Ruth and her clothing in the ground: 'I grew things on her grave after that.'[36]

Would a girl as pretty, young and vivacious as Ruth really fall in love with Reg Christie, a poor, middle-aged, balding married man? Or did he, like he did with other victims, lure her to the flat with promises of free medical treatment or an abortion? Ruth's missing person report in the *Police Gazette* said: 'It is known she is in bad health,' but without any details.[37] She may have been pregnant again and unwilling to have another illegitimate child. In the blackout darkness of dead-end Rillington Place, no one saw her go into the house, and no one but her landlady, Mrs Julie Walter, missed her not coming home.

Christie's job as a War Reserve constable, which he got despite a record for theft and assault, ironically made it easier for him to murder Ruth and not get caught. His official duties included keeping traffic moving smoothly, and he tried to stop cars parking in Rillington Place to deter potential observers from congregating in the street. He also had to keep track of enemy aliens and hunt down deserters and other criminals, so he knew all the cheap lodging houses and dark corners of Kensington. The respectability of the police uniform also gave him authority and made him seem trustworthy.

Christie's murder of Ruth Fuerst was also made possible by the disruptions of war: the passage of strangers in and out of Kensington, the number of vulnerable women and the darkness of the streets. War had unravelled the social fabric of London neighbourhoods and created unprecedented anonymity in its streets. Hidden by the blackout, shielded by bombed-out houses and the threat of random death from the enemy, a new type of murder emerged in wartime London. At the darkest end were the wartime serial killers, of which Christie was only one. Gordon Cummins murdered four women in a six-day spree in 1942, and John Haigh, the 'Acid-Bath' killer, murdered Donald McSwan in 1944. Haigh told McSwan's parents he had fled to Scotland to avoid conscription. When they started to ask questions about when he would come home, Haigh murdered them too.

Ruth Fuerst, a vulnerable, uprooted woman, was murdered in 1943, during the dingiest and most depressing years of the war. She was one of two wartime victims of Christie's. In 1944, he murdered Muriel Eady, who he had met at his work at Ultra Radio, Park Royal. She was an older and more retiring woman, and Christie lured her to 10 Rillington Place by offering her treatment for catarrh. Instead, he gassed her until she became unconscious, raped and murdered her and buried her alongside Ruth Fuerst in his back garden. Muriel did have family and friends who missed her, but they thought she had been killed by a V-1 rocket and did not look for her for long. The conditions of war protected Christie again.

Ruth and Muriel lay together in the back garden of 10 Rillington Place for ten years, forgotten victims of the war. By the time of their dramatic discovery in 1953, along with four other women's bodies, few were left to remember Ruth. She was identified by the description in her missing person report and by her Central European dental work. The housekeeper of Ruth's lodging house who filed the report, Mrs Julie Walter, had died in 1950, and the police could not trace anyone who had lived in the house in 1943. Any friends and lovers she had had melted away. Ruth had disappeared into the darkness of the wartime city.

MOVING THE ACCUSED ASIDE

Ever since the discovery of Ruth's body in 1953, the story of her life has been overshadowed by that of her killer. She is not alone. The whole system of criminal justice focuses on the accused: press, police, prosecution and punishment. This silencing of victims is recognised even by people in the system. When Bertie Manton was on trial for murdering his wife Irene in 1943, the judge, Mr Justice Singleton, warned the jury that Irene could no longer speak for herself: 'It may well be a fact for you to bear in mind when you are filled with pity for a man on his trial that not much has been said about the one who is dead. You have had an account of the man of his family life. We know they parted once or twice. We only have his account of why they parted. We don't know what the woman would have said had she been alive. You may wonder if she was as black[-hearted] as he has said.'[38] The victim was silenced forever, and the accused became a larger-than-life figure in the dock, their actions and demeanour reported in minute detail by reporters and observers in the courtroom galleries.

It can be hard to discover even the bare facts of the lives of murder victims. Almost all historical sources about twentieth-century murders in London focus on the accused. Newspapers and popular literature fixated on the criminal or the trial, such as the Notable British Trials series which ran from 1905 to 1959 and the Old Bailey trial series edited by C.E. Bechhofer Roberts, along with dozens of individual histories of memorable trials. The memoirs of police detectives, trial lawyers, coroners, forensic scientists and forensic pathologists unsurprisingly concentrated on their most notorious cases and how they brought murderers and criminals to justice.[39] Historians, me included, have mirrored this perspective, focusing on the criminal investigations that start after the victim's life has already been extinguished, and in which they are reduced to bodies, vehicles for expert forensic and police investigation.

There is also a gendered aspect to focusing on the suspect, usually a man, which marginalises the experiences of women. In the 1940s, the criminal justice system was almost entirely masculine: police, detectives, pathologists, lawyers, officers of the court, judges and reporters were almost all men.[40] Women most often appeared in murder cases as victims, already silenced; they accounted for only 15 per cent of people charged with felonies.[41] Women only began to serve on criminal juries from 1919 and did so only in small numbers. We can know little about jurors: the common-law rule of jury secrecy meant that jurors could never speak about their deliberations or decisions.[42] In the 1943 Manton case, newspaper reporters noted that the jury was absent for two and a half hours, and when they returned with the guilty verdict, one of the two women jurors was in tears.[43] Were they tears of frustration, or of sympathy, and if so, for whom? As with the life of Irene Manton herself, historians have to imagine and extrapolate women's experiences in the criminal justice system from the few sources available.

My aim in this book is to offer a new perspective on wartime murders, by telling the stories of the people involved: both victims and perpetrators. This shift has been achieved, ironically, by my twenty years of crime research in the other direction, focused on the institutional systems of crime detection. It has also been made possible by newly digitised social history sources – censuses, birth, marriage and death records, immigration records and newspapers – that can help trace ordinary people's lives in a way never before possible. A more humanistic, nuanced approach to criminal history focuses on the social context of the crime, breaking away from the heroic 'blue gaze' of the detective narrative that begins with the discovery of a dead body, to refocus on a wider view.[44] By placing the stories of murders into the context of the war and into the geography of the wartime city, this book provides a more three-dimensional look at both the lives of the victims and the motivations of the perpetrators.

TRACING THE VICTIMS

Researching the people involved in acts of violence in wartime London presents some serious challenges. During the war, millions of people moved house, children were evacuated and re-evacuated, and soldiers, internees and refugees moved in and out of the city. People could die where they were not known, such as the 480 unidentified bombing victims found in London shelters or in the streets during the war.[45]

In February 1942, a thirty-five-year-old woman whose ration cards were registered to 'Peggy Richards', also known as Margaret McArthur, was thrown from the unfinished Waterloo Bridge.[46] The police file only had depositions from two people who knew her. Peter Docherty was the bar cellarman at the Hero of Waterloo public house where she sat drinking with two Canadian soldiers the night she died, who did not know her name but who said 'I could guess what she was'. Joyce Smith, a local woman, had seen 'a woman I knew as Peggy' in the neighborhood: 'I did not know her by any other name.' The appalling behavior of her alleged killer, Joseph McKinstry, who was found rummaging for change in her handbag in Waterloo Station later that night, provided copy for newspapers and trial testimony in a way that the shadowy victim did not. McKinstry was reported as telling his friends, 'Good-bye. I will see you again if they don't hang me', and later: 'I am not going to remember too much of what happened on that goddam bridge.'[47] When he was acquitted, the papers described how McKinstry smiled and bowed to the judge before he was discharged.[48] Nothing at all was written about Peggy in the press, and all that Peter Docherty and Joyce Smith could say about her was that 'she was of a very quiet disposition'.

The police records (usually closed for thirty to seventy-five years) sometimes give more background details about the victims and their circumstances than appeared in the press or at trial. The London Metropolitan Police kept a ledger of deaths by violence during the war, recording each case chronologically, with details of the date and place of the discovery of the body, the circumstances, the suspect, if any, the result of the inquest, if any, and the final verdict and the sentence.[49] The individual police-case records are much more detailed and generally include a summary of the crime and depositions from witnesses, and sometimes post-mortem reports, photographs, editorial comments by other police detectives or superintendents, and occasionally newspaper clippings or anonymous letters. They often include depositions from witnesses who didn't appear in court, descriptions of housing and family circumstances, details on clothing and possessions, and other clues to the victim's background and circumstances.

Records of coroners' inquests can also be revealing, although they survive today only in newspapers and published accounts.[50] The Coroners Amendment Act of 1926 made inquests subordinate to police inquiries, so inquests were adjourned during police inquiries. If a police investigation led to a criminal trial and conviction, that verdict was recorded by the coroner and the inquest closed. But if the police did not bring charges, the coroner could reconvene the inquest and continue his independent investigation, for example in the 1942 murder of Maple Church described in Coroner Bentley Purchase's biography.[51]

Together with newly digitised genealogical records, these sources allow historians to understand murders in a new way. My approach in this book refocuses the frame of criminal history away from the detailed examinations of people's bodies, towards the particular circumstances of their lives. Framing their stories against the backdrop of wartime London helps us understand the war, and deadly crime, from a fresh perspective.

HOW DID THE WAR CREATE A NEW CHARACTER OF MURDER?

The doubled danger of wartime London made its murders unique. The Second World War brought a new level of risk to civilians, endangered by bombs and rockets from an unseen enemy in the air. The heightened atmosphere of tension and fear brought out the worst in some people. As James Sharpe observed: 'Tucked away in all of us, [there is] a potential for aggressiveness, destructiveness, violence and cruelty, which most of us manage – for the most part – to suppress.'[52] People tend to curb their aggressions with empathy, moral principles and fear of punishment. But in a world of darkness, fear and contingency, destructive behaviours were unleashed. Londoners had to fear not only the enemy without, but the enemy within.

The murder rate shot up during the war. Up to 1939, the yearly average was around 250–300 deaths a year in England and Wales. The numbers climb from 288 in 1940 to 406 in 1942, to a seventy-five-year high of 492 in 1945.[53] The rise in national figures was echoed in London, which had 46 recorded deaths in 1939, 50 in 1940, 59 in 1943 and a high of 66 in 1945.[54] Indictments for all forms of criminal violence also rose sharply, including the near-doubling of numbers of felonious and malicious wounding from 1939 to 1945.[55]

There may have been many more murders left undiscovered. Two hundred bombing victims were never claimed or identified, along with dozens of bodies found floating in the Thames.[56] Many more people just disappeared.

The wartime ruptures that split families, friends and neighbours apart made murders easier to commit, and easier to hide. Yet at the same time, the war expanded police powers and created a new bureaucracy of ration books and identification cards, which police used to trace movements of missing persons and perpetrators. Civil Defence personnel supplemented the Metropolitan Police in observing the streets and keeping records of suspicious activities.

It has taken the distance of years for a clear picture of these murders to come into view. During the war, crime reporting had to compete with war news. The focus during the war was on survival, and many, as Quentin Reynolds had observed when looking at the empty spectator seats at the Old Bailey, were too distracted to pay attention the way they had in peacetime. Only after the war did Londoners of all classes write about their experiences of wartime crimes, including famous barrister J.D. Casswell, Sierra Leonian seaman and Commonwealth Club owner Ernest Marke, London policeman George Daley, Murder Squad detective Edward Greeno and career criminal Billy Hill.[57] In the 1990s, many of the police case files at The National Archives began opening to researchers, although records of many of the more sensitive crimes remain closed.

The passage of time allows historians a richer retrospective of wartime crime. We can trace patterns and make connections that were not visible in the moment. But distance from the past also creates new problems. Many of the more recent popular retellings of notorious crimes are anachronistic and often wrong. For instance, while the wartime serial murderer Gordon Cummins is often described as 'the Blackout Ripper', he wasn't called this until the 1990s.[58] The only wartime references to a Blackout Ripper were to someone who attacked and stabbed two women in a dark street in Smethwick, Birmingham in 1939.[59] Historians have to navigate many of the assumptions and errors that have accrued to notorious cases' true-crime retellings. The best way to do this is to go back and dive deeply into the original sources and reconstruct the atmosphere of fear, excitement, deprivation and sadness that people endured in wartime London.

CHAPTER I

LONDON AT WAR

She had great anxiety about the war. Her mind was set on an idea that we should have to suffer at the hands of the Germans like the Czechs and the Poles. She worried about what would happen to Pamela.

Stanley Wright, husband of Lily Wright and father of Pamela[1]

Neville Chamberlain's sober, defeated voice came over the wireless at 11.15 a.m. on 3 September 1939, straight into the anxious ears of millions. He told listeners that although Britain had demanded that Germany promise to withdraw their troops from Poland by 11 a.m., 'I have to tell you now that no such undertaking has been received, and that consequently this country is at war with Germany'. He paused, and then in a quieter, somewhat petulant tone went on, 'You can imagine what a bitter blow it is to me that all my long struggle to win peace has failed.'

Britons could imagine. It had only been twenty years since the heart-breaking losses of the last war. Most people met the announcement of war with a sense of dread and disappointment, with none of the wild elation of 1914.[2] But at least there had been warnings; since the Munich crisis, civil defence preparations had been ramped up, including the mass distribution of gas masks for adults, children and babies in September 1938. With the advances in airplane and bombing technology demonstrated by the German Luftwaffe in the assault on Guernica in 1937, and the attacks on Poland on 1 September, civilians knew this would be a different kind of war, and one that put them immediately in the front line.

Within minutes of Chamberlain's announcement, the shrill wail of the air-raid warning sounded throughout London. Believing an apocalyptic bombing offensive was about to begin, people gathered their children and rushed to the shelters. Although it was a false alarm caused by an allied aircraft and the all clear sounded within minutes, people remained frightened, listening for the siren to go again at any moment. Londoners were especially afraid, believing that their city, as the seat of government, empire, finance and shipping, was particularly vulnerable. Local authorities had planned for enormous death tolls, with casualties predicted to be as high as 30,000 to 35,000 a day. The London County Council assumed there would not be enough timber to provide coffins and discussed mass dumping of the dead in lime pits or even in the English Channel.[3]

None of this happened. No attacks would come in the first year of war, during what became known as the Phoney War. But one of the effects of the unbearable tension of waiting for aerial bombers, along with the first family separations of war, was a wave of wartime murders in London. Unlike the later violent meetings of strangers fighting over sex, money and racial tensions, murders in the first year of war were often characterised by unbearable anxiety and fear: of family separation, loss of home, German invasion, injury, bereavement, death. Wartime fear was an immediate instinctive response to danger, such as that triggered by the air-raid siren, but also a longer emotional state of profound anxiety.

It's difficult to look back now and understand how frightened Londoners were, because it was against the law to say so. Spreading 'despondency' could be prosecuted under the Emergency Powers Act, and hundreds of people were charged with uttering defeatist talk.[4] 'Carrying on' was considered vital to the war effort and an important aspect of British national identity, as in Churchill's famous 'Finest Hour' speech on 18 June 1940: 'I do not at all underrate the severity of the ordeal which lies before us; but I believe our countrymen will show themselves capable of standing up to it . . . and will be able to stand up to it, and carry on in spite of it . . . every man and every woman will have the chance to show the finest qualities of their race, and render the highest service to their cause.'[5]

The wartime public regime of stoicism added to the psychological tensions of war as civilians sought to minimise or repress their fears.[6] As psychoanalyst Edward Glover stated in a 1940 BBC radio broadcast, a big part of civilian fear was worrying about maintaining their self-control:

The whole atmosphere of modern war is likely to revive those unreasoning fears that the human race has inherited from its remotest ancestors; gas masks that make us look like strange animals; underground shelters; . . . enemies overhead and unseen; wailing sirens; screaming air bombs . . . Small wonder, then, that we are afraid lest in the face of a real danger our first impulse should be to behave like little children . . . We are afraid of being afraid.[7]

With no socially acceptable outlet for their feelings, adults could only confide in their diaries or talk about their physical symptoms of fear and anxiety, such as stomach aches, skin problems or losing their hair in clumps. As diarist Vivienne Hall wrote, 'True, when you are with other people, you keep a grip on your nerves, and carry on at least with a pleasant face. But when you are alone, you are full of fear. You want to cry, but you dare not least [sic] someone should catch you.'[8]

Psychologists and government planners were pessimistic about the ability of civilians to withstand the experiences of bombing and expected a wave of shell-shock cases as seen with First World War soldiers on the

Western Front. In the first year of war, emergency medical stations were set up to deal with the expected civilian panic, and special wards were established in several London hospitals to take in civilian psychological casualties.

LONDON IN 1939

London in September 1939 was a tense and fearful place, literally plunged into an inky darkness. From 1 September, all doors and windows had to be covered with dark material and all streetlights and external lights extinguished or dimmed. Car and bus headlamps had to be fitted with slotted covers that directed their beams to the ground. The goal was to make the city invisible to nighttime bombers, but the effect was disorienting and dangerous. One volunteer diary writer for the social research project Mass Observation described the impression of the blackout as:

> psychological rather than physical. How weird! How rather exciting! How like the unseen forms of indigestion dreams! This groping through familiar streets now unfamiliar, all around you shadows which might turn out to be people or pillar boxes, while sudden shapes of cars crawl up to you with eyes no more than cats. This contradiction in our civilisation, the unlit city, continues to bewilder for the first thirty seconds every time you go out of doors at night. On dark nights it is really a matter of groping one's way, with nerves as well as hands held out into the future of the next second.[9]

Unsurprisingly, road deaths in London increased from 554 in September 1938 to 1,130 in September 1939, mostly of pedestrians.[10] To frustrate potential enemy invaders, street signs were also taken down, and maps and cameras were forbidden in the capital. Air-raid shelters were quickly improvised: trenches were dug in parks and signs were painted in luminescent white letters pointing towards public shelters in basements and church crypts. Propaganda posters blanketed exterior walls and were also posted inside banks, post offices, trains and Tube stations, reminding Londoners about the new wartime rules to be followed and their burden of civic duties.[11]

On 1 September 1939, as German forces began to move into Poland, all the trains leaving London were taken over for the evacuation of London schoolchildren into safer areas. The state-sponsored scheme, run by the London County Council, evacuated 390,000 unaccompanied schoolchildren and their teachers, 250,000 mothers and young children, 5,500 pregnant women and 2,400 disabled people, around one fifth of London's population.[12] Many thousands of children were evacuated privately, to relatives in the country or to Canada and America. In England as a whole, over 3 million people evacuated in the first months of war. In order to keep track of its moving population, the government instituted a National Register of civilians in England and Wales, taken on 29 September 1939. The information was used to produce identity cards, to administer military conscription and direct labour and to issue ration books. The names, addresses, ages and occupations of over 40 million people in England and Wales were recorded.[13]

Because of concerns for keeping up morale, civilian fear was rarely publicly represented in wartime, which has made it harder for historians to trace. But there is one place that we can find stories of the war's effects on families and vulnerable people: criminal trials and coroners' inquests on suicides and family murders. Many of these cases occurred because people were afraid for themselves and their children in case of bombing and Nazi invasion or could not face wartime separations. The murder-suicide of five-year-old Marion Allalemdjian and her nurse Claudina Valeriani in 1939 and the murder of nine-year-old Pamela Wright by her mother Lily Wright in early 1940 show the desperation that people could be brought to by their wartime fears, in killing the person that they loved the most.

MARION ALLALEMDJIAN

Two people that appeared in the Wartime Register were five-year-old Marion Allalemdjian and her fifty-year-old nurse Claudina Valeriani. They lived alone in a comfortable Victorian semi-detached house at 147 Dartmouth Road in Willesden.[14] Within three months, they would both be dead.

Marion was part of a well-travelled and cosmopolitan family. Her father, Kevork, was an Armenian fur merchant, like his father Mihran. Their family had migrated from Armenia to Turkey, then to Germany at the turn of the century. After the First World War, the family dispersed again, one brother moving to New York to set up a fur business, while another cousin started an offshoot in Australia. Kevork moved his father's Leipzig fur company to London in the 1920s, where it traded at 21 Garlick Hill, Cannon Street, until the 1980s. Kevork and his German wife, Ilse, had their four children in London: daughter Elbis in 1922, daughter Araxi in 1924, son Mihran in 1928 and baby Marion in 1934. By 1939, the family had scattered again, leaving only Marion in Claudina's care. Marion's grandfather Mihran lived nearby, in a large red brick home at 26 Lyndhurst Road in Hampstead, with his second wife, Sidonie.[15]

Claudina had been Marion's nurse for about three years. The Allalemdjian family subscribed to the continental and middle-class approach to parenting, in which the children were raised by a nurse and sent away to school at seven. Marion's emotional upbringing was particularly bleak. Her mother, Ilse, had struggled with her mental health for years. Sent to France for treatments, she committed suicide in 1938. Marion's older siblings had all gone to boarding schools, the sisters to a strict Catholic one, and she would have seen them only during school holidays.[16]

In August of 1939, Kevork decided to take the children on a family holiday to a Swiss resort with their family friends the Pozers. Marion, considered too young to sit up properly at the table, was left behind with Claudina. When Germany invaded Poland on 1 September, the family was stuck in Switzerland, unable to get back to England. Kevork decided to send the children to Swiss schools while he tried to get them out of Europe.

Marion's nurse, Claudina, was depressed. The past few years with Marion had been some of the happiest she had ever known. She had never married and had no children, and her family life had been mostly miserable. The exigencies of the war would push this already fragile person to breaking point.

Like Marion, Claudina's grandfather was an immigrant. Epaminondas Valeriani, who had an Italian background, had immigrated to England in the 1860s and set up shop as a foreign provisions importer at 24 Cranbourn Street, near Leicester Square. He had a close brush with the law in 1874, when a man who worked for him was accused at the Central Criminal Court at the Old Bailey of counterfeiting Moët & Chandon champagne by affixing false labels.[17] Despite this negative publicity, his business prospered.

His eldest son, Leone Valeriani, aged only fourteen, ran away and joined the navy.[18] He served for ten years on twenty-two ships in various naval engagements. After returning to London, he managed several hotels, including the Empire Music Hall in Leicester Square, now the Empire Cinema.[19] Leone married Emita Mary, with whom he had Claudina on 14 November 1889. But in March 1892, just as his son Basil Norman was born, Leone abandoned his family. He set sail for South Africa, where he joined the Matabeleland Mounted Police in Johannesburg. During the infamous Jameson Raid in 1896, 'Valley' was captured by Boers. During the night, he stole one of their horses and slipped away from the camp, only to find his own escaped horse following him. He jumped into the fresh saddle and made it to Johannesburg and safety. This story, reported in the London newspapers, prompted the *Daily Graphic* to commission and print a portrait of 'Dr Jim's Despatch Rider'. Wounded and tiring of combat, Leone was prompted by his father's death to return to England.[20] He was also thinking about his inheritance – his father had left an estate worth over £16,000.[21]

Leone reunited with his wife in England, but not his children. In the 31 March 1901 census, Basil and Claudina are listed as 'boarders' with George and Elizabeth Lillywhite and their twenty-three-year-old daughter in a small, six-roomed house at 24 Hoe Street, Walthamstow. Leone Valeriani and his wife settled in Bexhill, where they had four more children. There Leone ran two tobacco and cigar shops, and later the West Parade Shelter Hall rooms, as well as a series of illuminated fetes in the park.[22] All of these commercial ventures failed spectacularly.

With no share of her father's wealth, Claudina lived in meager circumstances. In 1909, when she was nineteen, she stole a pair of boots from a shop in Walthamstow. George Lillywhite, described in the newspaper report as 'an elderly man who had looked after the prisoner', pleaded to the magistrate for leniency for Claudina, 'as she had had an unhappy life'. As a result of his intervention, she was put on probation, instead of being sent to prison, and saved from the lifetime shame of incarceration.[23] In 1914, George died, and Claudina's brother, Basil, enlisted as a rifleman with 8th Battalion of the Rifle Brigade. He was killed in 1915 and buried in Belgium.

Meanwhile, things were looking up for Claudina, who had missed the high points of her father's extravagant life in Bexhill, but escaped the low points of his subsequent bankruptcy and disgrace. At the time of her arrest in 1909, she was 'described as a nurse'. She was never formally registered with the General Nursing Council (set up in 1919), and there are no employment records of her in any hospital, so she likely worked as a private children's nurse, a combination of companion, nurse and nanny. She was lucky to have escaped a prison sentence for theft; a record would have made her unemployable in a profession that depended so much on good 'character'.[24]

Claudina surfaces in the historical record again in 1926, crossing the Atlantic on the Cunard Line luxury ocean liner *Aquitania*. In 1927 she made the voyage again, on the White Star Line's luxury flagship, the

Majestic, as the nurse for a three-year-old American girl, Mara Lucy Elizabeth Di Zoppola.[25] The opulent surroundings and delicious food on the luxury liners were a long way from Claudina's Walthamstow upbringing. The Allalemdjians were also well-off, and Claudina must have been considered a good nurse to have kept her position for three years. She and Marion shared a comfortable home and must have been happy together, left mostly to themselves.

But once war was declared, all that was about to end. Kevork Allalemdjian, who had lost his wife only the year before, was determined to get his children out of harm's way. Stuck in Switzerland, he decided not to try to get back to England but to take the children directly to join his half-brother Souren in New York. He applied for passports for all the children, and Claudina feared what was to come.

At the inquest, Kilburn coroner Reginald Kemp asked Marion's grandfather Mihran Allalemdjian about their relationship.

Q: 'She was very fond of the child, was she?'
A: 'Yes.'
Q: 'She thought the child was going to be taken away from her?'
A: 'Yes.'
Q: 'Had anything been arranged to that effect?'
A: 'Not at present.'
Q: 'She had a sort of obsession about it, I suppose?'
A: 'Yes.'[26]

That autumn, Claudina and Marion had moved temporarily to Littlehampton in West Sussex to escape the threatened bombs. Grandfather Mihran visited them there on Thursday 20 November and noticed nothing wrong.

On that Saturday, Claudina decided to return to London. She wrote three letters, one to her friend Mrs Nellie Tilley, who worked as a secretary at Allalemdjian Furs, telling her how afraid she was to be parted from Marion.[27] The second was to her friend David Carruthers, a solicitor who lived in Kilmarnock in Scotland and who testified at the inquest.[28] He told the coroner and eight jurors that Claudina had had an operation five years ago to 'remove a nerve' and that she was a nervous and high-strung woman. He went on: 'Since the death of the baby's mother, she had come to regard herself almost as its mother.' The third letter Claudina wrote to Mihran Allalemdjian, telling him she was going to kill herself and Marion.

The following Saturday morning, the postman delivered Claudina's letter to Mihran. He immediately called the Willesden Green Police Station, hoping it was not too late. Police Sergeant South rushed to the house on Dartmouth Road and let himself in with the spare key. He smelled gas immediately and saw a note on a small table by the door that read, 'Light No Match'. He went back through the ground floor to the kitchen. The door was locked with the key on the outside, and with cotton wool packed under it. He opened it and found the room in darkness. When he turned on the light, he saw Claudina and Marion lying on the settee in their nightclothes. The oven door had been opened and the gas turned on full. They were both dead, clasped in each other's arms. The doctor who had been called to the house, Dr Clifford Tenten, testified that they had died about midnight the night before. The coroner summed up the inquest by saying it was a clear case of wilful murder by Claudina, who had 'an obsession that she could not leave the child and dreaded having to let it go'. It was, he concluded, 'a very painful case'.[29]

A shadowy sense of Claudina's personality emerges from these stories. A child rejected by her parents, who lived on the edge of her family's prosperity, then infamy. A woman who had to steal a pair of boots, but whose profession allowed her to travel in luxury and live in comfort. Claudina was essentially a lonely person, whose job made her keep moving from child to child. She was a fifty-year-old woman, with no close family, who had raised Marion from the age of two and loved her desperately. The outbreak of war forced them from London and would soon separate her from Marion, who would be likely to stay in

America for the duration once her passport was approved. The wealthy families who had employed Claudina for Atlantic voyages would no longer be travelling, and Claudina faced the prospect of being alone, unemployed and homeless. The First World War had claimed the life of her brother, and now this war would take away her ward, leaving her truly alone.

And yet we could also see how Claudina rationalised her actions. Some in the family understood that Claudina was not only trying to save herself from losing Marion but also to save Marion from losing her. Marion had already suffered from the distant parenting of a father that had sent her siblings to school and left her behind on the 1939 family holiday. She faced an immediate future of upheaval, immigration, boarding school and the lack of any mother figure in her life. Having already been deprived of the love of one mother, Claudina didn't want her to be hurt again.

In losing Marion, her family lost not only the child she was but the person she would have become. It's difficult to trace what Marion was like from the slight traces on the historical record. At five years old, would she have liked drawing, dancing or playing in the park? Was she learning to read? Did she have playmates nearby? Or was Claudina her only friend?

Surviving family photographs taken a few years before show her as a rounded, laughing child with a blonde bob. In one 1937 photograph, she stands proudly in the waves on a beach as Elbis helps her and another child with a net and bucket. A formal portrait from this period shows her smiling openly at the camera, her light dress arranged around her chubby legs in knee socks. In another series, she stands proudly with her sisters and brother wearing play clothes in a garden, while Kevork stands unsmilingly behind. Her good humour and irrepressible energy are evident in these pictures, as is the affection her older siblings had for her. In many of them, an older sibling holds her shoulders gently to keep her still for the picture. But the events of 1939 separated them forever.

What would she have been like? Her surviving siblings can give a clue to what her life may have been. In November 1939, Kevork took his three other children to New York, where they settled at 37 Brompton Road, Great Neck. Her brother, Mihran, died at fifteen years old in 1943 after a short illness, but Araxi and Elbis went on to live full, rich lives, both dying in their ninetieth year. Their father, while emotionally distant, supported their academic careers. Kevork put Elbis through Albany Medical School in the 1940s, unusual for a woman at this time. There Elbis met her husband, pharmacist John Schoales. They moved to Marion, New York, where he opened a pharmacy and she ran a private family practice for forty-five years, delivering hundreds of children. She had four children and five grandchildren.[30]

Araxi, fascinated by languages, went on to become a teacher. Gifted academically, she graduated from Smith College in 1946, and then did a joint MA with Middlebury College and the Sorbonne. While in France she met and married Stephane Prevot. While he was doing his military service in France, she moved to London and lived with her grandfather Mihran. She had her first child there. Araxi went back to the States to teach in Andover, Massachusetts, and was joined by her husband, and they had two more children before eventually divorcing. She went on teaching into her sixties.[31] According to her son Roger, she was a wonderful, self-sacrificing mother. She was able to intellectualise what had been absent from her upbringing and choose to be a more nurturing parent.[32]

In 2011, Araxi gave an oral interview as part of a project for Smith College Alumnae. She spoke of her arrival in New York, and how the family always planned to go back to England after the war. In the summer of her first year, she took a sculpture class with Mr Johnson: 'I learned sculpture from him. It was partly therapy; I made a sculpture of my brother and younger sister, who had [stumbling over the words], had both, both died in recent years.'[33] Her voice choked and her eyes welled up: 'That was very helpful to me, that summer.' When Araxi spoke of Marion, her son Roger told me, she was 'as sensitive and emotional as my mom could get'. For her, overshadowed by her elder

3. *Bomb damage in London, undated.*

sister, and with an ill mother, Marion had been an incredible gift, someone on whom to shower love and affection. Marion had been a much-loved child and, ironically, that love, threatened by the conditions of war, led to her death.

LILY WRIGHT

Ten miles away from Willesden, in the North London suburb of Wood Green, another loving family was about to be torn apart. The Wrights, Stanley and Lily and their nine-year-old daughter, Pamela, lived in a semi-detached villa at 178 Devonshire Hill Lane. Pamela was an adored only child, and had recently returned from evacuation because her mother could not bear to be apart from her.

On 16 February 1940, at just after 6 p.m., their neighbour Harry Wilks heard banging through the attached wall in the house next door. Since he and his wife were friendly with the Wrights, he went over to see what the matter was. Wilks opened the door to see Stanley in the hallway struggling with his wife, who was wearing a nightgown and no shoes or socks. Stanley shouted at him, 'For God's sake go upstairs, Mr. Wilks, and see if it is too late. Pamela is done in.'[34]

The house smelt strongly of gas, and the lights were all out. Wilks took his torch, which he had handy for use in the blacked-out streets, and went upstairs. He found Pamela in the master bedroom, lying on the edge of the bed with her head on the pillow. She had no covers on and was wearing a short, sleeveless frock. Wilks touched her hand, which was cold, and was satisfied she had been dead for some time. He came back down the stairs and Stanley Wright begged him: 'Fetch a doctor, quick!', to which Lily replied, 'Oh don't, Mr. Wilks.'[35]

He went to call in the local doctor, Dr Standen, and came back to the Wrights' house. He didn't mention it in his statement, but either he or the doctor must have also called the local Wood Green police. Lily had quietened down and they were still standing in the hallway, now with Mrs Wilks as well. They moved into the dining room and sat down to wait for the doctor. According to Mr Wilks, Lily said several times, 'I don't know what made me do it, I wish I hadn't done it now.' Nobody said anything in reply. Fifteen minutes later the police came.

Police Constable (PC) John Thomas Proudfoot arrived at the house just after 6.30 p.m. He went up to see Pamela and used a resuscitator on her until Dr Standen came at 7 p.m. He examined Pamela, found her cold and rigor mortis well established, and estimated she had been dead about five hours. He called the police surgeon, Dr George Finnegan, who arrived shortly afterwards, and he also confirmed that Pamela had been dead for hours.

The scene at 178 must have been chaotic. The police were inspecting the layout of the house, the gas taps and meter and the contents of the kitchen, as well as the bedroom where Pamela lay. Lily was being questioned by both Police Inspector Cecil Rhodes and Dr Finnegan about the circumstances of Pamela's death. At some point the Wilkses left, and a telegram was sent to Stanley's brother, Cecil Wright, and his wife, who arrived at 8 p.m. Cecil also identified the body of his niece. Lily was questioned, off and on, for close to four hours. Inspector Coates said the actual taking down of Lily's statement only took twenty or thirty minutes, but that Lily kept interrupting it: she 'went upstairs three times, then into the kitchenette, she went there twice, made tea, and lighted a fire'.[36] Her first statement was taken and signed at 11 p.m., before Dr Finnegan ordered her removal to the hospital: 'I thought the accused seemed rather not to comprehend the position, i.e. the death of her own child. She appeared rather dazed and generally vague.'[37] Whether Lily was also suffering from the effects of gas was never clarified.

According to the statement taken that night, Pamela had had an ordinary day. Lily had got up at 7 a.m., after Stanley left for his work as a scientific instrument maker, and had gone downstairs.[38] Pamela had come down for breakfast then gone back up to play in the front bedroom in the morning. The weather had been unseasonably harsh that winter, so cold in January that the Thames had frozen, so it was not surprising that neither of them would want to go outside. According to Lily, Pamela had come back down at 1.30 p.m. for egg and chips, made on the hob. Lily had put a penny in the gas meter at 8 a.m. to boil the kettle for tea, and a shilling before dinner. She said she had not used the oven all day. After the midday meal, Pamela had gone to lie down, and at 2.30 p.m., Lily had gone to check on her: 'She was singing to herself and quite happy.' Lily lay down with her for a few minutes, and after Pamela had gone to sleep she had got up to see to her washing and knitting. Lily had checked on her at 5 p.m. and she had seemed to be sleeping: 'I just let her lay there until her father came home and [we'd] all have tea together.'

By 5.15 p.m., the sun had set. Lily put the blackout curtains up in the dining room in preparation for dinner. At 5.45, she went upstairs to get dressed and saw Pamela was in bed: 'I looked at her and thought she looked funny. I thought she was ill. This was nearly six o'clock, I held her hands which were cold, I started rubbing them. My husband then knocked on the door and I let him in. He looked at my daughter and sent for the doctor.' Lily added that when she had come into the kitchen at 5 p.m., she noticed the two taps on the top of the gas stove had been left on, she did not know how. She had not smelt any gas, she added, because she suffered from catarrh, for which she had been gargling Hall's wine and ammonia potash.[39]

Lily's statement seemed odd from the beginning, because it did not match the time that Pamela likely died, around 1 p.m. in the afternoon. Also, the upstairs bedrooms were not serviced by gas, and the gas supply in the kitchenette was at the back of the house, separated by a floor and several walls from the front bedroom where Pamela was found. It seemed unlikely that the small amount of gas that could have made its way upstairs could kill. The other possibility was that Pamela had died in the kitchen, although Inspector Rhodes' statement notes that the oven was full of pots and pans and did not show any sign of having been used. The day after Pamela's death, the police called in the gas inspector of the Tottenham and District Gas Company, who found the cooker and gas system in good order, with no cracks or leaks.[40]

There was also no sign of any meal having been prepared, and the post-mortem performed by Francis Temple Grey found that Pamela had no food in her stomach. PC Henry Weightman also came to take measurements and drew up a plan of 178 Devonshire which showed the layout of the house and the distance between the stove and the bedroom. The police clearly suspected that Lily had either gassed Pamela in the kitchen or had lain down with her in the bedroom with the gas turned on. Since Pamela only weighed 4 stone, she would have been affected by the gas much more than Lily.

After five days in hospital, Lily was arrested and taken to Wood Green Police Station to be charged and cautioned. When the charges were read to her, she told the officers, 'I didn't do it.' The next day she appeared in Tottenham Police Court to be formally charged. She again pleaded not guilty. The chairman, Major Garland, told her, 'You will be remanded until tomorrow week. Do you understand? You will probably go into a hospital to be looked after.'[41]

Lily was transferred to hospital at Holloway Prison. During her time there, the governor and medical officer J.C.M. Matheson observed her behaviour, inquired into her family background, read over the depositions and police reports and interviewed her husband. From the turn of the century, prison medical officers had played a key role in observing, testing and reporting on prisoners on remand. They would submit a report to the Director of Public Prosecutions on the mental state of the accused, and whether they were fit to stand trial.[42] Matheson reported that Lily's family background seemed to show a propensity for ill health and weakness; her parents and older brother had died young, and her six sisters were described by Stanley as 'nervous'. She also had two uncles who 'appear to have been certified as Insane: one dying in a mental institution under certification, the other has recovered and apparently now is well'.[43]

Matheson described Lily's health as good and her mood as rational and cooperative, although rather depressed: 'This depression was, in my opinion, not abnormal considering her position.' She was underweight but in good health: 'She is not a strong character and appears to be given to much worrying and readily becomes anxious.' However, he concluded that she had been sane when she entered prison, continued to be sane, and was fit to plead and stand trial.

Lily's trial began on 3 April 1940, in the Old Bailey. The first witnesses were the Wilkses, the gas company inspector, Divisional Detective Inspector (DDI) Coates and Dr Francis Temple Grey. On the second day of the trial, Lily herself took the stand and was cross-examined by prosecuting lawyer Mr Byrne. He pressed her about her repeated denials of guilt: 'Is this not the true state of affairs: she and you in bed all the morning with the gas turned on, she in consequence killed by it, as she was a child, and you only rendered stupid by it? Is that what really happened?'

Lily replied shortly, 'No.'

Mr Byrne went on: 'Are you telling the jury that Mr and Mrs Wilks are both wrong when they say that you said to them, 'I don't know what made me do it?'

At this point, Lily dramatically burst into tears. Reversing her months of denial, she cried out, 'Yes, I did do it, I'll tell the truth!'

There must have been a brief pause here while Lily collected herself. Then Mr Byrne went on: 'And they are friends of yours, are they not?'

Lily answered, 'I could not tell you if they are friends or not.'

'You always thought they were friends?'

'Yes.'

'Next door neighbours for two years?'

'Yes.'

'Always on good terms with them?'

'Yes.'[44]

The court journalists did not report on the conversation about the Wilkses. According to the newspaper accounts, after Lily's sudden confession, she collapsed in the stand and had to be carried back to the dock, and then taken to the cells to get medical attention. Court was adjourned for fifteen minutes until she could return and proceedings start again.[45]

After Lily's confession, Stanley took the stand and spoke of Pamela as a much-loved only child. He described Lily as a 'very lovable mother.

She idolised Pamela and did everything possible for her, but after the outbreak of war, when we had to evacuate Pam, there was a decided change in her.' When they visited Pam in the country, he told the court, Lily cheered up, but when they got home, she started to cry.

Within months, Pamela was brought home again. She wasn't alone – without any raids, a third of London schoolchildren were back home by January 1940.[46] Lily was too worried about Pamela's safety to send her to school. She believed the German invasion was imminent, and, according to Stanley, 'Her mind was set on an idea that we should have to suffer at the hands of the Germans like the Czechs and the Poles. She worried about what would happen to Pamela.'[47] The night before the tragedy, newspapers reported, she told Stanley that the police or the Nazis were after her, and she did not want them to catch her asleep.

Stanley then burst into tears on the stand, as he described kissing them both goodnight for the last time. For a man to display emotion publicly was very unusual, particularly in wartime, when the emotional standard was a 'stiff upper lip' reticence.[48] Stanley's tears of grief and sorrow impressed the court reporters and would have impressed the judge and jury. They reinforced his words of loyalty and compassion for his wife, despite what she had done to him.

The next witness was governor and medical officer of Holloway Dr J.C.M. Matheson. He testified that Lily had been sane when she was admitted to prison but that, in his opinion, at the moment of killing Pamela she had been suffering from defective reasoning due to disease of the mind, and that she had not known that what she was doing was wrong.

This medico-legal language followed the legal definition of insanity set out in the wake of the 1843 trial of Scottish woodturner Daniel M'Naghten. M'Naghten was acquitted of killing civil servant Edward Drummond, whom he mistook for Prime Minister Robert Peel, by reason of insanity. The case had established a new legal defence. Defendants who could prove that 'at the time of the committing of the act, the party accused was labouring under such a defect of reason, from disease of the mind, as not to know the nature and quality of the act he was doing; or, if he did know it, that he did not know he was doing what was wrong' were not guilty under the law.[49] They were not to go free, however, but were sentenced 'To be detained at His (or Her) Majesty's Pleasure', meaning an indeterminate sentence, usually in a specialist institution rather than a prison. The 1883 Trial of Lunatics Act changed the wording of the verdict to 'Guilty but Insane', although the penalty was the same. Mrs Wright was accordingly found 'Guilty but Insane' and sentenced to be detained indefinitely.

The 'Guilty but Insane' verdict was often used in cases of infanticide or of parents killing their children, out of compassion by the courts. While infanticide was no longer a capital crime, the legal definition only applied to children under twelve months. In the case of older children, and where there was clear evidence of guilt, which Lily's outburst provided, a guilty verdict would be an automatic death sentence. The judge would put on a 'black cap', or square of black cloth, over his white wig, and pronounce the death sentence, telling the accused when and where they would be hanged. Even if it were likely that the defendant would be granted a compassionate reprieve, the ritual had to be carried out. This ordeal was considered cruel to vulnerable parents, and the 'Guilty but Insane' verdict offered a way around it. The punishment was also more compassionate, and allowed the prisoner to avoid prison, receive treatment and be released in a comparatively short time. Women from respectable families who were happy to have them back were likely to be detained for the least amount of time, sometimes only a few months, especially if there were no other children that could be in danger.[50] This was the case for Lily.

It's not clear when Lily was released, as Holloway Prison records for this period are still closed. But when Stanley died in 1960, Lily was listed as his wife and executor. Lily married again six years later and lived until 1984.[51] Whatever memories there were of Pamela are now gone. Photographs and mementoes of Pamela's would have been a painful reminder for Lily, and with no siblings or cousins, the details of Pamela's personality can only be guessed at. It was the Wilkses who spoke most about Pamela, both testifying that the Wrights were a 'happy and devoted family, and Lily was devoted to Pamela'.[52]

The Wright case was followed more sympathetically in the press than Marion's murder had been. Most of the newspapers avoided publishing Lily's name until after she was found guilty; two London papers mentioned only Pamela's death and 'a woman' being charged on 21 February.[53] The *North London Observer* followed the case most closely, but even its reporting of the most damning testimony was framed by sympathetic portrayals of Lily. Its reporter described Lily in her first court appearance as a 'pathetic figure' whose 'face was white' and who 'looked worried'. She wore a black hat and a black coat with a black fur collar: 'The darkness of her clothes accentuated the whiteness of her face.'[54] During the trial, the paper called her a 'devoted mother', who often burst out crying in the dock during testimony about her daughter's death, sobbing on the shoulder of the Court Matron who came to sit next to her.[55] Their headline reporting on the final verdict in the case was 'Feared Nazis, Killed Baby'.[56]

One element in the case not reported by the mainstream newspapers was the evidence given by Mr and Mrs Wilks. Yet it was the questions that Mr Byrne asked Lily about their testimony that made Lily break down and admit her guilt on the stand. Mr Byrne asked her if the Wilkses were her friends, to which Lily answered, 'I could not tell you if they are friends or not.' Because, although the Wilkses testified that the Wrights were a loving family, they also told the police of the words exchanged in the kitchen on the night of Pamela's death.

While Mr Wilks had been fetching the doctor, Mrs Wilks had gone to open the back door in the kitchen to dispel the gas fumes. She had noticed that the oven door was open 8 or 9 inches. According to Mrs Wilks, Stanley had asked Lily, 'You never put Pamela in there, did you?' She had not answered. But a few minutes later, she said, 'I told you not to go to work, didn't I?'[57]

The murders of Marion and Pamela are tragic, in the way that the deaths of all children are tragic, and doubly so because of the lifelong grief they left behind for their parents and siblings. They are also heart-breaking because they were occasioned by the nervous anticipation in the first year of war.

Ironically, once the bombing raids started in September 1940, the expected wave of civilian panic and 'bomb neurosis' did not come. The emergency stations for psychological casualties closed, and the War Neurosis wards turned their focus to other patients.[58] Psychologists and psychoanalysts such as Glover celebrated Londoners' impressive mental adaptability.[59] Most people were able to control their fears.

Claudina and Lily were exceptional because their apprehensions led them to violence. Both feared a German invasion and were terrified by the prospect of being separated from their beloved girls and unable to protect them. The tension of all the wartime horrors that were expected but hadn't yet materialised, which were not alleviated by any military news or action, built up to create an unbearable psychological pressure in both women. They were not alone; in the same period in London two fathers gassed their children and themselves, a mother killed her five-month-old baby and a husband slit the lodger's throat as he missed his evacuated children and was consumed by jealous thoughts of losing his wife to the other man.[60] These parents could not maintain the tight emotional control demanded by wartime ideals of civilian morale. Belief in an ultimate British war victory was not enough to control their fears of separation and death and to stop them from acts of despair and violence.

The darkness of the blackout had brought a corresponding gloom to London. But the darkness was about to be lit up, by the long-feared bombs of the Luftwaffe.

CHAPTER 2

BOMBSITES AND SHELTERS

I have had a miserable life with my husband, who hasn't lived with me except every now and then. He is supposed to pay maintenance, but I hardly ever get my money . . . What I want is my money regular, and my husband does not want to pay, and he has come to the police now to try to get me into trouble.

Rachel Dobkin, statement to police on 9 August 1939, murdered by her husband in 1941[1]

After the tension of months of dread and anxiety, the military stalemate in Europe was shattered by the German invasion of Norway on 9 April 1940. Within weeks, the Germans had overwhelmed Belgium, Luxembourg and the Netherlands. As German troops entered France, British troops were forced back into a hasty retreat to the coast. Using troopships and private boats, over 338,000 British troops and 113,000 French soldiers were evacuated from Dunkirk by the end of May. Europe had fallen to the Nazis.

At home, Britain's failure to protect Norway led to the fall of Neville Chamberlain and the appointment of Winston Churchill as Prime Minister. France's official surrender at the end of June left Britain and her empire alone to face Germany. As Churchill vowed that Britain would 'never surrender', Britain braced itself for attack. From 11 May, RAF Bomber Command began to lead small-scale attacks against German residential areas, as Churchill had no 'conscientious or legal objections' to civilian bombing.[2] It was even rumoured that Churchill wanted the Luftwaffe to bomb civilian areas, to divert their attention from RAF airbases and factories and allow Britain's depleted military resources to recover.

Londoners knew they would be the first target of civilian bombing. The feeling of being under attack, as much as the bombing raids themselves, was their defining experience of war. Trying to maintain everyday life with the constant sense of an invisible, impersonal threat would take an emotional toll for years to come. The Blitz also left behind empty bomb shelters and destroyed buildings where assaults and murders would be committed, and bodies hidden. Wartime London was a dusty, dark and grimy landscape of fear.

The bombs began to fall sporadically on London on 7 September. In the first raid, 'Black Saturday', 348 German bombers and 617 fighters dropped high explosives and incendiary bombs on the East End of London. Docks, gasworks and homes erupted in flames and lit the sky with a bright orange glow visible all over the city.[3] That night, guided by the fires, a second group of bombers returned to London, attacking the city until 5 a.m. Four hundred and thirty people died. The London Blitz had begun.

London was attacked fifty-six nights in a row. Bombs rained down on the city, focused on the industrial areas of East and South London but hitting every London neighborhood. Londoners carried on, listening for the sound of the warning siren, walking over the rubble and broken glass, in sight of ruined buildings, smelling the poisonous tang of burnt wood, dust, damp earth and stale water. The attacks tapered off in November, as the Luftwaffe targeted other British cities, but intensified again in the winter of 1941, peaking in two massive attacks, one on 16 April, and the last on 10 May.

While the death toll of the Blitz was considerable – over 43,000 Londoners killed and 50,000 more seriously injured – it was nothing like the millions of deaths forecasted. The problem Londoners faced was not how to bury the dead, but how to keep living in a devastated city. Over 300,000 Londoners' homes were destroyed, and electricity and gas supplies, telephone services and public transport were disrupted. By day, people navigated a city strewn with bombsites, broken glass, rubble and shrapnel as best as they could, hurrying home before darkness fell and the sirens began.

At night, bombed houses and empty shelters became dark pockets in city life, used for secret meetings and illicit activities. Shelters were relatively safe when full, but empty shelters and bombsites, hidden from view and in the darkness of the blackout, were scenes of terrible violence in 1941. The strangling of Maple Church in a bombed-out house was never solved. The murder of Rachel Dobkin, an unhappy woman whose body was discovered a year after she disappeared in the basement of a bombed church, was only brought to light and linked to her estranged husband by chance. Unlike Lily Wright and Marion Allalemdjian, who were killed ostensibly to 'protect' them from the horrors of war, these women were killed for personal reasons – sex, anger and gain.

AIR-RAID SHELTERS AND BOMB SITES

Before the war began, air raids on London were predicted to be short, devastating daytime raids with very high casualties. With this vision in mind, local London authorities focused on providing temporary, inexpensive shelters. Open trenches were dug in local parks and reinforced with sandbags, and steel-reinforced basements, church crypts and railway arches were requisitioned. These shelters were designated as Day, Day and Evening or Day and Night, and were identified by white luminous painted signs and arrows. Some of these painted signs survive on London buildings today, noticeably in Upper Brook Street in Mayfair and Longmoore Street, SW1.[4]

To encourage people to shelter at home, local authorities also distributed more than 2 million Anderson shelters to householders who had back gardens. Not until the first winter of the war, in December 1939, did local authorities begin to build new surface shelters: large concrete structures built in the middle of London streets, identified by painted white diagonal crosses or bands.[5] Many people felt surface shelters were likely to collapse under a direct hit, or be crushed by surrounding buildings. So, when the long, intense nighttime raids of the Blitz began in September 1940, Londoners forced the government to open Tube stations as shelters. People crowded in as dusk fell on the city and slept on platforms, staircases and between the rails.[6] Parts of the platforms were eventually roped off for shelterers, who brought their blankets, suitcases of valuables and flasks of tea. Most of these public shelters lacked all basic amenities in the early months of war, such as toilets, water and beds.

Metropolitan Police constables, and later specially appointed shelter welfare marshals, tried to maintain order and guard against petty crime and breaches of public morality, such as displays of bad language, nudity, sex or drunkenness.[7] The shelters were also policed at night by a special squad of policewomen called the 'Girl Protection Patrol' on the lookout for sexual immorality.[8] Plain-clothes policemen patrolled shelters in the daytime to prevent them from being used for gambling or to hide stolen goods.[9]

The most common crime in the shelters was opportunistic theft. The large numbers of people crushed into a small space with their valuables was very tempting. Thieves were generally caught by victims who were startled awake. Frances Higgins heard a noise in the middle of the night in the air-raid shelter at 4 Bishop's Road, Fulham, and shone her torch to see Owen Parker, an army deserter, opening her handbag.[10] Thieves would also steal clothes and shoes that had been taken off by sleeping shelterers.[11]

As the Blitz wore on into 1941, the conditions in public shelters were slowly improving. Most trench shelters, which were prone to flooding, were filled in, and other shelters added bunks and toilet facilities. In December 1940, a ticket system for regular shelterers in the Tube was introduced, so that local people were guaranteed a spot and didn't have to queue. With fewer transient shelterers, petty crimes in shelters decreased.

During periods of intense bombing, such as the London Blitz of 1940–41 and the V-1 and V-2 raids in 1944 and 1945, the shelters were full and well supervised. Likewise, in the aftermath of raids, many people had eyes on bombsites: the Air Raid Precautions (ARP) wardens, firemen, demolition men and others who helped in the clearing up. Looting was a serious problem, but crimes of violence were not.

After the raids had ended, shelters and bombed-out buildings stood empty and dark, visual reminders of the destruction of war. Ruins had many symbolic meanings, pointing towards London's past, present and future. The destruction of so many historic churches and buildings was a reminder of London's thousand-year-old history and a signal for the need for postwar reconstruction.[12] In the present, bombsites and ruins presented a host of very real dangers. There were so many bombsites in every London neighbourhood by 1941 that they formed a shadow city, uninhabited and

4. Ruins in Paternoster Square, with the Old Bailey Courthouse behind, 1940.

pitch dark in the blackout. From 1940 until well into the 1960s, London housed a secret world of bombed-out buildings used for children's games, illicit meetings, sexual encounters, criminal activities – and murder. Because no one was watching, many of these murders were never solved.

MAPLE CHURCH

On the night of 12 October 1941, a bus made its way down Hampstead Road, just south of Mornington Crescent. Formerly a busy road with houses lining each side, the block had been badly damaged by bombs, and the buildings were in the process of being demolished.[13] As the bus passed over the darkened roadway around 10 p.m., a soldier passenger heard a 'loud and unpleasant scream'.[14] He looked out the window but saw nothing in the blackness. A road surveyor who lived nearby also heard a scream around 9.45 p.m. He went to his door but heard nothing more and decided it was only a drunken woman. Around 11 p.m., before going to bed, he went to the door again and saw the shadowy figure of a man walking and holding a lighted cigarette.

The next morning, Charles Smith, an elderly labourer from Dalston working as a demolition man, changed into his work jacket in one of the bombed houses on Hampstead Road and climbed the debris-covered steps to number 225 ahead of his four workmates. The door to the room on the right was ajar, and as he passed, he saw something lying on the thick plaster dust that covered the floorboards. It was a woman's slip. When he peered into the room, he saw two legs protruding from the corner with bare feet facing outwards. A young woman was lying dead on the floor, naked except for a black coat and some cami-knickers thrown across her body. Scuff marks in a corner, where the floor was more stable, seemed to show where she and the murderer had been standing, and her dusty feet showed she had taken off her shoes prior to death. One of her shoes had fallen through the damaged floor-boards and was found in the cellar. Her gas mask, handbag and torch were scattered around the room, but her money was gone.

The woman was identified through her identity card as Maple Church or Churchyard, a nineteen-year-old clerk for Hackney Borough Council.[15] A studio photograph of her released by Scotland Yard showed a slim young woman, with dark hair and an oval face. Her smile was open and vivacious.[16] She lived with her parents in Carleton Road, Tufnell Park, in North London. She also worked nights as a helper in a services canteen in the West End.

Maple was a popular girl with her workmates and had spent the weekend with a friend, Vera Whyman. At the inquest, Vera told the coroner, Bentley Purchase, 'Maple and I were at school together at West Ham and often used to meet in London and have tea and outings.' They had been to the cinema in Leicester Square, and Maple had put her friend on a train to West Wickham at Charing Cross at 9 p.m. Vera believed Maple was going to take a bus straight home from Trafalgar Square. Purchase asked her, 'Do you think she was likely to go into a public house and have some beer on her own?'

'Oh no,' she replied. 'I should be very surprised.'[17]

But the post-mortem conducted by pathologist Bernard Spilsbury, pictured in a press photograph leaving the bombed house, showed that she had a large quantity of beer in her stomach. How Church had got from Trafalgar Square to Hampstead Road was not clear, but the police thought that she had probably picked up a man in a pub and gone willingly to the bombed house for sex. Contraceptives had been found in her bag, and a married former lover had made a statement to the police, one of two hundred collected in the investigation.

Another witness, a deserter from the navy who had been living in St Martin's Crypt, told police that his friend, a deserter from the air force, had bragged about being with a woman like Maple on that night. He had also boasted about having sex with women then stealing their handbags. The airman, when questioned, denied knowing Maple and said he had left his girl on Shaftesbury Avenue. There the leads dried up. A year later, when serial killer Gordon Cummins was arrested for a series of murders in February 1942, police noted that he had been stationed in Wiltshire at the time of Church's murder and had been a frequent visitor to London.

It was not unusual for women like Maple Church to be out alone in the blackout. Women had more opportunities for independence in wartime: more options for paid work and volunteering, and more access to pubs, dance halls and other spaces of sociability. Dark streets, ruined houses and empty shelters offered secret spaces for passionate meetings, but they were also places of extraordinary danger for women. Women were attacked in the streets, in darkened train carriages and in public shelters.[18] Mrs Lucy Wirtz, who lived in the flats opposite the bombed houses on Hampstead Road, told police it was an area known for criminal activity, and that men took advantage of the ruins to try to entice women in the darkness: 'Men hang about at night and I have been accosted three times within a distance of 100 yards . . . I often hear screams and the sounds of running feet. I suppose the sounds I hear are of girls who have been molested running away in the blackout.'[19] Church's experience shows both sides of the freedom that the war offered: the excitement of spontaneous encounters, and the vulnerability that led to her unsolved murder.

RACHEL DOBKIN

Bomb sites were also places to hide crimes years in the making. The discovery of Rachel Dobkin's body in the basement of a bombed-out church basement exposed the layers of unhappiness in her twenty-year marriage and foiled her husband Harry Dobkin's nearly successful attempt to evade detection. After the trial, police and forensic memoirs framed the case as a victory of detection for Detective Inspector Hatton and forensic pathologist Keith Simpson. But it was the missing woman's sister, Polly Dubinski, with the help of both lawyers and psychics, who relentlessly pushed the police investigation that led to the identification of her sister.

On the afternoon of Friday 11 April 1941, Harry Dobkin, a short, heavyset man in his forties, walked along Navarino Road, Hackney, where he lived in a flat with his parents. According to his later state-ment to police, he saw his estranged wife Rachel waiting for him and said, 'Please don't hang around in the street and cause trouble for me, my mother is very ill.' This, he said, was the fourth time she had accosted him near his home in two weeks. They arranged to meet at 5 p.m. in a café across from the Metropolitan Hospital at 374 Kingsland Road, Haggerston. Rachel agreed to bring their twenty-year-old son Stanley, who was home visiting from his engineering job in Slough.

They parted, and Dobkin, a market trader like his father before him, went to Chapel Market in Islington to try to sell some aprons, then picked up nine single pockets (a wartime fashion for women) from a seamstress.

At 5 p.m. they met at the café. Stanley wasn't there. Rachel said that her brother Nathan was to be married on Sunday, and she wanted Harry to return to her and go to the engagement party with her. She also asked him for money for wine and matzo for the party. He refused, and according to him she said, 'If you don't make peace with me, I'll make trouble for you.' He calmed her down and said he would consider it. Then, he said, she told him she was going to her mother's to listen to the wireless, in 16 Laleham Buildings, Boundary Estate, Shoreditch. Rachel had a flat on the same estate but ate all her meals with her mother, a Russian widow who lived with Rachel's siblings (sister Polly, thirty-eight, a shorthand typist, sister Mary, forty, and brother Nathan, forty-three). Harry said he saw her get on the number 22 bus going towards Shoreditch at around 6 p.m. She was never seen again.

At the trial, the prosecutor, Mr Byrne, asked Dobkin if he had told his wife to calm herself, and that he would make peace with her if she went home. Dobkin told the court he had.

Byrne: 'When you said that to her you had not the smallest intention of making peace with her, had you?'
Dobkin: 'No.'
Byrne: 'It was merely a question of getting rid of her?'

Dobkin: 'It was a method of avoiding her.'

. . .

Byrne: 'You had no desire to see your wife at any future time, had you?'
Dobkin: 'My wife, I had been warned not to speak to my wife.'

At this point Justice Wrottesley intervened: 'That is not the question. Listen to the question.'

Byrne: 'Had you any desire of ever seeing your wife again?'
Dobkin: 'No, sir.'

The judge repeated the question: 'You had no desire to see your wife again. Is that right?' Dobkin answered, 'I always tried to avoid her.'

Mr Byrne followed up one more time: 'Is this right, "I have no desire to see my wife again?" And that was true on the 11th of April, you never wanted to see her again after the 11th of April?' Dobkin replied, 'No, sir – yes, sir, rather; I did not want to see her again.'[20]

Rachel and Harry Dobkin fought their battles against the backdrop of a vibrant Jewish East End, which was about to disappear in the bombing raids. In 1941, the Jewish community in the East End was at its peak, with twenty-seven synagogues, six Jewish schools, eight almshouses, twenty-one charitable organisations and at least twenty-six benevolent societies and seventy-four social groups (or 'friendly societies'). Multiple Zionist societies represented various strands of political and religious Zionism, and fourteen trade unions represented the rights of Jewish workers. The East End was also home to a host of Jewish writers and artists, an active Yiddish theater, a Jewish art gallery on Whitechapel Road, the first English Jewish newspaper, *The Jewish Chronicle*, and a number of Yiddish newspapers.[21] Harry and Rachel lived in various flats in buildings built by Jewish philanthropic organisations, formed to combat the slum conditions created after an influx of Eastern European Jews between 1880 and 1905. These 'model' tenement blocks transformed the East End of the 'Jack the Ripper' murders into one of poor but respectable Jewish inhabitants.[22] Navarino Mansions, where Dobkin lived with his parents, was one of the buildings built by the Four Per Cent company in 1904 to accommodate 300 Jewish artisans.

Dobkin was a Russian Jew who had been brought to England in 1891 with his parents when he was only a few months old. In September 1920, he married Rachel Dubinski at the Bethnal Green Synagogue, on Bethnal Green Road. Their marriage had been arranged by a marriage broker, according to his sister, on the promise of a large dowry which never arrived. It was a failure from the beginning. When Dobkin was asked in court when he had stopped loving his wife, he replied, 'On the day that I was married.'

The newlyweds moved into a fourth-floor flat in Brady Street Buildings, a Victorian tenement in Whitechapel, but separated after a week. Dobkin moved back in with his parents, then enlisted as a ship steward on several trips to America. Rachel applied for a maintenance order against him at Old Street Police Station and was granted an order of £1 a week, later reduced to 10 shillings. Dobkin resented the order, was always in arrears and was sent to Brixton Prison three times for non-payment. Their son was born nine months after they married, but they only lived together again briefly twice. The first time her family paid him £8 to return. The reconciliation ended when Harry accused her of stealing his ship steward's papers, and she accused him of stealing a brooch and had him arrested. He appeared at Old Street Police Court, but the case was dismissed. The second time they reconciled, in 1937, Rachel paid him £7, but he only stayed a week.

Their final meeting in the café in 1941 was typical of their twenty-year relationship, but their acrimony was increased by the stresses of the war and of the Blitz. Rachel was unemployed, and her public assistance was in danger of being cut off. Harry had made a good living as a trader before the war, but rationing of fabric and other wartime shortages had forced him to take on work as a firewatcher at a paper store in South London. After tea with Rachel, he took a bus to his job at Kennington Lane, which began at dusk with the blackout.

Rachel did not go to her mother's. Her family waited for her all night, then in the morning Polly went to Rachel's flat, to find her bed hadn't been slept in. Polly went right away to the Commercial Street Police Station to report her missing. That same morning, 30 miles away in the Guildford Post Office, Rachel Dobkin's handbag was found on the floor and handed in to the staff. It contained her identity card, unemployment card, ration book, an outpatient's card for the London Hospital and her rent book. It also held an RAF badge, a metal ring, a comb, a mirror, three letters and a plain envelope, and a copy of *Old Moore's Almanack*. The only money was 2 pence in change. In the bag were also two Underground railway tickets whose dates had been erased. One had been issued at King's Cross to Westminster on the morning of 12 April. Rachel had seemingly been alive on 12 April, the day after her meeting with Harry, and had taken the hour's train ride south-west of London before losing her handbag and disappearing.

Three days later, on 15 April, Polly Dubinski came back to the police station and accused Harry Dobkin of killing her sister. She was not dissuaded when DDI Davis, in charge of the missing person's case, pointed out the seriousness of her allegations. But the police didn't believe her. A report to the Divisional Superintendent insisted that 'considerable patience' had been extended to Dubinski during the lengthy interviews, but that her main evidence was her trust in psychics: 'On each occasion she has talked at great length of the opinions and views of spiritualistic mediums whom she has visited in connection with the disappearance of her sister. She seems to have great faith in "mediums", and in view of their varied explanations, it has a depressing effect on her with the result that she comes to the police.'

Rachel had also been interested in psychics and had consulted Mrs Hilda Nerva of Stepney, a medium connected with several Spiritualist churches. After Rachel went missing, Polly Dubinski arranged a séance with her. Nerva went into a trance and saw 'country surroundings with water conditions' and experienced a choking sensation. She told Dubinski that her sister had been murdered. Dubinski became very upset, and Nerva took her to another medium, Mrs Lydia Kain of Stepney, who told her the same story. According to Dubinski, 'I had never met the clairvoyante before, but I was so convinced that I went straight to the police station, where two days before I had reported my sister missing and told them I was positive she had been murdered.'[23] Police believed it was Nerva who first put the suspicion of foul play into Dubinski's head. (When the police interviewed Kain, she vehemently denied telling this story. This was not surprising: claiming to have supernatural powers was still illegal under the 1735 Witchcraft Act.)

The same night that Dubinski made her allegations to the police, a mysterious fire broke out at around 1.30 a.m. in the Baptist chapel next door to where Dobkin was a firewatcher. The eighteenth-century building was at the corner of Kennington Lane and St Oswald's Place, with a Sunday School behind it. Dobkin didn't put it out or call the fire brigade. At 3.30 a.m., a passing police constable saw it and called the fire service. Dobkin was there, very flustered. By 5 a.m. the fire was extinguished. The Baptist Church minister, Henry Burgess, went down to the cellar to investigate and saw the remains of a straw mattress, with the cover ripped open and straw strewn around the floor. It had not been there before. He questioned Dobkin, who seemed very jumpy and had straw sticking to his freshly painted ARP helmet. When Burgess returned later in the day, the straw had been tidied up and a garden fork lay nearby. Burgess suspected, he confided to his diary, that the fire had been set by enemy agents. That night, a heavy bombing raid hit London: beginning at 9 p.m. and continuing until 5 a.m. the following morning, 500 German aircraft flew over in continuous waves, raining an esti-mated 450 tons of bombs across the city. More than 1,000 people were killed, and the damage was devastating. The Kennington Lane chapel was again severely battered by the attack, which tore up the bones in the adjoining graveyard and left twenty-three locals dead and fifty-five seri-ously injured. The chapel fire of the previous day was forgotten.

The police investigation was coloured by their belief that Rachel was mentally unstable, and that Harry Dobkin was stupid. A 1941 report stated: 'Both Mr. and Mrs. Dobkin are persons of low mentality . . . they are very vindictive towards each other. There is no doubt that Harry Dobkin tried to avoid payment of the maintenance order, and she in turn molests him whenever possible.' Harry Dobkin was interviewed by police on 16 April. He gave very detailed accounts of his movements on 11 April then wrote to police and gave his whereabouts for 12 April, the day the handbag was found in Guildford, without being asked. He made two more payments on his maintenance order at Old Street, even after being told his wife was missing. His house on Navarino Road was searched, and his sister and mother were questioned. The neighbours were also interviewed: 'The consensus of opinion was that Mrs. Dobkin was inclined to be mentally deranged.' The premises of 302 Kennington Lane (site of the chapel fire) were searched on 28 April and 1 and 2 May, and police even dug up part of the ruined basement, which seemed to have been recently disturbed. They found a freshly dug shallow hole 6 feet long and 2 feet wide. But it was empty.[24]

The police thought Rachel might have committed suicide or fallen in the river, so they arranged with Thames Division to view all the bodies that could fit her description. Polly Dubinski was shown two unidentified and decomposing bodies, then refused to see any more, 'owing to the gruesome sights'. After that, Detective Sergeant (DS) Hearn, who knew Rachel Dobkin well, visited mortuaries along the Thames and examined another eighteen bodies, an extraordinary number of unclaimed drowned women in one year. Rachel's photograph was circulated in the *Police Gazette* and published in the *News of the World*, with no result. It was also sent to the Central Casualty Bureau, which kept records and photographs of unidentified bombing victims. Inquiries were also made in hospitals and mental institutions.

Polly Dubinski must have sensed that the police, despite their wide-ranging search, were not taking her seriously. She paid a lawyer, Mr Shield, to write a letter to the Police Superintendent of G Division to ask about the inquiry at the Commercial Street Police Station. In his response, DDI Davis dismissed Dubinski's claims:

Reviewing the case, it will be seen that every avenue of enquiry has been exploited, but there is not the slightest indication that Harry Dobkin has murdered his wife, as indicated by the missing woman's relations. Had this woman found her way into a mental or other institution, there is little doubt that she would have been identified . . . The fact still remains that with this woman's mental history, she may have committed suicide, possibly by drowning, and her body has either not been found, or has been buried as unidentified.

Dobkin's story was believed:

If Dobkin's story is true, it can now be assumed, that Mrs. Dobkin was alive on the morning of 12th April 1941. The only alternative can be that she had been murdered and her handbag taken to Guildford and left there to hamper any investigation . . . I feel that the allegations against Dobkin have no foundation in fact . . . It cannot be feasible that a man would wait 20 years if he intended to do her harm. From my observations and that of PS Daws, who has been with me on this enquiry, it appears that he is a man of low mentality as mentioned in former papers. He does not appear to have sufficient intelligence to murder his wife without leaving some tangible clue as evidence, although that cannot be placed outside the bounds of possibility. His whole demeanour is against it, and he swears that he has never been to Guildford [where Rachel's bag was found].[25]

But Polly Dubinski didn't need a psychic medium to suspect a violent husband. Harry had been summoned for assault against Rachel four times, although each time the magistrate had dismissed the charges. Polly claimed that Harry had viciously punched Rachel in the head after they met in the street in 1937, and that she was so badly injured she was admitted with a loss of memory to St Clement's Hospital in Bow. After this, Rachel was no longer able to work. Dobkin himself admitted that the police at Old Street had warned him to stay away from her. In August 1939, Dobkin had gone to the Commercial Street Police Station and accused his wife of threatening to undergo an 'illegal operation': an abortion. The police investigated immediately, tracking Rachel down to her cousin's house, where she was sitting, crying. She said she didn't really want to have an illegal operation but was trying to frighten him, and later accused him of trying to force her to undergo an abortion.

Rachel told police that he had forced her to have intercourse with him in his workshop two weeks earlier and that, as her period was five days overdue, she thought she was pregnant. She was taken to the police station and medically examined. Dr Hannah Billig of Cable Street, Stepney, described her as 'an extremely nervous, excitable woman of a low order of mentality'. She had a bulky uterus suggestive of fibroids, but 'no signs of any interference'. The next day, Mrs Dobkin returned to the police and told them that her period had come and made a statement to that effect. DDI Davis ended this report with the statement that 'Mr. and Mrs. Dobkin are persons of such low mentality, that their statements cannot be relied upon', and the case was closed. What's striking about this story and Polly Dubinski's statements is that the police reports into her disappearance don't even comment on the accusations of forced intercourse or assault: a history of violence wasn't considered unusual enough to suggest that Harry might be responsible for Rachel's disappearance.

Nothing more was seen or heard of Rachel, until more than a year later. In July 1942, demolition men were clearing away the debris around the damaged historic buildings in Kennington Lane where Harry Dobkin had worked as a firewatcher in 1941. Across from the paper store was the Baptist chapel and, further along, St Peter's Church and Rectory, and the Lambeth Art School.[26] Across the street was the Imperial Court building, headquarters of the Navy, Army and Air Force Institutes.[27] The area had been heavily bombed: between 1940 and 1942 there were twenty-one air raids within 250 yards of the chapel.

The entire block surrounding the chapel had been extensively damaged on the night of 15 October 1940 after nine high-explosive bombs fell on it. One hundred and four people were killed, sixty-nine seriously injured and sixty-four slightly injured. There were no unidentified bodies. The doors and windows of the chapel were so badly damaged that looters later stole many of the fittings, including the organ pipes.

By 1942, the chapel was in a sorry state. Molly Lefebure, pathologist Keith Simpson's secretary, described it in her memoir: 'The roof was full of holes, through which the rain dripped onto the rows of dirty mute pews below, where hassocks and old hymnbooks mouldered together. On the dais at the end of the building, a battered harmonium lolled like a lunatic and pages of holy music lay scattered around it like grimy snow. The place seemed to be waiting for a congregation of Baptist ghosts.'[28] The rotting floorboards allowed glimpses of the basement below, where all that remained was an iron staircase and a rotting wooden chest in the corner. Two feet of dirt and debris covered the floor. On 17 July, demolition worker Benjamin Marshall's shovel hit something hard: a paving stone. He later recalled, 'I stood the stone up on its edge near the side of the wall. When I did that, I looked, and of course, I was mesmerised at the time . . . I see a body there.'[29] Thinking it was an air-raid victim, Marshall lifted the bones onto his shovel and set them to one side. They were taken in a paper bag to the local mortuary, St George's, where the Southwark coroner, Hervey Wyatt, asked forensic pathologist Keith Simpson to perform the post-mortem on the 'bits of some old air-raid casualty'.[30] Simpson took the remains to his laboratory at Guy's Hospital.[31]

According to his memoir, Simpson never believed the body was that of an air-raid victim, 'considering she had been lying neatly buried under a slab of stone, neatly set into the floor of a cellar: this was no bomb crater'.[32] The body itself also suggested that she was a murder victim. Her head and limbs had been cut through cleanly, and the lower limbs and lower jaw were missing (and never found). All the tissue had been taken off the skull except for a small patch of brown and grey hair.

But the killer had made a terrible mistake. Rachel's body had been sprinkled with slaked lime, which had preserved the tissue around the throat and the uterus. Simpson found a dried blood clot around the upper horn of the right wing of the voice box, showing bruising and pressure while still alive. Under the bruising was a fracture of the upper horn of the wing. Such small and specific injuries only happened during manual strangulation.

Because there were no clothing or personal items with the body, her identity had to be discovered using the physical features of the skeleton.[33] Simpson calculated height and age using the remaining bones. He X-rayed the uterus and found it full of fibroid tumours.[34] The profile matched missing person Rachel Dobkin. By this point the police investigation had shifted to Southwark, and DDI Hatton and his detective DI Keeling took over the case. They tracked down Rachel's medical and dental records and her photograph. She matched all the identifying features of the body.

To provide a final powerful image linking the body to Rachel Dobkin, Simpson turned to Mary Newman, a nurse and photographer at Guy's Hospital, to try a superimposition technique. Newman, a nurse in her forties, had been trained by her photographer father and had worked with him for years. After reading about the 1936 Buck Ruxton murder investigation, in which the bodies of two women had to be separated and identified, she had become interested in forensic photography.[35] Using the detailed instructions set out in Glaister and Brash's *The Medico-Legal Aspects of the Ruxton Case* (1937), Newman superimposed a photo of Rachel Dobkin onto a photograph of the skull.[36] The photo of Rachel had been taken by an itinerant photographer while the family was on holiday, and her sister had had it enlarged and framed. The photograph showed a wan, dispirited woman with sagging cheeks and dark hair, who could only manage a slight smile at the photographer. Because of the poor quality of the photograph, her eyes were dark and lifeless. But Simpson rejoiced: 'The portrait fitted the skull like a mask.'[37]

Harry Dobkin appeared at trial on 17 November 1942 at the Old Bailey before Mr Justice Wrottesley. Despite the fact that there were no witnesses to the murder and no direct evidence that Dobkin had committed it, the circumstantial evidence and the medical and scientific proofs of identity and cause of death were strong enough to make a firm case. John Slee from the *Daily Herald* described Dobkin as 'a gorilla-like man with wide nostrils and a short, massive body. His arms hung loosely from shoulders.'[38] He cut a 'grim figure' in the dock, and he had a habit of hanging his head, then raising it quickly after any damaging point from the judge to dart his eyes fearfully around the courtroom.

Just as Dobkin had tried to use the conditions of war to hide the evidence of his crime, so his defence tried to use them to explain away the medical evidence. First Mr F.H. Lawton, the lawyer for the accused, suggested that the body had been disinterred from the chapel graveyard by the bombing and was actually that of a Victorian parishioner. Lawton had visited the British Museum and other archives to trace the history of the chapel grounds and had found evidence that seventeenth-century Dissenters may have buried their dead under part of the land now occupied by the chapel. But there was no evidence that any graves were near the cellar. Lawton then suggested that the effects of the blast might be responsible for the dismemberment of the body, and that Rachel Dobkin might have died as a result of being propelled by an exploding bomb into a kerb or a piece of masonry, or from a tiny bomb splinter passing into her neck and crushing her voice box. In each instance pathologist Keith Simpson stood by his evidence and emphasised the medical authority of his experience in over 11,000 cases.[39]

The prosecution did not present any theory about how Rachel got to Kennington Lane, whether she went of her own accord to press Harry for money or a reunion, or whether he enticed her there. No bloodstains were found in the cellar or next door, and some time must have been taken to dismember her body. What happened to the other parts of the body also remained a mystery. Instead of developing a plausible theory of how the murder was carried out, the prosecution relied on the near impossibility of the body of Dobkin's wife ending up buried in a disused cellar next door to where he was a night watchman, so far from where she was last seen in Dalston.

The jury took only twenty minutes to come back with the verdict: guilty of murder with no recommendation for mercy. Dobkin then read a statement accusing the police of having fabricated his case: 'I have something to say that this charge against me is very poorly invented, and that is why I do not like giving evidence against the police, but I claim that this charge of murder, as I have mentioned, is simply invented by showing photographs.'[40] Dobkin had made other allegations of threats and intimidation against the police, including being left alone in Detective Hatton's office for an hour with threats that if he didn't confess to the murder of his wife, the detectives would hang him. Gordon Cummins had made similar allegations in almost exactly the same words. He told the judge that detectives had told him they had 'a noose around your neck'.[41] In the final police file report, DI Hatton assured the Superintendent that no violence or threats were made, and that 'to the last he remained what he had always been, an arrogant and persistent liar'.[42] It was certainly a change in tone from the missing person's inquiry, when the police had taken Dobkin's word over Polly Dubinski's. The Metropolitan Police's dismissal of Dubinski's claims was part of a long history of discrimination against women, which included coercing and intimidating female suspects.[43]

Dobkin appealed his conviction on 12 January 1943 but lost. From prison, he wrote scores of letters defending himself, and the Baptist Chapel minister Herbert Burgess became his unlikely champion. Burgess organised a petition for clemency that garnered 28 signatures from South London and wrote to the Home Secretary Herbert Morrison. The petition argued that the evidence was only circumstantial, and the proof of murder was not strong enough to hang a man. But it was all to no avail. Dobkin was executed at Wandsworth Prison on 27 January 1943, and Simpson himself conducted the post-mortem.[44]

After the war, Rachel and Harry's son Stanley returned to the East End and changed his last name to Britain. As the only nephew of the Dubinskis, he stayed close to his family. He lived with his aunts Polly and Mary and uncle Nathan in Bethnal Green until his marriage in 1951. He and his wife had two children and lived into their eighties.

During the war, British censorship controlled how ruins were shown to the public. Conscious that showing too much damage might call into question Britain's survival, the censors carefully edited images and descriptions of bomb damage. Only in literary representations could the deep anxiety caused by London's ruins be expressed. Fiction like Graham Greene's *The Ministry of Fear* (1943) or Elizabeth Bowen's short story 'The Demon Lover' (1941) expressed the sense of menace in bomb-scarred London, haunted by malevolent ghosts and sinister spies.

But the real menace was much more prosaic. During the Blitz, when Londoners flocked to shelters, they were vulnerable to death from enemy planes and to thefts and petty violence. Once the bombers had retreated, leaving behind swathes of bombed houses and pockets of empty shelters, people had more to fear from the murderous impulses of their fellow Londoners. The deaths of Maple Church and Rachel Dobkin show how the secrecy of these dark spaces helped to hide murders, and shield murderers.

In the years after the war, bombsites and empty shelters remained for years, reminders of the war's destruction. Freed from their role in wartime propaganda, British filmmakers used London's ruins as back-drops for a new postwar criminality. In films like *Hue and Cry* (1947), *Good-time Girl* (1948) and *They Made Me a Fugitive* (1947), bombsites were used as hiding places for criminal gangs, postwar deserters and black marketeers. The reality was even darker. In 1947, the body of a newborn baby was found in a derelict Anderson shelter in Hounslow, West London, in a lot where the house had been destroyed by bombs. In 1948, two more newborn bodies were found, one on a bombsite in

Shepherd Street, Mayfair, and one on the windowsill of a bombed house in Islington.

It wasn't only babies, but women and children as well. In 1948, the body of thirty-one-year-old Edith Dorland was found with head injuries in a bombsite at Mint Street, Southwark. She was the mother of three young children, living with them and her husband in the Newington Institution 'Rest Centre', a former workhouse that had been converted into rooms for the postwar homeless. Her knitted purse with money in it was found nearby. The body of five-year-old Eileen Lockart was found that same year in the basement of a bombed-out building in Finsbury, 3 miles from her home in Bow. None of these murders were ever solved.[45] The bombsites gave up their dead, but not their secrets.

CHAPTER 3

PUBS AND CLUBS

Little Hubby [Harry Distleman] was really devoted to his wife and family and was inordinately proud of his kiddies. He carried their photographs around with him and was eager to show them to his friends and acquaintances. He spent as much time at home as he possibly could. You see, [pointing to the mantel shelf and sideboard] the room is full of photographs he took of the kiddies.

Relative of Harry Distleman to a *Holloway Press* reporter,
9 May 1941[1]

During the war, pubs, clubs, theatres and other places of entertainment offered a respite from the darkness and rubble of London's streets. The lights, company, music and drinks helped to distract people from the anxiety and fear they felt in the face of bombing raids, family separations and the battles yet to come. The West End, which had drawn pleasure-seeking crowds since the eighteenth century, was filled with people driven by an intense, and sometimes reckless, search for pleasure. As typist Vivienne Hall wrote in her wartime diary, the streets were as crowded as ever: 'people jostling each other in good-humoured tolerance and everyone determined to have a good time, despite the fate hanging over us'.[2]

With newcomers from Allied nations and armies pouring into the city, by 1941 London nightlife was in full swing again. From humble pubs to the Streatham Locarno Dance Hall to glamorous night clubs like the Café de Paris, people wanted to drink, dance, be in company and forget their worries, even if only for a few hours. Dance halls were especially popular as they were fun, colourful, brightly lit and cheap. Mecca's Paramount Dance Hall on Tottenham Court Road had a 9-foot wall of sandbags built around its entrance, and the manager was also the local air-raid warden. After the evening dancing session, up to 1,000 people could shelter all night, and even rent a bunk for a shilling.[3]

Nightlife in wartime London centred around Piccadilly Circus and radiated outwards. Although the advertising signs were not lit, and the famous statue of Eros holding his bow was boarded up to protect it from bombs, visitors milled around and passed the time sitting on its steps. Male and female prostitutes looked for clients, and the streets around bustled with pubs, restaurants and theatres. East of Piccadilly was Covent Garden, home since the eighteenth century to a huge fruit and vegetable market which operated from midnight until noon, and after dark to taverns, pubs, theatres and houses of prostitution. To the north of Piccadilly was Soho, another eighteenth-century neighbourhood known for its seedy nightlife and its vibrant immigrant community.

The dark and treacherous streets led Londoners to indoor places of entertainment that could offer lights, colour, sociability and usually drinks. Alcohol was the lubricant of the wartime West End social scene, and places selling it did a brisk business. Spirits and wine were hit by import shortages during the war, but beer was still available and enormously popular. During the war its consumption rose by a quarter, although it was watered down in most places to meet demand. Rising wages for women and working-class men, and the presence of soldiers on leave in the capital, kept the taps flowing.[4]

Pubs and nightclubs catered especially to male patrons, although not always. Maple Church, who was found strangled in a bombed-out house, had a stomach full of beer. Peggy Richards, also known as Margaret MacArthur, had been drinking in the Hero of Waterloo Public House with Canadian soldiers shortly before she was thrown off the unfinished Waterloo Bridge. The relaxation of licensing hours in the West End after 19 April allowed some venues to serve liquor until 2 a.m., including restaurants like Maison Lyons Corner House.[5] The war also saw the mushroom growth of new drinking establishments: unlicensed 'bottle parties' and special 'clubs' preying on naïve servicemen who paid exorbitant amounts to sip watered-down beer with hostesses who tried to get them to empty their wallets as fast as possible.[6]

As meeting places where alcohol and wartime anonymity lowered inhibitions, pubs and clubs saw higher levels of violence during the war, and the death of two men in 1940 and 1941. Morris Sholman, a veteran of the Great War who had been working with his brother in a pub in Covent Garden, was killed in a botched robbery by a Canadian deserter who wanted money to run away with his girlfriend. Harry Distleman, a former Soho club manager with a lengthy criminal record, was knifed in a gang fight in a billiards club by rival Antonio Mancini. Their deaths point to a moment in the war in which gangs still fought with broken billiard cues and knives, while an increasing number of servicemen with guns were getting violent.

COVENT GARDEN

The Coach and Horses pub in Covent Garden was no wartime fly-by-night. Nestled between the Theatre Royal and the Royal Opera House at 42 Wellington Street, it had been serving customers since the eighteenth century, and it survives to the present day. It was divided into two rooms with separate entrances: a saloon bar on one side with a few more comforts, and a public bar on the other. Between the two rooms was a large two-sided bar with metal and glass screens and shelves for the alcohol and glasses. The barman stood in between and served both sides. The screens between the bars could be closed for privacy.

The rooms had wooden wainscoting and a coffered ceiling. Colourful propaganda posters were tacked up next to the framed prints – one on the public side exhorting men to join first-aid parties: 'A Real Man's Job', and on the other side warning drinkers: 'Don't Help the Enemy! Careless Talk May Give Away Vital Secrets'. From the saloon bar, steps led down to the basement storage and toilet, and upstairs to the private rooms.

The Coach and Horses was perfectly situated to attract drinkers at various times of day, serving market porters and other workers from Covent Garden in the morning and theatre patrons in the evenings. It was also steps away from Bow Street Police Station and Magistrates' Court building, which dealt with the local petty criminals, as well as high-profile committals for the Old Bailey, including Oscar Wilde, Dr Crippen and, later, the Kray twins. Witnesses, complainants, police or those defendants lucky enough to be acquitted were only steps away from a pint. It was also a four-minute walk to the headquarters of the Canadian Provost Corps in Henrietta Street, on the fringe of Covent Garden. Hundreds of British, Canadian and other soldiers were billeted near the area.

Although some theatres did continue to perform in wartime, the drinkers in the Coach and Horses in 1940 were less likely to be theatregoers than in years past. The Theatre Royal next door had been closed since 1925 and was being used by Greene King to store their beer barrels. Across the street the Royal Opera House was leased for the duration of the war as a Mecca Dance Hall, one of the most popular wartime venues in London.[7] When all places of public entertainment were initially closed at the outbreak of war in 1939, some theatres sent their troupes on tour in less dangerous areas or leased their premises as shelters or first-aid stations.

Only gradually did theatres reopen in London, and often only for matinees or early evening performances until the worst raids of the Blitz had passed.[8] Trade journals like *Theatre World* commented somewhat snidely in October 1940 that due to the Blitz: 'The choice of the

Londoner is now restricted to the delights of the Revudeville at the Windmill and the lunch-time ballet hour at the Arts Theatre Club, to which must be added the brave venture of Shakespeare at the Vaudeville [in the Strand] – matinées only.'[9] Only the Windmill, in Great Windmill Street off Piccadilly Circus, could proudly boast that they were the only theatre which had never closed. Their 'Revudeville' was a series of continuous variety acts staged from 2 p.m. to 11 p.m., whose highlight was nude 'tableaux vivants'. The theatre manager was allowed to bend the strict rules forbidding on-stage nudity by convincing the Lord Chamberlain that the motionless nude dancers were no different from the classical statues that filled museums and galleries. The 'if it moves, it's rude' rule was further bent by stagehands periodically letting a mouse loose on the stage, making the nude dancers scream and run. The Windmill and the Mecca were two of the most popular venues for soldiers on leave, and the Coach and Horses was within easy walking distance.

MORRIS SHOLMAN

The Coach and Horses' licence had been owned by Mrs Dinah, known as Daisy Phillips since 1925. She and her husband Hyam, known as Harry, worked the bar with Daisy's nephew David, and all three lived upstairs. When the war broke out, the Phillipses moved to the Strand Palace Hotel and visited the pub during the day. David's brother, Morris Sholman, was out of work, so they hired him to work with David. David, Morris, his new wife Dorothy, known as Dolly, and the maid, Miss Julia O'Keefe, lived in rooms upstairs.

The Sholmans were from a tight-knit Jewish family. Their father, Jacob, known as Jack, immigrated to London from Russia in the 1890s and married Rosetta Martin (Daisy Phillips's sister) from Bethnal Green. They had three children in London before moving to Queens, New York in 1905 to move in with Jack's half-brother Harold. They all lived together at 229 Home Street, in the Bronx: Harold with his wife and five children, Jack and Rose with their three children, including eleven-year-old Morris, and Rose's younger brother Aaron. Harold kept a store and Jack was a baker.[10] Five years later, the family had moved to 115 Orchard (St) in Queens, with a new younger sister. Jack now described himself as a peddler, and sixteen-year-old Morris was a shipping clerk.

Morris joined the Middlesex Regiment (Duke of Cambridge's Own) in 1917 when he turned eighteen. He served in the 19th Battalion as a private and served in France and Italy.[11] He was awarded a British War Medal and Victory Medal for service in a theatre of war.[12] After the war, Morris moved back to London and lived in a Victorian terraced house at 75 Blantyre Street, Chelsea.[13] His brother David lived there with him from the mid-1920s through the 1930s, and when he and his brother moved out, their parents moved in.

In 1938, Morris was living with widow Dorothy Manno and her nineteen-year-old son Harry in Battersea at 16 Watford Villas. She was using the name Sholman, although they were not married. In the 1939 Register, Morris is listed as a barman and Dorothy as a bookkeeper. Her son Harry was an operator at BBC Television, who later joined the Number 12 Commando D Troop and worked for the BBC Broadcasting unit in the British Army of the Rhine.[14] Morris and Dorothy officially married in July 1940.

During nights of heavy raids, the four occupants of the Coach and Horses slept in a nearby shelter – the basement of Page's at the corner of Wellington Street and York Street. Although Wellington Street and Covent Garden market itself was not damaged during the Blitz, the surrounding area was fairly heavily hit, with high-explosive bombs falling directly behind, on Catherine Street, and in the streets to the north and south. On the night of 19/20 December, the sirens were quiet, and the Sholmans and Julia O'Keefe slept in their beds.

They didn't sleep late: the Coach and Horses had an early morning licence from 5 a.m. to 9 a.m. that let them serve the market porters and local workers. A large sign on the wall alerted any visitors to the fact that 'Men in uniform of His Majesty's forces will not be served with refreshments between the hours of 5 a.m. to 9 a.m.'.

At 5.10 a.m., hours before the sun rose, the Sholman brothers unlocked the doors and brought up the spirits from the basement to place on the bar shelves. David put the regular float of £20 in change near the till. Morris went behind the bar and David carried the empty liquor boxes back down to the cellar. As David went towards the stairs, he saw the first customer of the day come into the public bar. John Anderson was a regular, who came in for a pint or two every morning before work. He was a fifty-four-year-old lift attendant at the Parker Street Lodging House, the first London County Council model lodging for men, which opened in 1893 and catered for hundreds of poor working men.[15] Although Dorothy and David did not know Anderson's name, they recognised him by his unique appearance – he only had one arm.

John Anderson asked Morris for a pint of ale and paid for it with a £1 note. Morris made some comment about the dirty condition of the note, and Anderson sat down to have his drink on a chair in the public bar. After a few minutes, Anderson heard the door open to the saloon bar and a man walk in.

He heard the man say, 'Hands up! Paper money!' Anderson, alarmed, stood up to look across the bars into the saloon and saw a medium-height man wearing khaki with a muffler wrapped around his head. He saw Morris with his hands in the air, but he didn't hear him say anything. Then he heard two loud gun shots in quick succession. He dived behind the bar for cover, then immediately got back up in time to see Morris lying on his back in a pool of blood on the floor behind the bars, and the other man running out the door of the saloon bar.

Anderson acted bravely: 'I ran out of the public house into the street which was in total darkness. I could not see or hear the man then. I shouted for Police and a Policeman came and went into the saloon bar with me. I did not look over at the dead man anymore.' Anderson told police that he did not notice if the robber had any accent, and because he was wrapped in a muffler, he would not be able to recognise him again. He also had not seen if the revolver was military issue: 'I only saw it glisten in the light.'

At that moment, Dorothy Sholman had been coming down the stairs with two cups of tea for Morris and David. When she heard the shots, she was frightened, and froze. Julia O'Keefe also heard the shots from her room and ran downstairs, pushing past Dorothy, at the same moment that David was running up the basement stairs to help his brother. He heard John Anderson outside: 'The man with one arm was

5. *Interior of the Coach and Horses pub, Covent Garden, 1940.*

shouting for help. Morry was on the floor bleeding from the front of his neck. I tore his collar off and called "Morry, Morry." He did not speak.' Morris was already dead.

By this time, Dorothy had made it into the bar, where she saw a bullet on the floor, picked it up and put it on the bar counter. Julia ran back upstairs to telephone Mr and Mrs Phillips at the Strand Hotel, and Anderson came back with a War Reserve policeman attached to the Bow Street station. Within a few minutes, the policeman had sent to Bow Street Police Station for reinforcements. A doctor was finally called, who pronounced life extinct. The second bullet was found on a shelf of the public bar.

No one in the family had seen the robber, and no money had been taken from the till. The entire incident had taken only a minute and had left very few leads. David told police: 'I can't think why anyone should have done this. I have no enemies and as far as I know neither has Morry. He was a quiet man. None of us usually go out of the house in our spare time.'

With the only clue to the shooter being that he was a 'man in khaki', Divisional Detective (DD) Inspector Rudkin and Inspector Capstick of E Division of the Metropolitan Police decided to enlist the help of the local depots of military police. There were hundreds of Canadian and British soldiers billeted near Covent Garden, in London on leave or passing through Charing Cross or Waterloo Stations. The Metropolitan Police's job was made more complex by the fact that British military men were officially under the jurisdiction of the Corps of Military Police (CMP), and Canadian military men were policed by the Canadian Provost Corps.[16] American forces would also have their own military police in place from 1941. The military and civilian forces had to find ways to work together to investigate crimes that affected civilians and trace soldiers who were absent without leave.[17] When the crimes involved murder, the suspect was most often turned over to British civilian criminal courts.

At the same time that the police were arriving at the Coach and Horses, Lance-Corporal John Westley Osbourne of the Canadian

Provost Corps was on night duty at the headquarters on Henrietta Street. At 5.45 a.m. he got a phone call from his friend and fellow soldier James Caie Forbes McCallum.

'Is that you Ossy?'

'Yes, is that you, Mac?'

He answered, 'Yes, can you come up and see me; I'm at Bloomsbury Square, Southampton Row.'

Osbourne asked Sergeant Stewart for permission to leave the station, which was first refused. Only when Osbourne told him that 'McCallum says that it is imperative that he sees me right away and he is crying' did the sergeant finally tell him to 'keep out of trouble' and go to see McCallum. Osbourne returned to the phone, and they arranged to meet at the corner of Bloomsbury Way and Southampton Row.

Osbourne was an older man, who had served in the First World War and had been in the Canadian Army since 1936. He had been stationed in London since August 1940, along with over 23,000 troops of the Canadian Army in the UK. Their role in the war was not clear: a plan to defend Norway was cancelled, they were not able to join the British Expeditionary Force in France, and the first Canadian First Infantry Brigade, which landed in Brest in June 1940, was immediately withdrawn when the French government requested an armistice with Germany. With little to do, Canadian soldiers had a reputation for hard drinking and lawlessness. They went on rampages in Brighton and other southern towns and were involved in assaults, robberies and other violent crimes.

Osbourne had been a friend to the new recruits, many of whom were away from home for the first time: 'I was acting as a friend and advisor to many of the younger men and they came to me with their troubles.' He was particularly drawn to McCallum, who was only twenty years old and, along with his brother who was also in the Canadian Army, supported his widowed mother in Montreal.

McCallum was well liked and known as a hard worker but had recently been troubled and distracted. He had asked Osbourne to lend him money, and Osbourne had been with him in the Canadian Beaver Club two days before when McCallum got a telegram from his mother. The Beaver Club, next to Canada House in Trafalgar Square, was a place for Canadian soldiers to get meals, supplies, mail and help finding billets in London.[18] McCallum had been greatly upset by the telegram, and Osbourne had spent the evening with him buying him drinks in a nearby pub and trying to cheer him up.

When Osbourne got to Southampton Row, McCallum was standing near the phone booth. Osbourne asked him, 'Hello Mac, what's the trouble, has someone been knocking you around?'

McCallum answered, 'No, it's worse than that, I've shot myself.' His left arm was hanging down, with his hand in the pocket of his greatcoat and his sleeve bloodied. Osbourne took him to his own room, number 14 at the Bedford Road Hostel, in Bedford Place. There he took McCallum's service weapon, a .455 Smith & Wesson revolver, took out two spent cartridges and put it on a shelf, helped him off with his coat and treated his arm. There were two bullet wounds in the left arm, one on the inside of the arm, and one on the outside, near the wrist.

Osbourne cleaned the wounds, bandaged them with a field dressing and helped McCallum back on with his coat. At 6.40 a.m. the two men left the room and started walking towards Covent Garden. They crossed over Bloomsbury Square and onto High Holborn towards Drury Lane. Osbourne was not pressing for an explanation, but McCallum finally blurted out a kind of confession: 'I've always been with the law, Ossy, but this time I've shot against the law.'

Osbourne asked him, 'What have you done?'

'I've shot a man high.'

'Is it serious?'

'I don't think so.'

'Where did all this happen?'

'Not a minute and a half from Bow Street.'

Osbourne didn't press him for more details but told him to go and see a doctor. McCallum refused but asked Osbourne to come to see him later. They separated at Covent Garden, and McCallum went back to the cheap room he was renting at the Craven Street Hotel, while Osbourne returned to duty at the Canadian Provost Corps in Henrietta Street.

A few minutes after Osbourne got back, at about 7 a.m., a plain-clothes police officer came into the office and announced that a murder had been committed in a Covent Garden public house. He asked for help identifying any Canadian soldiers who were absent without leave or in public houses that morning. The same request was made to the Provost Corps of Military Police at Great Scotland Yard. Osbourne did not at first connect this news with what he had been told by McCallum.

At 7.30 a.m., Osbourne and other military policemen, under the direction of Inspector Capstick, went around public houses in Covent Garden to check on the men in them. In all, seventeen soldiers were detained and questioned, then taken to military authorities. Osbourne was directed to take one of the men to Waterloo Station.

When he retuned, it was 9 a.m. and he signed off duty. By this time, he was remembering McCallum's confession: 'It was not until about 9 am when I was thinking over the events of the morning I recalled his statement of about a minute and a half from Bow Street that I connected him with the murder.' He lingered at the station for a few minutes but: 'There was not a commissioned officer in the place, and I walked out to think the matter over. Eventually I decided to see Detective Inspector Capstick.'

Osbourne walked to Bow Street Police Station and found Capstick, and together they went to the Craven Street Hotel. McCallum was in bed with his nineteen-year-old girlfriend, Irene Turnbull. Osbourne turned to McCallum and said, 'The man is dead, Jimmy. This is Inspector Capstick.' MaCallum answered dazedly, 'Dead?' Irene then began pleading with Osbourne, although he didn't say what for, and he missed the next things that were said. Within a few minutes, the three men went to Osbourne's billet to get the gun and cartridges. The khaki scarf that Anderson had seen was actually a balaclava and had been issued to Canadian soldiers as a comfort item on the ocean journey. McCallum had thrown it away as he ran from the Coach and Horses.

McCallum was arrested and taken to Bow Street Police Station. He admitted the shooting but claimed he had been out all night drinking and only vaguely remembered going into the Coach and Horses. He told Capstick that he thought someone had tried to take his gun away: 'I think I had it out of the holster and was holding it. The man in the pub was trying to take the gun from me and during the struggle the gun went off and hit me in the arm.' This evidence was contradicted by his girlfriend, who said he had spent the night with her and left early in the morning 'to borrow money from a friend' and by Osbourne and the doctor who treated his arm that morning, who said he was sober. John Anderson had seen or heard no struggle in the pub and had seen Morris Sholman with his hands raised and unmoving. Anyone standing behind the saloon bar would also be protected by the counter and the glass screens. Two water bottles on the bar were not disturbed.

McCallum had been driven to such inept desperation because he needed money to get married. He had met Irene Turnbull in October. She was an orphan living in London and working as a waitress. They had moved into the Craven Street Hotel and McCallum had begun supporting her. He was always short of cash and had borrowed money from all his friends. He had been so distracted that he was demoted from Corporal to Acting Lance Corporal in November.

In December, Irene had told him she was pregnant. He had requested permission from the Canadian Army to marry. They had also needed money to pay their mounting hotel and living debts, as Irene told police: 'We were to have been married on 18 December, but we experienced some money difficulties and were awaiting a letter from Jimmy's mother.' On the morning of 18 December, McCallum had received a telegram from his mother to the Beaver Club. 'As a result, we did not get married on 18 December. Jimmy wanted to get married on the 19th of December, but I would not agree and the wedding was postponed until January 1941.' She told police that he had told her that morning that he was going to borrow money from a friend. He had said as he left, 'I won't be long,' but he had looked worried. He had returned with a bandaged arm and a bloody coat, around 7 a.m., and she had put him to bed: 'I must have fainted because the next thing I know the police came and took Jimmy away.'

The telegram McCallum's mother had sent to the Beaver Club opposed the marriage absolutely: 'Ridiculous Idea Stop Don't Not During War Seems Very Thoughtless to Me I Need Your Help signed Mrs. McCallum.' Mrs McCallum was a widow living in Verdun, Quebec, who depended on her sons' military allowances. She had moved with her husband and young James from Scotland to Montreal in 1922, but in 1931, her husband had died, leaving her with James and a younger brother. She had opened a boarding house, but it had failed, and she had resorted to cleaning offices. Her sons had volunteered for the Canadian Army the day after war was declared; James had become a military policeman in London, and the younger son, John, had been stationed at Aldershot. James had been seen as a sober and industrious soldier and had been quickly promoted to Corporal.

The police report traces all James's subsequent troubles to his having met Irene Turnbull: 'She is of very strange behaviour and is probably mentally deficient, or an extremely cunning "gold digger".' She tried to disappear after James's arrest, but police found her and put her in lodgings where she could be supervised until the Director of Public Prosecutions decided he didn't need her evidence. Then she was found employment in the chamber of the defence counsel C.G.L. Du Cann, until the day he asked her to give evidence for the defence. Then she disappeared until a month after the trial, when she was admitted to Charing Cross Hospital with pyelitis of pregnancy. With no evidence proffered, the police notes dismiss her as a 'prostitute' and her actions as a 'mild form of blackmail'. Although Irene was suspected of no crime, her information was forwarded to Superintendent Dorothy Peto of Metropolitan Police Division A4, the Women's Division, which combined welfare and policing.

McCallum's trial for murder took place at the Central Criminal Court, from 11 February to 13 February. He pleaded not guilty by reason of insanity. His defence was that a bomb had exploded 100 yards from him in Henrietta Street in October, and that since then he had suffered badly with nerves. He had seen the company doctor, Captain Conn, and been prescribed a tonic. This medical evidence was rebutted by Dr Grierson of Brixton Prison, who found no evidence for insanity. The jury retired but returned with two questions. John Anderson was recalled, to answer that he was not hard of hearing and had heard 'hands up, paper money', and Captain Osbourne was recalled to demonstrate the shooting of a service revolver, telling the jury that Canadians were not trained to rest the gun on their left arm.[19]

The jury eventually returned a guilty verdict with a strong recommendation to mercy. McCallum's youth, the pressure of money worries and the strain of the war and the fact that the shooting was almost certainly accidental likely influenced their decision. The entry and exit wounds on his left arm suggested that he had shot himself when trying to swing the glass screen to get at the cash register behind the bar or to cover Sholman. If so, then the second fatal shot may have been caused involuntarily by his reaction to his wound. It would also have been impolitic to hang a Canadian soldier tried under British civilian law.

Two weeks later, McCallum's death sentence was commuted to penal servitude for life. It was too late for Mrs McCallum. She died suddenly in Montreal, the morning her son was reprieved, before she got the news. McCallum was transferred to Camp Hill prison in Newport, Isle of Wight. There he worked and waited out his sentence. Meanwhile, public opinion about the disruptive behaviour of Canadians in England was transformed by their bravery in the ill-fated Dieppe Raid in August 1942. Of an attacking force of 6,000 men, 5,000 of whom were Canadian, half were killed or taken prisoner in the attempted landing.[20]

During his years in prison, James was visited by his brother John McCallum, who served in the Royal Canadian Army Service Corps, then the 1st Canadian Parachute Battalion, every two or three months. A letter that James wrote to John, who he called Russell, still survives in McCallum's prison file. Dated 26 June 1944, in it he writes that he has no idea where his brother is, but to write as soon as possible with any news. He seems quite despondent: 'Everything here is just as usual "rotten to the core" and although I have been here some time, I still cannot understand what kind of people are in here. Some, the court martials, are fairly decent, but of the others the majority is reversed. So roll on the end of the war and let us get back to Canada . . . Your loving brother, Jimmie.'[21] A 1945 report from the Prison Governor to the High Commissioner of Canada gave a more optimistic report on McCallum's state of mind. McCallum was learning to cook and hoping to qualify as a cook in the Merchant Navy on release. The governor reported that McCallum was industrious, showed genuine repentance and no bitterness over his sentence or imprisonment, 'realising his sentence is a just one'.

From 1945, McCallum was also visited by Mrs Londsdale of the Women's Voluntary Service Club, Southampton. She remembered him from the London Blitz as he used to come into the St Martin's in the Field Canteen and 'was very popular with us all as he always behaved so very well and seemed so young for such a responsible job as policeman'. In her letter to the prison governor, she recalled how she had offered to speak at his trial but had been told that all that could be done for McCallum was being done. She wanted to visit him to remind him of happier times and came to see him seven times.

In June 1946, he was released from prison. He was handed over to the Canadian military for repatriation to Canada, with no further conditions on his release if he did not return to the UK.[22] His brother went on to be a successful journalist in China and Canada and to teach journalism at Ryerson, but James died young in 1971.[23] He was buried in the Cimetière Mont-Royal, close to his mother.

McCallum's gun may have gone off accidentally, but Sholman's death showed the new deadliness to assaults and robberies in the capital. With so many soldiers and deserters in London, many of whom had personal firearms, the potential for deadly violence was much greater. For example, a thirty-one-year-old man named Philip Ward who had been called up and trained as a gunner in the army went on a shooting spree in 1941. Ward had ordered a double-barrelled shotgun from a London firm in January. On 8 November, he was granted seven days' leave, and on 11 November, he drove a rented car to the homes of members of the Chiswick Junior Conservative Club who had asked him to leave four years before.[24] He rang their bells and shot them at close range as they came out, then drove away. He shot eight people and killed three before the police ran him off the road in Watford, covering him with a rifle as they pulled him from the driver's seat.[25] When he was brought to court to face murder charges, Ward was restless, smiling and disruptive. A few weeks later, the medical officer of Brixton Prison told the court that Ward was too ill to stand trial. He was suffering from paranoid schizophrenia and had been for the past ten years. Ward was declared unfit to plead and confined to an asylum. But the unasked question was surely: how had a man with such a severe mental illness become responsible for artillery systems in the army? And how many more unstable men would use their military weapons training against others?

SOHO

A ten-minute walk from Covent Garden, across Leicester Square and north of Piccadilly Circus, was another distinctive London neighbourhood troubled by wartime violence. Soho had for years been the cosmopolitan home of recent immigrants, first French, then Italian, Greek and Eastern European.[26] The area was less fashionable than other West End districts, and its inhabitants crowded into streetscapes which were essentially unchanged since the seventeenth century. Soho's main industries were to offer its exoticism to Londoners – those looking for foreign food, cheap fashion in the Berwick Street market and shops, and Soho's famous nightlife of dancing, music and sex.[27] By the 1930s, there were more than fifty cabarets and dance clubs in Soho, which catered to all tastes.[28] The popularity of jazz clubs, which drew African American and West Indian musicians and clientele, added to the cosmopolitan mix. Soho was also known for its commercialised sex. Male and female sex workers walked the streets, or worked in brothels, theatres, restaurants and nightclubs. It was a highly profitable local business, intertwined with many other more 'respectable' ones. For instance, the upscale Café Royal (at the junction of Air, Glasshouse and Regent streets in Soho) was used by prostitutes seeking clients, who would pay waiters for referrals.[29] Soho, more than any other London neighbourhood, transformed itself after dark, from a 'grubby, foreign daytime scene' into streets of bohemian nightspots.[30] The construction of mass-market leisure along Soho's edges, such as a Lyons' Corner House on Coventry Street, a Maison Lyons on Shaftesbury Avenue, the Astoria Dance Hall and Cinema on Charing Cross Road, and Marks and Spencer's on Oxford Street, also helped to draw more people into Soho.

The outbreak of war and the temporary closing of entertainment venues dampened the enthusiasm for nightlife for a few months, but Soho pubs and nightclubs quickly filled again in the summer of 1940. After the fall of France in the summer of 1940, Soho became home to even more exiled European nationals. German and Austrian refugees were joined by Free French and Polish soldiers and people working for exiled Allied governments or the BBC Foreign Service at nearby Broadcasting House.[31] Soho was also a favourite haunt for soldiers on leave, first British and Commonwealth soldiers, and later American GIs, both white and Black.

But Soho was not a utopia, and local and international tensions exploded in race riots and gang violence during the war. On 14 June 1940, a day after Mussolini declared war on Britain and the Allies, anti-Italian violence broke out in Soho, as well as in other Italian neighbourhoods in Edinburgh, Glasgow, Cardiff and Newcastle. Curious onlookers crowded the narrow streets and threw stones at premises they believed were Italian-owned. They watched as police began arresting some of London's 7,000 Italians, under orders from Churchill to 'Collar the Lot!'[32] Within hours, police had detained 600 Italian and British-born Italian men in London on Scotland Yard's 'blacklist', suspected to be fascists, and sent them to internment camps. Newspapers reported that overnight, posters reading 'British Owned', 'Under British Management' and 'British Staff Here' 'appeared almost magically on the windows of many Soho shops during the day'.[33] Even the Spaghetti House in Old Compton Street declared itself to be 'a British restaurant'.[34]

Soho was also the central London neighbourhood most associated with organised prostitution and gang violence. The magazine *John Bull* went so far as to call it 'Murder Land' in 1936: 'To the men who pore over crime statistics at Scotland Yard, Soho is the place which for its area has a worse record for blood and violence and for the darker forms of crime than any other in Great Britain. Decent, hardworking, clean-living foreigners, as good citizens as any Briton, living cheek by jowl with the scum of Continental gutters. And now the mixture is getting a bit too strong for anybody's taste.'

Crowded in Soho were over 300 'clubs', run by men with criminal records and protected by criminal gangs. Some of the gangs were remnants 'of those dangerous race[course] gangs which were broken up by the police some years ago. Some of the worst, the foreign elements, in these gangs have got together again, this time to prey on night club proprietors instead of bookmakers.'[35]

Gangs had been part of London life since at least the 1880s. At horse and greyhound racetracks in London and South East England, gang members set up gambling pitches, protected bookmakers from theft and violence from other gangs, pickpocketed wallets from the crowd and fought other gangs. Gangs were also involved in running illegal West End nightclubs and gambling dens, and in protection rackets to which bottle parties, clubs, public houses, cafés and shops had to pay protection money or risk being attacked or informed on to the police.

Gang violence was loosely associated with territories, or sets of territories, but loyalties to family, ethnic community and neighbourhood were also important.[36] Unlike the impression given by the media that London's gangs were predominantly Italian or 'the scum of continental gutters',[37] gangs in London were more mixed, including English, Irish and Jewish Londoners, as well as Italians. And unlike media portrayals of American gangs, London gangsters rarely used guns in this period but confined themselves to knives, boots and razors as weapons.[38]

Billy Hill, a London gang leader from the late 1920s, described in his autobiography how his trademark was to slice an X or a V across a victim's cheek: 'They remember that, and wherever you saw anyone wearing one you knew it was Billy Hill who had done it. But I never chivvied anyone unless I had to. There's no point cutting up people if it's not necessary . . . I was always careful to draw the knife down the face, never across or upwards. Always down. So that if the knife slips it don't cut an artery. After all, chivving is chivving, but cutting an artery is murder. Only mugs do murder.'[39] During the war, he switched to carving a V for Victory into victims' faces.[40]

Marking with the knife was part of wider gang culture in London. *Daily Mail* crime reporter Arthur Tietjen wrote that 'Charing Cross Hospital must surely employ a special staff of medical seamsters to deal with the gaping wounds made by these weapons'. According to him, recipients were 'stoics well trained in silence'. One man had ninety-nine stiches from ear to ear, and all he had to say was, 'The bastards would do it when I've got on my new suit!'[41]

No one gang dominated Soho during the interwar or wartime period. Instead, competing factions rose, fought and fell as their members were arrested. The main gangs with interests in Soho in the 1930s and 1940s were the Whitechapel-based Yiddisher gang, including Jack 'Spot' Comer, the Hoxton mob, based in Soho, led by Jimmy Spinks, and the Clerkenwell Gang, also known as the Italian Mob.[42] In the 1920s and 1930s they were dominated by Charles 'Derby' Sabini and his brothers, and other associates from the Anglo-Italian community, including Antonio Mancini.[43]

The conditions of war opened new vistas of opportunity for London gangs. The blackout shielded their activities from police scrutiny, and forging food and petrol coupon books and identity papers for deserters gave them a new revenue stream. Gangs were also involved in the selling of black-market goods and large-scale organised thefts, even using ARP uniforms or vans disguised as ARP vehicles or ambulances.[44] Billy Hill, self-styled 'Boss of Britain's Underworld', waxed nostalgic about the war in his 1955 autobiography: 'Some day someone should write a treatise on Britain's wartime black market. It was the most fantastic side of civilian life in wartime. Make no mistake. It cost Britain millions of pounds. I didn't merely make use of the black market. I fed it.'[45]

The war also provided the police with a new method for breaking up gangs: internment. The six Sabini brothers, who had dominated Soho protection and gambling rackets and racecourse crime, were arrested and interned in June 1940 with other Italian-Britons, although their mother was English, their father was dead and they spoke very little Italian.

It was left to Antonio 'Babe' Mancini, a long-term Sabini man who had 'graduated through the police courts and obtained a degree in the Criminal Records Office files at Scotland Yard' to represent the gang's interest.[46] He had started his career as a bookmaker, before becoming a greyhound dealer in 1927.[47] He also had a less reputable career. In 1935, he was convicted of loitering at the all-tennis ground at Wimbledon and sentenced to three months' hard labour. Police detectives said they had seen him try to pick four pockets, 'but it was very difficult to catch a clever pickpocket'.[48] After this stint in prison, he tried to go back to greyhound racing, but his business collapsed after an import tax was placed on dogs from Ireland, and he was forced to sell his house and kennels. He was arrested again in 1938 after he stole a man's wallet at a Folkestone hotel. He had sprinkled toothpaste on his victim's clothes, then offered to clean his coat, pocketing the wallet as he took it off.[49] He had ten previous convictions for theft, and one for unlawful wounding.

Mancini was not interned with other Italian-Britons in the 1940s, although both of his parents were Italian and had immigrated to London in the 1880s. Antonio was born in Holborn, with two brothers and two sisters. His brother Gerald ran a newsstand outside Holborn station and in May 1940 had discovered and rescued a kidnapped baby who had been abandoned naked in a telephone kiosk in the station.[50] Antonio was married to Catherine Slaymaker, daughter of a Covent Garden porter, and they had two children. In the 1939 Register, they were listed at 114 Lamb's Conduit Street, and Mancini was described as a hairdresser (the job he had done in prison) and Catherine as a factory hand.[51]

By 1941, Mancini was the catering manager of a Soho club, the Palm Beach Bottle Club, at 37 Wardour Street. That address was home to a long succession of shady Soho nightclubs. In 1935 it was a jazz club called the Shim Sham Club, known as 'London's miniature Harlem'.[52] Like other Soho clubs, the Shim Sham tried to avoid liquor licensing regulations by running as a so-called bottle party. Bottle parties were an invention of the Bright Young Things of the 1920s for their private entertainments. In the 1930s, they became commercial ventures ranging from elegant nightclubs to dingy basement bars, in which customers signed order forms filled by local all-night wine merchants. Because it was legally a private party and the club did not own the liquor (as upheld by a court case in 1932), revellers could drink as late into the night as they wanted and avoid the strict licensing hours of 11.30 a.m.–3 p.m. and 5.30–10 p.m., Monday to Saturday, with even shorter hours on Sundays.[53]

The Shim Sham closed after a raid and reopened as Rainbow Roof, whose management was also charged with unlicensed dancing and music in 1936. As one club was forced to close, another would open. In 1939 there were between 200 and 300 bottle parties operating in the West End, mostly in Soho. The Public Morality Council of London had many stories of the wartime depravity of the clubs.[54] In one month, the seventeen-year-old hostess of a Soho bottle party was suspected of having a corrupting association with the owner, referred to disparagingly as 'a man of colour', Sir Ronald Hunter was called 'Sir Galahad' and attacked by another patron outside the Kit Kat Club at 4.45 a.m., and the hostess of another bottle party was found to be an approved school runaway of seventeen.[55]

In the spring of 1941, three clubs were operating at 37 Wardour Street. The Palm Beach Bottle Party, where Mancini worked, was in the basement, the Cosmo was on the ground floor and the West End Bridge and Billiards Club was on the top floor. The Billiards Club had a main room with five billiard tables, and a smaller room behind in which thirty to forty men would gamble or play games of chance such as faro and chemin de fer. Mancini was a member, as were men from another rival gang, the Yiddishers, including Albert 'Hubby' Distleman and his younger brother Harry 'Little Hubby' Distleman.

HARRY DISTLEMAN

Harry Distleman also had a long history of run-ins with the law. His first adult conviction was for stealing socks, aged twenty, then for stealing cloth, for which he was sentenced to nine months' hard labour.[56] He was also involved in gang violence: in 1927, aged twenty-two, he was charged with causing grievous bodily harm to three constables who had come between two rival gangs in a fight in Hackney.[57] Although he had lived in Camden Town since he was a child, he was associated with the East End Jewish gangs, and later with the Hoxton gang in Soho. Mancini and Distleman met in the mid-1920s, though where is not known: most likely at a racecourse, in a club or in prison.[58]

Harry was from a Russian Jewish family and had ten siblings, the oldest three born in Russia and the rest in the East End. His father had died in 1920, leaving his mother a widow with four children under fifteen, including Harry. She got by renting rooms at 199 Hampstead Road, steps away from where Maple Church would be found strangled in a bombed-out house in 1941.[59] His older brother Albert or Abel 'Hubby' Distleman described himself as a property dealer and was involved in several share-pushing scandals in the 1930s. He was also suspected by police to be involved in brothel-keeping in the West End. He told police in 1941 that he was not close with his brother and did not know his associates, except for their childhood friend Eddie Fletcher, but Harry's nickname 'Little Hubby' would suggest otherwise.

Harry Distleman and other Jewish gang members did not just fight rival gangs in the 1930s, they were also fighting the popular political fascist group, the British Union of Fascists. Sir Oswald Mosley, formerly a popular Conservative, then Labour, MP, formed the violently anti-semitic British Union of Fascists in 1932, and the Blackshirts were the paramilitary heavies that policed the rallies and attacked critics. In 1933, Harry was charged with assaulting Kay Fredericks, a self-described fascist. Fredericks had been leaving a restaurant with a friend in Shaftesbury Avenue when a crowd, shouting 'Down with Blackshirts!', started following them. According to Fredericks, 'They made a rush at us . . . and the prisoner struck me in the face, fracturing my cheek-bone.' Distleman was sent to prison for a month.[60] Fredericks had been attacked a few months prior to this, again while wearing a black shirt. The magistrate asked him, 'Why do you dress up like that?', to which Fredericks replied, 'We belong to the Fascist movement.' John Feigenbaum, one of two young Jewish men convicted of attacking him, when asked if he had any feelings against Blackshirts, replied, 'I think that they are unjust in that they would intimidate and persecute people because of their race.'[61]

According to former lawyer and crime historian James Morton, Antonio Mancini was also an antisemite. He showed his dislike of Jews in prison by taking advantage of his job in the kitchen to spit in their food.[62] According to Morton, one day in 1939, a young Jewish gang-ster, named Jack Comer, refused to eat the food. When he was sent to the prison barber, also Mancini, they fought, and Mancini lost. This won Cromer the respect of other gang members in prison and would launch his postwar career.

Distleman, like Mancini, also managed Soho clubs. He ran the jazz club The Nest on Kingly Street for four years from 1934. The Nest was one of several basement jazz clubs along the street where visiting black musicians played and socialised.[63] In the two years since then, according to his brother, he lived off savings and his winnings from betting on greyhounds and racehorses.[64] He had married Ivy Tilford in 1926, and they had three daughters, Shirley, Trinda and Delia. In 1941, they were living in a small flat in Cranleigh Houses, in Somers Town.

The roots of the fatal confrontation had begun ten days earlier. On 20 April, Harry's best friend Eddie 'Fair Hair' Fletcher and Joseph Franks of the Yiddisher Gang had got into a fight with the doorman of the Palm Beach Bottle Party and had been beaten up and banned from the club. The owner, Nicolo Carriolo, had told Mancini not to let Fletcher back in the club.[65]

On Thursday 1 May, Harry Distleman kissed his wife goodbye and told her he would not be late. At around midnight, he was playing pool with Eddie Fletcher and other members of the Hoxton gang in the Bridge and Billiards Club upstairs at 37 Wardour Street, when in walked

6. Interior of the Bridge and Billiards Club, 1941.

Joseph Collette, Harry Capocci and Albert 'Italian Al' Dimeo, then AWOL from the RAF. Fists, billiard balls and pool cues started flying.

The fight was personal, but also part of an organised tactic of gangs targeting each other's property and profits. The light shades above the tables were smashed and bottles and glass were strewn around.[66] Fletcher took another beating, and he and Harry retreated to the Charing Cross Hospital to have stitches. About half an hour later, at 3 a.m., they were back at the club, apparently to retrieve Fletcher's overcoat.

What happened next was never clearly established. According to Mancini, he had been working downstairs when the manager told him to go up and protect the Billiards Club from further damage. When he got there, Fletcher and Distleman were fighting Collette and Dimeo again, and Mancini tried to intervene. He went over to Fletcher and grabbed him by the shoulder, and he and Fletcher began fighting. Distleman came over to help his friend. He grabbed Mancini's shoulder, and punched him, while Fletcher came at Mancini with a raised chair. Mancini, assailed on both sides, drew out a dagger, and stabbed Distleman in the shoulder, and slashed Fletcher's wrist. Fletcher called out, 'He's knifed me boys!'[67]

Both were seriously wounded: Distleman's stab wound penetrated under the left armpit, dividing his axillary artery and the accompanying vein and leading to rapid internal hemorrhage.[68] Distleman staggered back, and lurched to the door of the club saying, 'I'm terribly hurt. He stabbed me in the heart. Babe's done it!'[69] As he stumbled down the stairs, he said to someone else: 'I am stabbed. I am stabbed. I am dying.' He died on the pavement in the doorway of the club.

Fletcher, whose left hand had been nearly severed, was taken back to Charing Cross Hospital. When the police saw Distleman's body, sprawled in the doorway, his pocketknife was lying open next to him, but how it got there was never explained. In his pockets were £31 in a wad of notes, three National Service (Armed Forces) identity cards and a red billiard ball, wrapped in a handkerchief.[70]

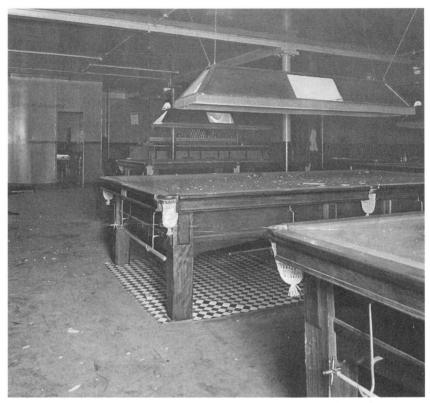

7. Interior of the Bridge and Billiards Club, 1941.

Meanwhile, Ivy Distleman waited anxiously all night for her husband to come home. Only at 6.30 a.m. did Harry's brother Hubby come and tell her he had been killed.[71] That afternoon, Mancini turned himself in to the police at the West End Central Police Station on Savile Row, in C Division. He told Divisional Inspector Arthur Thorp, who was put in charge of the case: 'I don't know what to say, I am entirely in your hands. I admit stabbing Fletcher with the long dagger which I found on the floor of the club, but I don't admit doing Harry Distleman. Why should I do him? They threatened me as I came upstairs, and I got panicky. In fact, I don't remember everything that happened.'[72] The next day, he admitted that the dagger was his, and that he carried it in his pocket wrapped in a rag because of threats on his life from the Hoxton gang.

On 3 June, he was charged with the murder of Harry Distleman and the attempted murder of Eddie Fletcher at Bow Street Magistrate's Court, steps from the Coach and Horses pub. Mancini pleaded not guilty. The origins of the fight and its destructive aftermath were given in testimony from the doorman of the club, the owner of the Palm Beach bottle party and Detective Inspector Thorp and in the forensic evidence from Dr Bernard Spilsbury. Mancini's defence counsel, Mr Addis, told the court that the charge should be reduced to manslaughter and not murder: 'If two persons quarrelled and fought in their passion, the killing in such a case would be manslaughter. The same argument applied if there was great provocation such as to excite a person. In this case there was no malice aforethought. Distleman first hit Mancini and attacked him in an unwarrantable manner.' The magistrate, Mr Pry, seemed to agree. He committed Mancini to the Central Criminal Court for trial on both charges but said 'it might very well be that the Jury would take the view that Distleman's death was due to manslaughter'.

Mancini, like McCallum, must have been shaken that a man died as a consequence of his actions. But McCallum, who had been pointing a gun at a man while trying to rob him when it went off, had a much greater chance of facing execution for murder. The fact that Mancini had been involved in a general fight, and that Distleman had attacked him first, gave him a reasonable chance of a lesser conviction. Before the trial, he told Inspector Thorp: 'I am sticking by the statement I have already made. I will take my chance on it.'[73] He had legal precedent on his side. In 1924, in a similar fight in a West End nightclub over cards, bookmaker Barney Litz was stabbed in the neck and died, and the doorman was also stabbed by the killer as he ran from the club. Alfred Solomon was charged with murder, but the jury found him guilty of manslaughter.[74]

At his trial in July 1941, Mancini's defence was that he had been attacked and had lashed out blindly and in self-defence. He was found guilty anyway. After the guilty verdict was passed, Mr Justice Macnaughten told Mancini, 'The jury have rejected, and in my opinion rightly rejected, your plea that you slew this man in self-defence.'[75] As the black cap was placed on the head of Mr Justice Macnaughten, Mancini 'squared his shoulders and received the death sentence calmly'.[76] Afterwards, Mancini turned smartly and walked down to the cells with no sign of emotion.[77]

Three factors pushed Mancini towards the noose. The first was the war. Just as the police had used the internment laws to 'clean up' the streets of Soho, so juries were fed up with the crime and lawlessness of the behaviour of London gangs, and they decided to make an example of Mancini. His Italian heritage may have also counted against him. British juries are forbidden to ever reveal their deliberations, but the fact that they came back with a guilty verdict after only fifty-five minutes suggests that they did not discuss a reduced charge of manslaughter. They also offered no recommendation to mercy.

The second was the ambition of Inspector Thorp, who used this case to propel his career forward. He was stationed at the West End Central Station at Savile Row as a Divisional Detective Inspector. In March 1940, before Mancini came to trial, he was promoted to Chief Inspector and moved to Scotland Yard to join the Murder Squad. The case gave him publicity and was so important in his career that he used it in a chapter in his 1954 autobiography, calling Distleman 'Scarface' and including a photograph of Mancini.[78]

And the third was the advocacy of Ivy Distleman, Harry's wife. Less than a week after his death, she gave an in-depth interview to the local paper, inviting them inside her flat and describing the sorrow of their three daughters. They wrote:

> In a neatly furnished flat in Cranleigh-Street, nine-months-old Delia Distleman looks up at her sad-eyed mother in black and smiles that pretty and contented smile which Daddy loved so much. And as her eyes roam around the room, there comes a faintly puzzled expression . . . She gurgles and a young mother looks down at her with infinite tenderness. Shirley, aged five, and Trinda, aged three,

now with their aunty, look puzzled too. 'Where is Daddy?' they lisp. But they will never see their beloved Daddy again.[79]

Harry was portrayed by the local paper as a beloved family man, perhaps because of the influence of his family, or because he was genuinely liked in the community. He was noted to be especially popular with the shelterers in the basement of their block of flats: 'He used to take tea and biscuits to them, and by his merry personality did much to cheer them during trying raids and through the long nights.' A neighbour told reporters, 'He was a very jolly man,' and a relative in the flat described how proud he was of his family, pointed to the mantelpiece and said, 'You see, the room is full of photographs he took of the kiddies.' Their account of Harry was very different from his depiction in other newspaper accounts as a violent criminal, in such headlines as 'Murdered Man had Fourteen Previous Convictions, Six for Assault'.[80]

Ivy also appeared in person in the Central Criminal Court to advocate for her deceased husband. On the third day of the trial, she was present in the spectators' seats, dressed in black. When the counsel for the defence, Mr Hector Hughes KC, told the court that Mancini was the father of two children, she jumped up and shouted: 'I've got three!' Police officers ejected her, but the message to the jury was clear.[81] And they listened.

Mancini's conviction for murder was a surprise to everyone. As crime reporter Arthur Tietjen wrote: 'When the verdict was known, a hush fell over Soho. A gangster on a murder rap was almost an unheard-of thing in the annals of gang warfare in that salubrious quarter.'[82] Mancini, in the condemned prisoner's cell at Pentonville, decided to appeal. What would follow was one of the most elaborate legal appeals to date. His first legal move was to appeal to the Court of Criminal Appeal on the grounds that the judge had not explained to the jury that if there was reasonable doubt as to whether or not the act had been provoked, Mancini was entitled to be acquitted of murder and found guilty of manslaughter instead. At the first hearing on 20 August, the three judges were unable to agree on whether Distleman had brandished his penknife, which was found beside his body. Another hearing before a full court was ordered and the case was reheard on 3 September before the Lord Chief Justice and four other judges. They dismissed the appeal. But their decision was so contrary to previous cases that the Attorney General asked that in the public interest the case be appealed again to the House of Lords. It was only the third appeal on a conviction for murder to reach the House of Lords since the passing of the Criminal Appeal Act in 1907.[83]

In the House of Lords, after a two-week discussion, the appeal was again emphatically rejected on 16 October 1941. The Lord Chief Justice, Viscount Simon, said in his remarks that since it could not be proved that Distleman had used his penknife, 'the only knife used in the struggle was the appellant's dagger, and this followed Distleman's coming at him and aiming a blow with his hand or fist. Such action by Distleman would not constitute provocation of a kind which could extenuate the sudden introduction and use of a lethal weapon like this dagger'. To be used as a legal defence, provocation had to be severe enough to temporarily deprive the person provoked of the power of self-control. A punch in the face was not enough.[84]

Neither Mancini, nor his wife or sister-in-law, who had listened in to many of the legal arguments, were present in court to hear the final verdict.[85] According to a reporter from the *Daily Mirror*, Catherine Mancini already knew the appeal would fail 'by womanly intuition', although she still believed there was hope for a reprieve: 'Though I have been told this is the last appeal that can be made, something tells me that Tony is going to live.'[86]

But it wasn't to be. The Secretary of State refused the appeal for clemency and told the governor of Pentonville Prison that the law must take its course. After four months in the tiny, condemned prisoner's cell, Mancini's time was at an end. On 31 October, he was hanged, the first execution by Albert Pierrepoint as the chief executioner. According to some accounts, Mancini said 'Cheerio!' as the noose was placed around his neck.[87] He left £101 to his widow, Catherine Mancini.[88]

After Mancini's trial, the three other men involved in the fight, Albert Dimes, Joseph Collette and Harry Capocci, were tried at the Old Bailey in July for maliciously wounding Fletcher. The recorder, Sir Gerald Dodson, noted that the incident took place 'under the shadow of a graver offence. One man had lost his life, and another man was under sentence of death.' Perhaps feeling that enough punishment had been handed out, he told Collette and Dimes: 'You were probably expecting prison and no doubt you deserve it, but I am going to bind you over.'[89] Capocci was acquitted. 'The case ought not to be magnified into something it is not. It is a disreputable brawl in an abominable haunt.'[90] Like the judge, the gangs in Soho also seemed to have had their fill of violence, and no more gang scuffles reached the news or the courts for the rest of the war.

Tragedy struck the Distleman family again six years later, when Ivy Distleman, then thirty-seven, died as a result of an illegal abortion. A friend of Ivy's had persuaded another woman, Mrs Lily Rose Bell, to help Ivy end her pregnancy. Mrs Bell, a respectable wife and mother, was not a professional abortionist – no money changed hands. But whatever procedure she used led to Ivy's death. Mrs Ball was prosecuted and found guilty of performing an illegal operation and sentenced to nine months' imprisonment to, in the words of the judge, 'deter others'.[91] Ivy's estate of £1,238 was left to Harry's mother Rebecca and his sister Janet Hart. Janet raised the three girls, now orphaned, to adulthood.

The deaths of Mancini and Distleman were, according to Arthur Thorp, 'severe blows to the gangs in the West End. They lay very low for a long time after that.'[92] But while there were fewer gang fights and attacks on clubs and bottle parties, criminal gangs continued to operate out of Soho, run by gangsters who had come up in the 1930s such as Billy Hill and Jack 'Spot' Comer. But the newest and most notorious gang were the Messinas, five Maltese brothers who, after being expelled from Egypt, had moved to Soho in the late 1930s to establish businesses in the sex trade.

It was at the Palm Beach Club at 37 Wardour Street where Marthe Watts met Eugenio Messina on 3 April 1941, just before Distleman's death. They would become the most notorious sex traffickers in London, arranging fake marriages with British men to bring European women into London to work as prostitutes. Marthe was a Belgian woman who had married an alcoholic Englishman, Charles Watts, for British citizenship. She moved to London, met Messina and lived with and worked for him.[93] Together with the other Messina brothers, they built up a prostitution empire worth over £100,000 until it was exposed in 1950.[94]

The West End offered a range of opportunities for wartime masculine sociability. Men could choose between the lower-class and relatively inexpensive pub, or the higher-end and more private club to drink, talk and relax. Bolstered by servicemen on leave as well as people looking for criminal opportunities, the unstable social mix in pubs and clubs challenged wartime standards of masculinity. As Sonya Rose has shown, the ideal wartime man tempered the martial qualities of heroic masculinity with the understated, restrained, self-deprecating and good-humoured courage of the 'little man', traits seen as quintessentially British.[95] The lack of self-control shown by McCallum and Mancini, as well as their ethnic and national backgrounds, marked them culpable both for the crimes for which they were convicted, and for failing to live up to the masculine ideals central to good citizenship.

Pubs and clubs were central to all kinds of wartime crime. McCallum's botched robbery was only one of many committed against pubs, shops and jewellers during the war by soldiers and deserters desperate for money. Pubs and clubs became the new headquarters for criminal gangs, from which they ran black-market schemes, gambling and prostitution rings, and protection rackets. The billiard ball, fake identity, papers and wad of notes found in Harry Distleman's pockets as he lay dead on the pavement showed the profits and the dangers of wartime racketeering. Rival gangs attacked each other again and again in wartime clubs, jostling for a piece of the lucrative crime markets that would dominate the West End into the 1960s.

CHAPTER 4

HOME

I had last seen Mrs. Watson at about 5 p.m. on Tuesday, 20th May 1941, when she was hanging out some washing on the line in the back garden. I waved my hand to her, but I didn't speak. She smiled at me. I did not see the child at that time, and I haven't seen her since.

Mrs Rose Burgess, 5A Goring Way, Greenford

I looked out over my balcony and saw that he [Watson] had dug a hole in the shape of an oblong, right beside the coal shed. He again came out of his flat at about 5 o-clock and started to dig again. I called out to him, 'Are you digging for victory?'

Mrs Lilian Bound, 9A Goring Way, Greenford[1]

'Keep the home fires burning', the First World War patriotic song urged, 'until the boys come home.' Home was the place of safety, privacy and comfort, protected by women, who were themselves defended by the men fighting on distant battlefields and dying in muddy trenches. Home was the lace-covered mantel where their uniformed portraits stood, yellowing over the long years of loneliness. Ironically, the woman who wrote the song lyrics, Lena Ford, was killed in March 1918 during a German air raid on her home in Warrington

Crescent, Maida Vale. Aerial warfare made those mantelpieces and everything they stood for vulnerable to enemy attack and destruction.

Some of the most affecting photographs of the Blitz were the bombed buildings with their rooms open to the air, with their patches of wallpaper, pictures and even some mantelpieces visible to passers-by. Bomber planes made all British homes vulnerable to enemy attack: the raids of the Blitz from August 1940 to May 1941 destroyed over 1 million flats and houses in London and killed 43,000 civilians. More people on the home front had lost their lives by 1941 than military personnel: 3,500 soldiers died in the Battle of France in spring 1940, and 544 pilots were lost in the Battle of Britain.

Even in homes that weren't literally exposed to passers-by, the regulations and restrictions of the war destroyed the privacy of their inhabitants. Where people slept, who they slept with, what they ate, where they shopped and when and where they travelled were all registered for government inspection. The local ARP kept a list of each household, including the bedrooms in which everybody slept, in case rescues were needed. Wardens could enter any home to make sure the blackout restrictions were being heeded. Ration books and identification cards registered people's addresses and where they moved. Refugees, already registered as aliens, had to appear before internment tribunals to have their security risk classified and face deportation or internment. The frequent hostility of neighbours added an extra layer of wartime scrutiny and fear, particularly for refugees with German names and accents.

Despite the enormous amount of surveillance and bureaucracy, the war offered new opportunities for people to murder and cover up the crime, claiming that the victim had been called up, had evacuated to the country or had gone to help relatives. These excuses were plausible, since millions of people were on the move in wartime: leaving bombed-out and damaged homes, conscripted into labour in another town or evacuating with their offices or their children. For example, John Haigh murdered William McSwan in 1944, dissolving his body in acid and telling his parents he had gone to Scotland to avoid being called up for military service. Lionel Watson was also a murderer who used the conditions of war to kill his wife, Phyllis, and her child in May 1941. Phyllis and Eileen died at home, in the place they should have felt most protected.

For refugees in London, who had already lost one home and feared for their families in Europe, home was even less safe. Jewish-German refugees felt particularly vulnerable. Irene Coffee and her widowed mother, Margarete Brann, felt particularly vulnerable. By October 1941, the German advance into the USSR, as well as conflicts with their neighbours, made them decide to kill themselves in their Maida Vale flat. Irene survived, only to be charged with her mother's murder.

These two stories, only a few months apart, show the fragility of home in wartime. Home could still provide joys and comforts, such as Phyllis showing off her new clothes to her neighbour the day before she died, or Irene and her mother having another woman over for tea in their flat that week. And the safety of home may have always been more ideal than real. But the war threatened even that, especially for vulnerable women and children.

PHYLLIS AND EILEEN CROCKER

Three weeks after Harry Distleman stumbled down the stairs of a Soho club at 3 a.m., clutching his side and calling out, 'I am stabbed, I am stabbed, I am dying', Mrs Lilian Bound saw her neighbour Phyllis Crocker for the last time. It was 20 May 1941, around 5 p.m. Mrs Bound lived with her daughter, Heather Thomas, and son-in-law in the upstairs flat of a mid-Victorian semi in Goring Way, Greenford, and Phyllis lived downstairs with her daughter Eileen. Phyllis was close with both mother and daughter, and they visited each other's flats and had tea every morning. At 5 p.m. Mrs Bound saw Phyllis, in her customary flowered overall, hanging out washing in the backyard: 'I called out. She turned and waved her hand and smiled.'[2] Phyllis was never seen alive again.[3]

Phyllis's mother, Sarah Alice, had been widowed when her daughter Phyllis was only a year old. In 1930, they settled in Acton, and Sarah took in boarders. Once Phyllis left school, she worked as an assistant at the Acton Town Hall canteen for five years. She became great friends with her supervisor, Mrs Ruby Tattersall.

In 1939, Phyllis discovered she was pregnant by one of her mother's boarders, a married man. After her daughter Eileen was born in October 1939, Phyllis and her mother decided to make a fresh start. They took a flat on the other side of Ealing at 9 Goring Way, Greenford, in May 1940. A new neighbourhood where they weren't known would help Phyllis and Eileen escape the stigma of illegitimacy, in a time when fatherless families were becoming more and more common. Phyllis took a new job at the Hoover factory in Greenford. Housed in a beautiful Art Deco building in Perivale Greenford (now luxury flats and a Tesco supermarket), the vacuum-cleaner factory was also making aircraft parts for the war effort.

Phyllis was a slight woman of about 5 foot 4, who wore glasses and had fair hair. She seemed to make friends wherever she went and was described by Mrs Bound as 'bright and jolly and good company – an exceptionally nice woman'. Eileen was well-built, with fair hair and a happy, sweet nature. No description survives of Sarah Alice, who was sixty-nine by this time, but after a lifetime of work and being widowed twice, she must have been tired and starting to feel the strain.

The start of the raids was the beginning of the end for her. As a suburb, Greenford was not targeted as heavily as Central London,[4] but sirens every night and the sounds of falling bombs terrified Phyllis's mother. As soon as the warnings began in late August, she went to Scotland for six weeks to stay with a friend. But it was only a temporary respite. As soon as she came back, the sounds of the sirens triggered a complete mental breakdown.

On the morning of 17 October, Sarah left Phyllis and Eileen and took a long bus ride to Twickenham, near the Thames. At 10 a.m., according to the Twickenham Police Incident Book, George Smoothy saw something floating in the water: 'I rowed down in my boat and found the woman on the Richmond side, her clothes keeping her afloat.'[5] He got her in the boat and called an ambulance.

Sarah told the police, 'I'm sorry but I have to fight against the feeling. I sit in the shelters and think horrible things. It's the sirens that made my head so bad. I ran away from my daughter and came over here.'[6] Although suicide and attempted suicide were crimes, the police did not proceed with charges. Mrs Smith came home for a few days but was clearly too much to handle. On 24 October, she was sent back to hospital with 'confusional psychosis'. She died there on 2 November 1940. She left her life savings to Phyllis, £130 in a Post Office savings account, and shares worth about £70.

Once her mother had left for Scotland, Phyllis would have found it too difficult to work without anyone to care for Eileen. She wasn't lacking for company, however, as she had met a man who also worked at the Hoover factory: Lionel Watson. Lionel was then twenty-nine years old, and a married man with four children. His wife had left him, and his three oldest children had been evacuated, while his mother took care of his youngest son. He had been living with his parents in Stonebridge, Harlesden, and working as a Bakelite moulder.

Lionel was a quiet, somewhat morose man, around 5 foot 11, with broad shoulders, a round face with dark eyes, a sallow complexion, a small dark moustache and dark hair. He did not smoke or drink but loved clothes and was a flashy dresser. He had five convictions for felony; in 1938 he had been convicted at the Central Criminal Court for office breaking, stealing cash and postal orders worth £226. He had received a sentence of eighteen months' hard labour. Lionel was also tempted by the company of women, and they seemed to like him, at least for a while. His wife Alice Frost had, according to her police statement, separated from him three times because of his persistent cruelty and his associations with other women.

Lionel's three oldest children were evacuated after the fall of France in June 1940, when it seemed like a German invasion was imminent.

They went to the seaside town of Weston-super-Mare in Somerset: Pauline, aged nine, and the boys, Brian, seven, and Norman, six. Lionel's son John lived with his mother, Eleanor. The three of them decided to visit the older children in September. Lionel told his mother he wanted to bring a girl he worked with and her baby on the trip, as 'the journey would do them good'. It was Phyllis and Eileen. The five of them visited the children, stayed overnight and made their way back to London.

But when they got into Paddington Station around midnight, there was a heavy air raid, and they had to spend the night in one of the air-raid shelters at the station. As the planes passed overhead, Eleanor Watson and Phyllis went to the ladies' toilet. While they were there, Phyllis foolishly confided in her that Eileen was the illegitimate child of a married man. Mrs Watson later told police, 'I thought it was wrong that she should have an illegitimate child and I told her so.' According to Mrs Watson, Phyllis replied: 'If I thought I was going to have another one, I would do myself in.' But Mrs Watson was still disapproving: 'It was obvious to me that the association between Lionel and this woman was not all that it should be.'

His mother's fears were confirmed when Lionel moved into the flat at Goring Way in September 1940, telling his parents it was closer to work. He promised Phyllis he would get a divorce and marry her. After the death of her mother, Phyllis asked the estate manager Mr Darcy if Lionel could take over the tenancy. As Darcy explained in his statement to police: 'Not being impressed with him, we declined to do so.'

Lionel and Phyllis's life in the flat seemed very happy, according to the neighbours and his family. Lionel continued to visit his parents once a week to see his youngest son, often bringing Eileen. His mother recalled he was 'passionately fond of the little girl', and his father said he obviously thought a lot of Phyllis. Phyllis's best friend, Ruby Tattersall, who visited them once a fortnight, 'was never much interested in Watson', but thought that he 'was a good husband and would do any mortal thing for Phyllis'. By his own account, he helped with the housework: washing up, buying food, helping with the laundry and tidying up.

The main observer of their lives was their upstairs neighbour, Mrs Lilian Bound. Phyllis and Lilian were close and communicated by tapping on the floor or calling through the letter box. Lilian had the upstairs flat, so she could see into the garden as well as the front door, and she was an exceptionally observant woman. She told police over and over again what a happy and pleasant woman Phyllis was: a 'very happy and bright sort of girl'. She described Eileen as a 'bright little soul', happy and well built, with very fair hair.

Phyllis's mother's death was followed by another crisis. At the end of November, Phyllis found out she was pregnant. Although she and Lionel appeared to the neighbours as a happily married couple, Phyllis knew how vulnerable her position was, as a partner to a man who already had four children, and with one illegitimate child whose father did not pay maintenance. Although it's not clear how, where and by whom she had it done, Phyllis underwent an illegal abortion in mid-December.

Illegal abortions were usually performed by inserting an instrument, chemicals or soap into the cervix to induce miscarriage. They carried a risk of death from immediate shock and a high risk from bacterial infection. Phyllis was unlucky. She became very ill and was admitted to hospital on 22 December for a septic abortion, where she stayed until 4 January. She told her neighbours she had had a gallbladder operation.

When Phyllis came home from the hospital, she was pale and frail. To ease the tensions between them and to cheer her up, Lionel lied to her and told her that he had got a divorce and that they could get married. The couple 'married' on 18 January 1941 at the South Ealing Register Office. Heather Thomas was the witness. Phyllis seemed very happy again.

Although Phyllis was more contented, Lionel was beginning to feel trapped. In April or May, he had asked a workmate whose invalid wife had to take sleeping pills, 'Can you give me some of your poison tablets? I want to kill a dog.' He was not given any. Next door to the Case Hardening Department where Lionel worked was a big drum of cyanide that was not locked. Another workmate saw him open the lid and pry off a big lump, saying he wanted to kill some insects.

In April, Lionel's visits home to his parents and payments for his children stopped. Phyllis was also pregnant again, and this time, believing she was married, told her friends she was happy about it.

On 13 May, Lionel's mother Eleanor decided she had had enough and went to the flat on Goring Way to confront him. She rang the doorbell, and when Lionel answered she told him off for neglecting his children: 'I must admit I was speaking rather loudly as I was angry, and Phyllis said, "Get away from my doorstep and stop shouting!"' Eleanor then called out that Phyllis was causing her son to lead a wrong life, and screamed: 'What sort of woman do you call yourself?' She then walked away, and Lionel, looking very sorry for himself, walked along with her, promising to visit the next day. He did not.

Around this time, Phyllis told Mrs Bound that Lionel had received a letter from a solicitor, asking for £10 in divorce fees. He wanted Phyllis to pay them out of the money her mother had left her. Phyllis told Lilian she was tired of paying his debts: 'I am getting very fed up about things, as the fortnight Lionel lost when the machine broke down at his work he was paid the first week but the second week he didn't bring any money home, and I had to draw money from the post office.' They had also gone to a solicitor to start proceedings against Eileen's father, who hadn't been paying the 10 shillings a week he owed for maintenance.

The evening of 19 May, Lilian came to visit Phyllis, who showed off some women's and children's clothes she had got from a clothing club. A few hours later, Heather Thomas came to visit Phyllis in her kitchenette. She said Phyllis seemed happy and talked about coming to work with her at Philco Radio in Perivale. Eileen was cheerfully running around the kitchen.

The afternoon of 20 May, a baker's roundsman called at the flat with the daily loaf of bread. Lionel came to the door and told him they were going away and not to deliver any more bread. At around 5 p.m. Lilian Bound saw Phyllis hanging out the washing in the backyard and smiled and waved to her. She was never seen again.

The next morning, Lionel knocked on Lilian Bound's door and brought her some milk. She asked after Phyllis. He, 'pale and agitated', with shaking hands, said she had gone to her aunt's in Scotland. The next day she heard him scrubbing downstairs and noticed a strong smell of pine disinfectant. She kept asking after Phyllis and wondering why she had not written. On 26 May, she asked him again, and he told her that Phyllis didn't want to hear from her, as she wanted to get right away. Mrs Bound 'felt rather hurt at that and went indoors'. She never mentioned Phyllis to him again.

That same day, Lionel walked into a pawnbroker in Ealing with a platinum eternity ring, a gold ring set with diamonds and sapphires, a gold pendant and a bracelet, and sold them for £4. He showed up on his parents' doorstep, paid his mother the arears in child maintenance and moved back in. Later that week he visited an old family friend and gave her a child's rolled gold bracelet and a silver serviette ring engraved with an 'E'.

On 27 May, one week after she had last seen Phyllis, Mrs Bound noticed Lionel digging in the back garden. She called out to him, 'Are you digging for victory?' – a popular propaganda slogan for planting a vegetable garden. He replied he was going to bury some rubbish. He dug an oblong hole 5 feet long and 2 feet wide. Although she did not see him bury anything, she noticed that he had placed six flagstones over the patch of turned-over earth. Over the next weeks, she and the other neighbours noticed him periodically digging in the garden and pouring pine-scented disinfectant around the flagstones.

Lionel was also seeking comfort in a new love interest. The Hoover plant, where hundreds of women worked on the production of aircraft electrical parts, was the perfect hunting ground for him. He set his sights on seventeen-year-old Joan Philby. On 30 May, he slipped a note into her hand asking for her to meet him for a drink. She did not reply and destroyed the note. He kept pursuing her, until eventually she consented to go out with him to the cinema and on various other outings. He showered her with gifts: powder, cosmetics, a ring and a gold bracelet. He also gave her a page of margarine coupons, which she did not notice were from the ration book of a child.

On 15 June, after they had been on an outing, he invited Joan into the flat at Goring Way. He took her into the bedroom, opened the closet and showed her Phyllis's clothing, including three fur coats. He told her they belonged to his divorced wife and asked if she wanted to have them. She refused and asked if they could leave as she felt uncomfortable. The next day he brought her some of the items she had admired in the flat, including an unfinished check dress and almost-new brown and white shoes Phyllis had bought just before she died.

These outings were not cheap, and Lionel was still short of money. He went back to the solicitors to see if Eileen's father had paid any maintenance for her. He also tried to get Phyllis's Post Office savings account signed over to him by forging her signature. It had already been drained from £130 to £47 in five months. They were suspicious and asked for the form to be signed in front of a Post Office official. Lionel did not pursue it.

It had been a hot June, the hottest of the war. By the third week of June, the residents of Goring Way noticed an offensive smell. On 30 June, Lilian Bound and her neighbour Mrs Rose Burgess went into Phyllis's empty flat to see if anything had been left to spoil. They found nothing. Then Lilian remembered that Lionel had said he was going to bury some rubbish in the backyard. The two women went into the back garden and prised up a flagstone. They saw earth mixed with a white powder which looked like garden lime. Lilian took a stick and poked around in the earth, until 'I touched something, and it went off with a hiss'. The smell then became so nauseating that they dropped the flagstone and went indoors.

When Mr Burgess came home, he and Mrs Bound went to Greenford Police Station. They were sent away with the advice to examine the pit themselves, and to complain to the local sanitary inspector if they found any rubbish. Mr Burgess went back with another male neighbour to dig up the pit. It only took a few moments before they uncovered what looked like human flesh. Mr Burgess informed the police of his suspicions, and they arrived within the hour, armed with shovels. Mr Burgess was still there when he saw them uncover a hand. Phyllis and Eileen were buried there, nestled together in a sheet.

The bodies were quickly removed and sent for autopsy. Sir Bernard Spilsbury, the famous Home Office pathologist, performed the postmortem, and he said the bodies had no injuries and no visible cause of death. He noted that Phyllis was three months pregnant. Tissue samples were sent to Dr Roche Lynch, the Home Office analyst, and he found traces of sodium cyanide in the organs of both, although he couldn't say exactly how much they had been given or in what form. Since cyanide disappears from the body, the fact that there was still some there after six or seven weeks of burial in hot weather in a shallow grave 'convinces me that a substantial dose must have been taken, and satisfies me that death in both cases was due to poisoning by cyanide'.[7] With such a large dose, they would have become unconscious in a minute or two and died within half an hour of taking it.

After the discovery of the bodies, the police, under the direction of Superintendent Yardell and DDI Deighton, searched the flat. They found a hacksaw and file in a box in the kitchen. Roche Lynch analysed those as well and found grains of sodium cyanide. The police also traced Phyllis and Eileen's ration cards. They hadn't been used, and there had been no application to move them to Scotland. Lionel had given Joan a page ripped from Eileen's margarine ration.

Lionel was arrested at work the next morning, at the front gates of the Hoover factory at 7 a.m. He was expecting it, as he said: 'I know. Don't show me up here. There is no need to hold me. I found them dead.' Lionel claimed that Phyllis had been so depressed she had killed Eileen and taken her own life. He was taken to Greenford station and arrested.

The trial began on 15 September 1941, at the Old Bailey. Mr Christmas Humphreys prosecuted, and J.P. Valetta acted in Lionel's defense. The circumstantial evidence against him was strong. Over four days, the prosecution put forward the forensic evidence for poisoning, witnesses to Lionel trying to get money from Phyllis, and workmates who had seen him with the cyanide. At one point, Humphreys held up a tiny test tube filled with cyanide to the jury and exclaimed: 'He comes away with a fistful when that much means death!'[8]

The most powerful witness against Lionel was his upstairs neighbour, Lilian Bound. Her love for Phyllis and delight in their friendship helped her paint a picture of a happy woman who, unlike her mother, was not terrified by the air raids and slept through them. She was happy about her pregnancy and was excited about a holiday she was planning in May.

Lionel took the stand in his own defence, which did not go well. He was not a charismatic speaker, and his description of Phyllis as depressed and worried did not ring true. His story was that, on the night of 20 May, he had gone out to see a film at 6 p.m. When he had returned home around 10 p.m., he told the court, he had found them both dead in bed. He had been immediately afraid, in his own words, that his lies could potentially be revealed: 'I was very upset. I was in a bit of a fix because I had bigamously married her. That occurred to me at the time. I could not call a doctor owing to that. I thought of my children and my people and my job.' He had taken off Phyllis's rings, 'because she had a wish never to have jewellery', covered her and Eileen with a blanket and sat up all night on the sofa, thinking of where he could secretly bury them: 'If the bodies had been found I would have been charged with everything, including murdering them. I am suggesting she murdered the child and took her own life.'

The prosecution, led by Mr H.A.K. Morgan, subjected him to a rigorous cross-examination. He had to admit to having lied to the police on several occasions, to having pawned the jewellery, including the rings he had removed from Phyllis's hands, to having tried to access her money and to having courted Joan Philby: 'I loved Phyllis passionately. I began to love Joan Philby after taking her out a few times.' His testimony revealed a man who was both a liar and monumentally callous: 'It was to save my own skin that I buried the bodies.'

The emotional effects of Lionel's testimony and the forensic descriptions of Phyllis and Eileen were devastating. There were three women on the trial jury, and during the judge's summing-up at the end of the trial, one woman fainted. She had to be helped from the room. When she came back, Mr Justice Cassels reached over the bench and handed her his own bottle of smelling salts, and she took her seat again.[9]

The jury was gone only twenty minutes before they came back with a verdict of guilty of murder, and no recommendation to mercy. When asked if he had anything to say, Lionel began, 'Sir . . .', then went silent. As the *News of the World* reported, 'Watson was unmoved when the judge donned the black cap. As he passed from the dock, he gave one glance to his father, who sat a few feet away.'[10] Watson's judicial appeal failed six weeks later, and a petition for mercy to the Home Office organised by his mother was also unsuccessful. He was hanged at Pentonville Prison on 12 November 1941.

The contrast between Phyllis's pre-war life and wartime troubles was stark. Phyllis, Eileen and Phyllis's mother had a happy domestic life, before the experiences of the air raids led to Mrs Smith's nervous breakdown and death. Phyllis was left vulnerable to the villainous Lionel, who lied to her, manipulated her, stole poison from the war works to murder her and her daughter, disposed of their bodies in the full view of their neighbours and then gave her clothes to his new love interest. The contrast between the peaceful life that Phyllis thought she had and the grotesque betrayal by her partner made her murder especially macabre.

Histories of family and domestic life in Britain have rarely examined the secret and darker side of relationships: divorce, sexual violence and domestic violence.[11] But cases of partner murder can reveal the social vulnerabilities of women and children, and their press coverage and trials can illuminate prevailing emotional norms and how these were shaped by race, gender and class.[12] Lionel Watson, whose crime was premeditated and motivated by gain, was shown no mercy by the jury, judge or Home Secretary. But, as we will see, men on trial for murder who could suggest their partners had been unfaithful were seen as having been provoked into violence, and shown much more leniency by the courts.

For Phyllis and Eileen, the home they thought was safe was not. And the same was doubly true for European refugees in London. Having escaped one unsafe home in Europe, refugees experienced more traumatic events, with the German air raids and threatened invasion, suspicion of neighbours and surveillance by the police, alien tribunals and potential internment, and fear for family left behind. Stories of refugee suicides appeared every few weeks in the London newspapers in the early years of war. German refugee Georg Israel Muller was found gassed by his landlady in his rooms in Primrose Gardens, Hampstead, in 1941. In his two years in London, Muller had been hit by a car in the blackout, been bombed out of his flat and feared for his wife and child trapped in Germany.[13] He could not go on. In October 1941, Irene Coffee and her mother Margarete Brann felt the same way.

MARGARETE BRANN

Margarete Brann, whose maiden name was Blaschke, was born in Germany. Her parents both died when she was a teenager, and in 1908, she married Alfred Brann and moved to Dresden. Alfred owned a prosperous grain and animal feed business, and the family was educated, middle class and Jewish.[14] They had two daughters, Herta and Irene. But their prosperous and comfortable life was torn apart in the 1930s. Alfred Brann, already ill, was devastated by the rise of the Nazi party. The Nazis were elected to the Reichstag and Hitler appointed as Chancellor in January 1933, and Alfred Brann died weeks later. In March 1933, the Reichstag passed Hitler's Enabling Act, which allowed him to pass laws without parliamentary approval and to override individual constitutional rights. By April, construction on the first concentration camp at Dachau had begun.

In 1935, Margarete and Alfred's eldest daughter, Herta, married a former employee of the family business, and they moved to Palestine.

The family had a falling-out of some kind, and Irene never spoke to or heard from her sister again. Margarete stayed with Irene in their apartment on Bankstrasse. Irene worked as a bank clerk, and the two women travelled extensively, to Egypt in 1936 and to Switzerland in 1937. There they met Eustace Charlton, a retired shipowner from Cheswick, Northumberland, and his wife Charlotte, and discussed their plans to immigrate to England. Irene kept the photo albums of these trips all her life, showing her as an elegantly dressed young woman with a happy, round and childish face, and short curly hair.

Despite their luxurious life, the women were desperate to find a way to get out of Germany. It was very difficult for refugees to get work visas for Britain without political connections or wealth. Most occupations were restricted because of fears of economic competition, and domestic service was one of the only options. In 1938, Irene applied for a work visa to work as a children's governess in the Isle of Wight and was accepted, but her mother's visa was denied. Irene decided to go anyway. In September 1937, Irene arrived in England. Her job as a governess lasted only a short time. A London lawyer and fellow Jew, Isaac Fine, helped her keep her visa by hiring her as a servant.

She was not alone in coming to London in search of safety. Between 1933 and 1939, over 78,000 refugees from Germany and Austria arrived in Britain, not including children. Of these, 57 per cent were women, over 20,000 of them taking advantage of domestic service visas.[15] For middle-class women, unaccustomed to domestic labour, servant jobs were difficult, and they were often unstable, dependent on the caprices of the employer. Former Jewish refugee domestics interviewed in the 1990s and 2000s told horrifying stories of their isolation, poor working conditions and, in some cases, of surviving sexual assaults and suicide attempts.[16]

For women, one of the best ways, if a risky one, around the visa problem was to marry a British citizen. The British Nationality and Status of Aliens Act (BNSA) from 1914 stated that 'the wife of a British subject shall be deemed to be a British subject, and the wife of an alien

shall be deemed to be an alien'. Marriage offered women a British passport and relative safety, although the police did try to track down fraud-
ulent marriages, especially when used to traffic foreign women for sex
work.[17]

Irene could not expect to find and fall in love with a British man in
the short time needed to ensure her mother's safety. So, like hundreds
of refugee women, she entered into a marriage of convenience. Because
these marriages were not legally valid, they were secret, and often seen
as shameful.[18] Historian Irene Messinger has recently traced over 100 of
such marriages in Britain, almost all of wealthy women with international family or political networks that would help them connect with
a citizen and ensure that the secret would not be revealed. While Irene
Brann was not in the highest social circles, she had money, and she had
a friend in Isaac Fine, who helped her arrange it.

In Stoke Newington Town Hall, on 27 November 1937, Irene
married twenty-eight-year-old Aaron Coffee, a Jewish printer. Irene
implied in a later letter that she paid him a fee.[19] He said goodbye to her

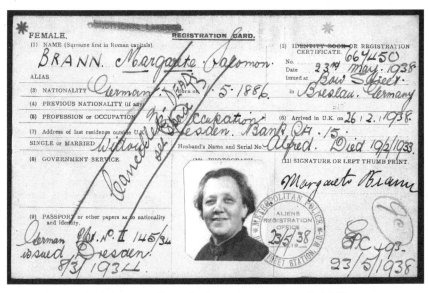

8. Margarete Brann's alien registration card, 1938.

116

immediately after the ceremony, and she only ever saw him again by chance, on the street in 1938. But despite the lack of love, Irene was euphoric. She had an English name and a British passport, and she could go back to Dresden and get her mother.

They made it back to England in February 1938. The two women found an apartment at 82 Sutherland Avenue, Maida Vale, on the top floor. Irene's excellent English and secretarial skills meant she could get a job that paid better than domestic service, and both women enrolled in classes in a polytechnic college.

When war broke out in 1939, mother and daughter faced new problems: the hostility of those around them, and Margarete's potential internment. The Aliens Department of the Home Office set up internment tribunals throughout the country to examine every UK-registered enemy alien over the age of sixteen. Their aim was to divide the aliens into three categories: Category A, to be interned; Category B, to be exempt from internment but subject to the restrictions decreed by the Special Order; and Category C, to be exempt from both internment and restrictions. Margarete had been called to appear, and the women were terrified that she would be sent to 'a kind of concentration camp' or be deported abroad. As Irene wrote to the Charltons: 'Mother says she is not in the least afraid of that, because in any case it is better than being in Germany, but maybe she could be released only if some English people of high repute would testify that she is no spy, and so on. And even I may need a reference badly when applying for a job and so on, especially in my peculiar case. You understand.'[20] Irene also asked the Charltons to take possession of their silverware in case their flat was bombed, and sent them the details of their wills and executors.

In London, the two women lived a life that was much diminished from their old one in Dresden. They had some savings, but their apartments were not luxurious, and they had few friends. They were no longer able to travel, or to host or entertain. They were not active in a synagogue, and they avoided socialising with most English people, concerned about their German accents. They were lonely.

When the bombing raids began in September 1940, they realised that their top-floor flat on Sutherland Avenue was too exposed and moved to Castellein Road. Their flat there was more cramped and less luxurious but had a small brick air-raid shelter in the back garden. What they could not have known when they took the flat was how unfriendly the neighbours were. Margarete and Irene, as both Germans and Jews, faced a double discrimination. Antisemitism ran high during the war, and their neighbours no doubt did not like to have Germans in the house as they were being bombed by German planes.[21] Margarete was the wife of a businessman, still wearing her beautiful pre-war clothes and with her elegant furniture from Dresden. She could be imperious and saw herself as a higher social rank than her neighbours, which must have annoyed them. Mrs Mahoney, the downstairs neighbour, insisted on being able to enter into the two women's apartment at any time to access the mailbox in their hallway. It led to a long-simmering conflict. The mistrust of the neighbours could also have serious consequences, if questions were asked about Irene's missing husband. The women lived in fear that the fake marriage would be discovered, Irene's British passport invalidated and the women deported back to Germany.

On 5 August 1941, Irene got a secretarial job at the Mercantile Overseas Trust, Ltd at 27 Old Broad Street, EC2, at a salary of £4 a week.[22] Her employer said she was 'cheerful and balanced' and never discussed her personal life or the international situation.

In the first week of October, the women decided that they could no longer stand living in their flat. Margarete called again at George Goslin Real Estate to inquire about available flats and was shown one on the Essendine Road in Maida Vale. She made an appointment to view the flat again with Irene. But on the morning of 11 October, Irene called the estate agent. She cancelled the appointment, telling the assistant, Violet Clark, that there had been a death in the family. But there hadn't been. Not yet.[23]

The women subscribed to the *News Chronicle*, a more liberal newspaper than *The Times*. The news of the war in October focused on the

German army's bloody advance towards Moscow. On 10 October 1941, the paper quoted the German press department's report that the Red Army had been encircled at Vyazma and Bryansk and that Moscow would fall in a few days.[24] Irene would later tell the police that she and her mother had been very worried and depressed by the news about the advance of the Nazis: 'On Saturday, October 11, we talked over the whole worry and decided to end our lives by taking a large dose of veronal and phanodorm. We brought them with us from Switzerland and kept them with the intention of taking them if we were ever sent back to Germany.'[25]

The two women had lunch together, then wrote a suicide note and letters to four friends. At around 7 p.m. they took off their wedding rings and put them in the safe in the hallway. They put on their night clothes and divided the pills between them. Margarete had twenty Veronal and twenty Phanodorm, and Irene had ten of each: 'We dissolved them in water, said goodbye, and then drank the drugs. We then snuggled up together. I do not remember what happened after that.'

Nothing was heard from the flat for days. On 15 October, after Irene had been absent from work for three days, the company sent a telegram. Hearing nothing, they fired her.

A week after the women first lay down, Irene stumbled down the steps of the flat into the street, still dressed in a nightgown under an open dressing gown. Her hair was dishevelled, and she had bloody wounds on her neck and wrists. She turned left and tried to walk down the street, but she was too ill. She leaned against the wall, and after a few minutes, a girl walked past, and Irene asked her to take a letter and a telegram for her doctor to the post office. Then Irene groped her way back into the house, pausing to hang onto the railings before going back into her apartment and closing the door. Her upstairs neighbour watched her – 'Her hair was blowing about, and she was very ill looking' – but did not speak to her. The neighbour later told the police that she rang the bell after Irene went back inside but, getting no answer, went back to her flat.

Dr Green got Irene's handwritten telegram at 12.30 p.m. It told him that 'We wanted to end our lives. We were too depressed. My beloved mother has succeeded but unfortunately, I have not. I do not know the date or hour [undecipherable] I too want to die and that [undecipherable]. I enclose a front door key. All is so awful in this world. I hope this is not too much trouble for you. May God bless you and your children always.'[26] When he got there, the basement tenant, Mrs Mary Mahoney, let him in the front door, and he entered the unlocked apartment. Mrs Brann was lying dead in bed, her head buried in the pillow. Irene was lying semi-conscious in the next bed, and he had to shake her awake.

As he went to call the police, the elderly upstairs female neighbour, Mrs Brandhendler, handed him an undated note she had found in the mailbox, that read, 'Please call Dr. J. Green at telephone 2414, but please [illegible]. We are both very bad, here is money.'[27] A coin was paper-clipped to it.

When had Irene first woken up? She was a woman of precise words – had her mother still been alive at that time? Had the neighbour seen the note and done nothing? It seems unlikely she had not checked her mailbox for days. Mrs Brandhendler's police statement emphasised that she was French and her husband Polish, and that they had lived in England for twenty years. She also said that she was not on visiting terms with Mrs Brann and Mrs Coffee and 'I never saw the husband'. Was it the suspicion of the neighbour that led to Margarete not getting medical help?

In the bedroom, the twin beds were pushed together, and the large window looking onto the garden was blacked out. There were some chests in the corner and, on a table, five letters written by Irene before they took the pills. Suicide letters, as Ella Sbaraini has shown, are key to understanding the intentions of people in their own words.[28] Irene's letter delicately referred to the discrimination that she and her mother faced, and emphasised that their motivations were entirely political:

11 October 1941. We are writing to state that we owe no money or anything else to anybody – either in this country or abroad. We have

120

no debts of any kind. With our deadly enemies, the Nazis, conquering one country after another, we feel that the world is going to take an awful turn. All that is good and decent seems to be going down, and it is very difficult to try and help a country when so many people think, because one was born in Germany, one is the enemy of Britain, when the contrary is the case.

The letter went on to list the details of their executors and wills and the location of other important papers. Their money was left to Isaac Fine, and their household goods to the Jewish Refugee Committee. They had £400 in their bank account, as well as stocks and bonds.

One of the letters on the hall table was addressed to Isaac Fine, and another to Charlotte Charlton, leaving her Irene's gold watch as a reminder of their meeting in Switzerland: 'I cannot say how happy I am to have my mother with me at this hour, and as usual we are of the same mind. And what hopes are there for us for the future, with so many people even now doubting our devotion to this country? Not everybody is as enlightened as you.'

Another letter was to Madeline Pratt, a friend Irene had made at the polytechnic, the only person addressed by her first name. They were both interested in languages and logic and would often meet for lunch. A fourth letter was to Mrs Fanny Klatzko, an elderly Russian friend who also lived in Maida Vale, enclosing two hair nets as 'a little gift'. They had had tea with her on 7 October, and she had noticed nothing wrong. No letter was left for Margarete's sister Irma in Poland or Irene's sister Herta.

Irene was taken from the flat to the hospital, where she slowly recovered from the effects of the drugs. There she was guarded by a police officer. She tried to write letters there, although she didn't have her glasses, to tell her friends that she had lived but her mother had died, and that she was not sure what to do next.

On 27 October, DI Richard Deighton came to Paddington Hospital. He told her that he had been investigating her mother's death and that she was being arrested for murder as the survivor of a suicide pact. Irene did not understand. She said: 'I didn't murder my mother, we decided to end our lives together. I did not understand it was a serious thing to do. We were both very depressed about the Nazi persecution of the Jews. I will explain everything and then you will understand the position.'

When Irene was questioned at the police station, she elaborated a little on the events that had led up to their decision, still thinking her arrest was a misunderstanding:

I did not murder my mother. We decided to die together. I had no luck. Little did I know that doing this is a serious act. We were both very depressed and worried that the Nazis might invade England. We are Jewish refugees and the fact that the Nazis were invading country after country destroying everything that is decent and livable made us both anticipate what would happen if they came to England, although I felt confidence that Britain would eventually defeat them. My father died in Germany in 1933. His illness was made worse by the Nazi purges that year. The latest news of the war and the advance of the Nazis frightened us greatly, and there seemed to be nothing decent that had not been trampled and destroyed by them.

Despite her pleas for understanding, Irene was remanded to Holloway prison, to await trial for murder.

Suicide pacts – agreements to commit suicide together – were entered into by more than a dozen young couples in England during the 1920s and 1930s, showing the intense pressures faced by partners who defied social norms.[29] During the war, suicide pacts were more common among older people, who could see no future for themselves. Another German couple, Jenny and Max Lang, had also decided to end their lives, by gas poisoning, in 1940. Max died, but Jenny survived to be charged with murder. She died a short time later in prison of pneumonia.[30]

Irene appeared at the Old Bailey, Room 4, on 9 December 1941. She was defended by Mr Victor Durand, who told the court that Irene and her mother were victims of Nazi oppression. The Judge was Travers Humphreys, who wrote several books about his famous cases and even played himself in an early true-crime television show, *Murder Anonymous*, in 1955. But he never wrote about this case.

Irene Coffee was charged under a law from 1821, which stated that a surviving partner of a suicide pact was guilty of murder. It was enforced most strenuously if the survivor was male, or if there was any possibility of coercion. In this case, Irene's obvious misery made that seem unlikely. But, as Justice Humphreys told the jury in his summing-up: 'It is not for us to decide whether we approve or disapprove of a particular law, so long as the law is clear and indisputable . . . It is my duty to tell you what the law is, and it is your duty to apply the law to the facts as you find them.'

The jury found Irene guilty. Humphreys put the black cap on and read out the death sentence to Irene, although he tried to reassure her by telling her that he would forward the highest possible recommendation to mercy. After the verdict, Irene appeared stunned, and she kept repeating, 'I didn't murder my mother.'

Two female warders took her down the steps to the police car that was waiting to take her back to Holloway Prison, to the set of rooms called the new condemned suite in E Wing, built in 1937. It was made from five former cells. There was a visiting cell with a glass partition, a private bathroom and a day cell. There the lights were kept on twenty-four hours a day and the prisoner guarded round the clock by at least two wardresses. On one wall was a bookcase which hid the empty room between the day cell and the execution chamber a few feet away. The execution chamber was two storeys high, with a double gallows set over the drop room or 'pit'. There was an autopsy room adjacent. From this cell, Irene wrote desperate letters to her friends, and sank into a deeper and deeper depression.

The Charltons wrote a letter to the Home Secretary on her behalf, pleading for clemency and offering to take Irene in until she regained her feet. Within two days, Irene's lawyers had also submitted a petition for a stay of execution and parole. They set out twelve points in Irene's favour, pointing out that she had an exemplary character and had never been in trouble, and that she had not known that suicide was a criminal offence. She was also a loving daughter who had saved her mother from Nazi oppression, and a patriot who was sure of eventual British victory but depressed about the German advance and the 'affection of certain people to doubt her undoubted allegiance to the British cause'.[31] Despite the fact that the women had only escaped with one-twentieth of their belongings, and Irene worked as a shorthand typist, she had invested £150 in war defence bonds.

Their advocacy had results. On 15 December, the King granted a stay of execution: 'It may now be made known to you that, in light of certain circumstances which have been most humbly brought before Us, We are graciously inclined to bestow Our grace and mercy on said Irene Louise Valeska Coffee and to pardon her in relation to said conviction on condition of life imprisonment.'[32] Irene moved out of the condemned cell to the general population of Holloway, where she took a job in the prison library. But her mental health continued to deteriorate, and after continued advocacy from her friends, she was released on 3 March 1942.

Irene immediately left London and its painful memories. She lived with the Fines in Scotland for three months. After she felt stronger, she took a job in northern England as a secretary at a soap factory. When the factory moved to the Lake District, she moved too, living with a family in Penrith for two years.[33] At this time, according to the daughter of the house, she was still travelling with all of her mother's clothes. She kept their shared possessions boxed up and stored in her one small bedroom. At the end of the war, she moved back to the outskirts of London, then to Switzerland, then back to London, before deciding to immigrate to Australia in 1953.[34]

There Irene fell in love, possibly for the first time. She married Eduard Tell, a Swiss national, in 1955. He was a railway employee, and they lived in a charming cottage at 15 Melville Street, in West Ryde, in

9. Irene Coffee and Eduard Tell in New South Wales, 1955.

New South Wales. A photograph sent to his brother shows them smiling outside, with a pet bird in a cage at the window. Irene lived here for thirteen years.

But the war had long shadows. In September 1968, Irene took an overdose of amitriptyline. This time she did not survive.

Irene did everything she could to save her mother from the fate that she feared awaited her at the hands of the Nazis. Margarete's sister Irma was not so lucky. In late April 1942, Irma and her husband, Otto Stern Ransohoff, wrote a letter from Breslau to their son and daughter-in-law in Locarno.[35] On 3 May, they were deported to Lublin District.[36] They were murdered there in one of three Nazi extermination camps: Belzec, Majdanek or Sobibor. These camps murdered 2 million Jews between 1942 and 1943 – 99 per cent of the Jewish population of the Generalgouvernement (occupied Poland).

Londoners escaped this fate. Their homes were vulnerable to enemy attack but not to violation from their own government. Violence in the home was individual: exacerbated by the war, but still meted out by family members. Irene Coffee was an exception to this. Although guilty under the law, she did nothing to harm her mother and only acted out of love. The consequences would blight the rest of her life.

Yet her example would benefit others. The public sympathy for cases like Irene's would lead to a permanent change in law. In 1957, Parliament passed a new Homicide Act, which made the survivor of a suicide pact guilty of manslaughter, not murder. No one like Irene would face a judge in a black cap again.

CHAPTER 5

DARK STREETS

A couple moves through the blacked-out streets.
'You're taking me the wrong way round.'
'I want to kiss you goodnight. Are there any air raid shelters around
here?'
'I don't know of any. In any case, I wouldn't go in one with you.'
Conversation between Mrs Greta Heywood and RAF
airman Gordon Cummins, moments before he attacked her
in a doorway on St Alban's Street, Piccadilly, 12 February 1942[1]

Not everyone craved the security of home during the war, as illusory as
it was. For many people, the war offered new opportunities to move
around, for work and in the services. Particularly for the young, and for
women, the war provided freedom from domesticity, a kind of excitement laced with danger, as Londoners moved away from their home
neighbourhoods and mixed with strangers. The millions of British and
Allied soldiers passing through the capital added to the adventure of
London's wartime entertainments. The blacked-out streets made the
bright lights of packed dance halls, cafés and pubs even more dazzling,
and alcohol and anonymity helped to fuel many casual sexual encounters, to the dismay of civilian and military authorities.[2]

The darkness of wartime London led to a lowering of other kinds of inhibitions as well. Crimes of all kinds went up during the latter years of war, and especially crimes by servicemen and deserters. Although it was rarely acknowledged during the war, many of the violent crimes committed by soldiers in the capital had a sexual element. The murder of Evelyn Hamilton in the dark streets of Marylebone, the first in a spree of murders of women in London committed by aircraftsman Gordon Cummins in 1942, and the murder and robbery of William Raven in his flat by two Canadian soldiers he had invited home show the dark side of wartime sexual freedoms, fed by the destructive impulses let loose by war.

The anonymity of the blackout also made it harder to catch killers who were strangers to the victim. Cummins's crimes were predatory, as he targeted vulnerable women to rob and kill, while the murder of Raven was unplanned and opportunistic. In both cases, the murderers were only traced by the details of their uniforms and definitely identified by their fingerprints. Many other cases where soldiers or deserters were suspected were never solved. It was too easy for strangers to blend into the dark streets and disappear.

UNIDENTIFIED BOMBING VICTIMS

The bombing raids of the Blitz had shown how unsafe the streets could be. In the first few months of war, Londoners tried to confuse an invading enemy by removing all the street signs and ripping out street railings for war material scrap drives (although most of the metal ended up rusting in council depots or dumped in the Thames estuary). The first wave of casualties were road accident victims. Then, when the bombing raids began, thousands of Londoners died in surface, basement and Tube shelters and in the streets, crushed by falling buildings or debris, or killed by 'blast' – their lungs destroyed by the impact of bomb detonation.[3]

During an air raid, emergency services tried to get victims out of the bombed area as quickly as possible.[4] When a dead body was brought into a first-aid post, the staff tried to identify it before it was taken away.[5] But during intense raids, 10–20 per cent of bodies were still unidentified when they arrived at hospital mortuaries.[6] There, student volunteers tried to prepare them for searching relatives: 'A most important but very unpleasant duty is that of cleaning up these pitiful victims to make them presentable for those who come to identify them later in the night or the morning, of carefully collecting and making an inventory of their belongings and placing them in a bag, of discovering identity cards . . . and of searching for physical marks or other evidences which may assist what is sometimes a very difficult task of recognition.'[7] The bodies were then moved to a public mortuary, where their faces were photographed, wrapped in a white sheet. Their details and photographs were circulated in each London district.[8] Over the course of the war, 60 Unidentified Casualty circulars were compiled, listing 480 bodies. Of these, 200 were never identified: men, women, children and the elderly, mostly found in public shelters or on the streets after an intense raid.

For example, the bodies of two women in their early twenties were found by rescue workers in the Marble Arch Subway on 18 September 1940. One had light brown hair and a pink flowered dress and the other dark hair and a black cotton dress. The second woman had a sapphire engagement ring, but neither was ever identified. Two weeks later, a woman and a female baby were found dead in the Kennington Park trenches. The woman was wearing a wedding ring, so perhaps the child was her daughter. A handwritten note in the circular states that the baby was previously identified in error, a terrible reminder that another child must also have died that day. But these two also remain nameless.[9]

The blackness, the rubble-strewn streets, the anonymous dead and the emotional tension created an atmosphere of fear in London's streets. Even more terrifying was the thought of an anonymous killer lurking in the blacked-out streets, ready to strike the unwary, and escaping unseen down the darkened alleyways.

EVELYN HAMILTON

A neighbourhood of faded grandeur, Marylebone had sustained significant damage during the raids: the dusty bombed squares had huge
pockets of empty space where grand houses had once stood. Elizabeth
Bowen's novel *The Heat of the Day*, set in 1942, describes how the streets
were saturated with the awareness of those recently killed:

> Most of all the dead, from mortuaries, from under cataracts of
> rubble, made their anonymous presence – not as today's dead but as
> yesterday's living – felt through London. Uncounted, they continued
> to move in shoals through the city day, pervading everything to be
> seen or heard or felt with their torn-off senses, drawing on this
> tomorrow they had expected – for death cannot be so sudden as all
> that. Absent from the routine which had been life, they stamped
> upon that routine their absence – not knowing who the dead were
> you could not know which might be the staircase somebody for the
> first time was not mounting this morning, or at which street corner
> the newsvendor missed a face, or which trains and buses in the
> homegoing rush were this evening lighter by one passenger.[10]

But the London dead were not always killed by bombs.

Montagu Place, the street running across the top of the stately
Montagu Square, had suffered serious damage in the Blitz, and some of
its buildings were no longer inhabitable. Local hotels and lodging
houses still kept it a busy neighbourhood. On the night of 8 February,
nobody heard a scream.

The next morning, around 9 a.m., plumber Harold Batchelor and
his mate were passing down Montagu Place on their way to work when
Harold saw an electric torch lying in between two surface shelters on
the corner of Wyndham Place. As he glanced towards the entrance of
the middle one of three shelters, he stopped in his tracks. The body of
a slight, brown-haired, middle-aged woman was lying sprawled on her

back in the middle of the floor, her right leg raised and resting on some brickwork in the corner of the shelter, her left foot pointing towards the entrance. She was wearing a camel-coloured coat and a green jumper. Her brown skirt had been pulled up, her clothing torn and her right breast exposed, and she had bloodstains in her underwear. Her scarf was lying loosely over her face, and her gloves were lying palm upwards on her body, with the fingers pointing towards her face. She was still wearing her gold watch but had no handbag. She must have been lying there for hours.

Her shoes were scuffed and there was mortar dust near her body, but no one had heard a struggle. The local policeman on duty, War Reserve Constable Arthur Williams, had checked the shelters around 11.20 p.m. and found them empty. He had passed by them again several times that night and noticed nothing unusual. The only people he had seen on the street were soldiers looking for the nearby Church Army Hostel. None of the neighbours had heard anything: Mrs Cartwright, a housekeeper living in a nearby doctor's house, told reporters, 'I am a very light sleeper and I'm sure that if there had been any screams or unusual noises during the night or early in the morning, I should have heard them, but I heard nothing.'[11] That a murder could have happened in the darkest hours of the night with people sleeping all around was terrifying.

The woman had no identification – her handbag was never found. Detective Constable Carter took two photographs of the scene, and detectives took samples of the brick dust that covered the floor of the shelter. Then the body of the unknown woman was taken to the Paddington mortuary, where Sir Bernard Spilsbury performed the post-mortem. The woman had been strangled, and her right breast had a deep scratch. She also had bruises on her face and a cut over her left eye.

Detectives asked that a photograph of the woman be taken to be shown to people living near Montagu Place the next day. After a few hours of shaken heads and blank stares, Kathleen Rosser Jones, the manageress of the Three Arts Club boarding house at 76 Gloucester Place, recognised the photo. She told police it was a woman who had

10. Evelyn Hamilton, undated.

rented a room from her two days earlier. She had come by taxi around 10.30 p.m. and had asked where she could get a late meal. The landlady told her to go to Lyons' Corner House at Marble Arch. She had walked out the door at 11 p.m. and never returned. Her travelling case contained only clothes.

Her name was Evelyn Margaret Hamilton. She had turned forty-one years old on the day she died. She was one of four sisters raised by a widow in the village of Ryton in Tyne and Wear. She had attended Skerry's College in Newcastle and had graduated from the University of Edinburgh with a diploma in chemistry and pharmacology. Her career as a chemist and druggist had taken her to Ryton-on-Tyne near Newcastle, then to Hornchurch, Essex in November 1941, where she managed a chemist's shop. The shop had closed, and she had found a new post in Grimsby. She was only travelling through London; her train to Grimsby left from King's Cross the next morning.[12]

Evelyn was a serious, somewhat lonely person. She was single, with no children and few close friends. The photograph published in the *Daily Mirror* shows a composed, unsmiling woman, with shadowed eyes and hair pulled back tightly from her face. One of her sisters, nurse Kathleen Hamilton, came down from Newcastle to identify the body.[13] Kathleen described Evelyn to Inspector Clare as introverted and bookish: 'I have never known her to court anyone and I do not know any of her friends. As far as I know, she has never had a man friend. All her holidays were spent with various fellowships and worker educational societies. All her friends were what I would describe as intellectuals and her one hobby in life was to improve her knowledge and mind on all subjects. She was a keen socialist and studied very deeply the problems associated with this subject.' Her neighbour, Mrs Butler, said, 'None of us knew her well. She spent most of her leisure, alone in her room, reading books on chemistry and medicine.'[14]

One of the first enquiries made by the Marylebone Police was into Evelyn's background. Police went to Ryton-on-Tyne, where Evelyn had worked for twelve years as the manager of Wilson's Chemist Shop, living above it. She had been fired in April 1941 because, as the manager Mr Charles Hiles told police, she 'had developed rather a "sour" nature and this was affecting the business'.

Her friends told police she was of a 'reserved nature' and suffered from liver trouble and periods of depression. She was involved in the Worker's Education Association, the Soroptimists Club and the Tyneside Film Association, and enjoyed country walks at night. Her friend Florence Shyvers, a nurse who worked for the Newcastle Education Committee, described her as a 'reticent and shy woman, wonderfully clean living, rather religiously inclined, a lonely girl of studious nature who was rather unversed in sex matters and did not associate with men'.[15] From April 1941 to October 1941 she worked as a traveller for the Messrs Genatosan Manufacturing Chemists'

Association, before she was fired again. The manager, Mr Blackwell, thought she was 'mentally disarranged' and that she was herself fully aware of this, being under the care of two separate doctors in Manchester for nerve trouble.

Whatever battles Evelyn faced with her mental health, they didn't seem relevant to her death. She was last seen by Betty Witchover, a waitress in the first-floor restaurant at Maison Lyons, who noticed her walking alone down the aisle looking for a seat. The Maison Lyons, one of a chain, was a huge five-storey space, with differently themed restaurants on every floor, speedy twenty-four-hour service and a food hall packed full of as many delicacies as the war would allow. The waitresses wore a distinctive maid-like black and white uniform and were so efficient at dashing from table to table that they were called 'Nippies'. Evelyn's final drink was a small glass of white wine, to celebrate her birthday. Her final meal, in a year of strict rationing, was wholemeal bread and a main course of mostly beetroot. She probably left around forty-five minutes later. From the restaurant, it was a nine-minute walk to where she was found. Her torch and a box of matches were found scattered near the shelter entrance. Had the killer stopped her to ask for a match? Or had he waited in the street or inside the shelter for someone to pass by in the darkness?

After the nightly raids ended in the spring of 1941, many public shelters were left empty, mostly unlocked, and abandoned to the occasional supervision of wardens and policemen. Evelyn Hamilton lay for seven to eight hours in the Montagu Place shelter before Harold Batchelor happened to glance through the doorway.

Evelyn Hamilton's killer left no clues. Hamilton knew no one in the city, and she was not the type of person to strike up casual acquaintanceships. It was an opportunistic crime perpetrated by a stranger, motivated by sex and greed. There was nothing to connect her to her killer, and her murder would likely have remained unsolved – except that the killer, emboldened by the death of Hamilton, would strike again.

On 11 February, Mrs Evelyn Oatley, known as Nita Ward, was murdered in her Wardour Street room in Soho. The meterman discovered her, clad only in a coat, stabbed to death and her body mutilated. A publicity portrait of her from her actress days, published in the newspapers, showed a pretty, scantily dressed woman perched on a chair with a big smile.[16] Her husband, Harold Oatley, a retired poultry farmer from Blackpool, was devastated by her death and came down to London to help with the investigation. He told reporters, 'She was fascinated by West End life and would not leave it.' He had been to see her the week before, but as he said, 'We do not live together, and I had recently seen a solicitor about a divorce.'[17] Neighbours did not hear a struggle; Evelyn Oatley had likely invited her killer into her room.

Three days later, the bodies of two other women, Doris Joannet and Margaret Lowe, were also found in their homes. Margaret Lowe's adopted daughter, who had come to visit for the weekend from her boarding school, discovered her mother's body in their Marylebone flat. Doris Joannet was discovered in their Bayswater flat by her husband, coming home from his night shift as a hotel manager. Both women had also sold sex to support their families. In 1942, as American soldiers were pouring into the capital, it was the most lucrative short-term employment available for women.

The final intended victim in this string of murders was attacked on the street. On 13 February 1942, Mrs Margaret (Greta) Heywood began chatting with a handsome British aircraftsman while waiting for her date at the Universalle Brasserie, and they went for a sandwich in the Trocadero restaurant across the street in Piccadilly. She found him attractive and charming but slightly off-putting. He flashed a roll of notes at her and told her he had £30 and could show her a good time. She told him she would possibly go out with him but wouldn't make love to him, as she didn't do that for a living. But she wrote her number on a slip of paper and gave it to him.

After dinner, as he was walking her back to the brasserie to meet her date, he took her the wrong way through the blacked-out streets. They walked down the south side of Jermyn Street, away from the Universalle, then down the short St Lands Street towards the Captain's Club pub. Then the airman pushed her into a doorway and kissed her forcefully. When Heywood tried to push him away, he put his hands around her throat and strangled her into unconsciousness, while muttering: 'You won't, you won't, you won't, you won't.'

A moment later, a delivery boy named John Shine was passing with bottles of drink for the pub. He saw Heywood lying on the ground and a man rifling through her handbag with a torch and shouted at him. The man ran away but left his RAF-issue gas mask and haversack in the doorway. Shine ran to help Heywood as she regained consciousness. He offered to take her to the hospital, and she leant on his arm as they began to walk. After a few minutes, local policeman James Skinner noticed them, and he told them to go to the West End Central Police Station to make a statement first. Shine brought the mask and bag, which Greta insisted had belonged to her attacker. By 11.30 p.m., the RAF serial numbers had been linked to Gordon Frederick Cummins, a handsome and well-liked aircraftsman originally from Yorkshire.

Police interviewed Cummins the next day, 14 February. He claimed that his mask and bag had been stolen, and that he had spent the evening drinking with a corporal whose name he could not recall at the Volunteer Public House in Baker Street. Detectives did not believe him, and he was arrested and held on remand upon a charge of causing grievous bodily harm. Meanwhile, his billet was searched. In the kitchenette, police found a white metal cigarette case engraved with the initials L.W., which had belonged to Evelyn Oatley, as well as a picture of her mother. Detective Chief Superintendent Frederick Cherrill matched his fingerprints with those in Evelyn Oatley's room, and later they would be matched to those left in the rooms of two other murder victims.

On the day that Evelyn Hamilton had been murdered, 8 February, Gordon Cummins had visited his wife, Marjorie, who was secretary to a West End theatre producer and lived with her sister Freda Stevens in

Barnes. He had stayed for lunch and tea, telling his wife he was hard up and asking her for a pound. His sister-in-law said he was gone by 5 p.m. But the next night, on 9 February, Cummins went out with his friend Felix Johnson, and he showed him he had £19 in notes.

On 17 February, Corporal Gordon Freeman was looking for scrap in the kitchen dustbin in the billet and found a green and black propelling pencil and memo pad with 'L.A.C. Cummins' written on it halfway down. Knowing Cummins had been arrested, he handed it over to the police. Within a few weeks, the police traced the pencil to Patricia Gray, who had worked with Evelyn at Yardley Chemists in Hornchurch. Patricia had loaned it to her before the shop shut on 7 February, and Evelyn had not returned it to her.[18]

Cummins was charged with the murders of Oatley, Lowe and Joannet, and with causing grievous bodily harm to Heywood and attempting to murder another woman, Catherine Mulcahy, at her Paddington flat on 12 February. A month later, on 26 March, Cummins was also charged with the murder of Evelyn Hamilton. The pencil linked him to her handbag, and brick dust from the Montagu Place shelter had been found in his gas mask haversack.[19]

Despite this long list of charges, Cummins was only prosecuted for the murder of Evelyn Oatley. In an era of capital punishment, one conviction was enough to hang. After a four-day trial at the Old Bailey in April 1942, he was found guilty. Mr Justice Asquith put the black cap on his head and sentenced Cummins to death for what he described as 'a sadistic, sexual murder of a ghoulish type'. When asked if he had anything to say, Cummins bit his lip and said, 'I am absolutely innocent.'

His wife, Marjorie, rarely took her eyes off him during the trial and wept when he was sentenced to death. He appealed, challenging Cherrill's identification of his fingerprints, but the appeal failed. He was hanged at Wandsworth prison on 25 June 1942. His wife told reporters after his execution, 'I know the world believed him guilty, but until I die, I will never believe he was capable of the revolting murders for which he has been hanged. I believe in his innocence.'

In true crime accounts, Cummins was hanged during an air raid, a fitting end for the 'Blackout Ripper' – although he wasn't called that until the 1990s.[20] But there were no raids on London that day. It would have been appropriate for a man whose crimes fused wartime dangers with a cruel misogyny to himself die during an enemy attack. Cummins's crimes were the ultimate example of the new opportunities for murder offered by the war: he used empty air-raid shelters and the anonymity of the blacked-out streets to prey on women. And had he not dropped his gas mask, he may never have been found.

The fact that some of Cummins's victims worked as prostitutes helped to create his posthumous persona as the 'Blackout Ripper'. But selling sex was something that many women did occasionally in difficult economic times, and it was not necessarily a full-time job or identity.[21] As Hallie Rubenhold pointed out in *The Five: The Untold Lives of Women Killed by Jack the Ripper*, the assumptions of many contemporary writers of historical true crime echo Victorian attitudes about prostitution, sin and punishment, while their writings describe in detail the mutilations inflicted on the women's bodies by their killers.[22]

For women in wartime London, selling sex was one of the most well-paid jobs they could do. Even before the influx of American soldiers, Inspector Sharpe of the Flying Squad reckoned that most prostitutes worked four hours a day and made £80 to £100 a week compared to the £2 made by full-time London shop girls.[23] The *New London Survey of Life and Labour* estimated that the numbers of London prostitutes had doubled during the war, from 3,000 in 1931 to 6,700 in 1946.[24] Most solicited in the streets and brought the client to a rented room. The poorest solicited and had intercourse outside, in prewar times in unlit parks and dark alleys, and during the wartime blackout almost anywhere, prompting Quentin Crisp to declare that wartime London was 'a massive Hyde Park' and 'a paved double bed'.[25]

Prostitution was especially profitable during the war because there were so many soldiers in London looking for a good time. These thousands of rowdy soldiers also led to more violence in the capital. As

Cummins waited in his condemned cell at Wandsworth Prison, the War Office commissioned a secret survey comparing crimes committed by servicemen with those committed by civilians over a four-week period in London in July 1942.[26]

The results were shocking. In this one month, over one-third of the men charged with a crime were in the services (2,921 civilian men versus 1,045 military men). The real numbers were no doubt even higher: these statistics didn't include any crimes committed by US troops. The American Armed Forces policed its own men and only disclosed details to the Metropolitan Police in cases involving British civilians.[27] Many of these crimes involved sexual violence, although this was rarely publicly acknowledged at the time. Historian Robert Lilly has found evidence of rapes, gang rapes and other sexual assaults perpetrated by American soldiers in England, part of the estimated 14,000 rapes of civilian women by GIs in Europe between 1942 and 1945.[28]

The crimes committed by servicemen against Londoners were about to get even more violent. In the autumn of 1942, a wave of robberies and murders swept over London. Was the war creating a total disregard for the law and for human life?[29] The brutal murder of William Raven seemed a perfect example.

WILLIAM RAVEN

William Raven cared a lot about clothes. A well-kept and affluent man of forty-one, he prided himself on his appearance. He worked as a departmental manager for the Merchant Navy Supply Association, with a salary of £750 a year, as well as being a director of his own clothing company. His studio photograph shows a boyish-looking face, with fair hair, large eyes and a cheeky expression. His wife Muriel had divorced him five years earlier and lived in Cumberland with their two sons, John, eleven and Alan, fourteen.[30] He wrote to her regularly and visited the boys several times a year. According to his cousin, Benjamin Bell: 'In the legal sense he was the guilty party, but at no time has there

11. William Raven, undated.

ever been any suggestion, as far as I am aware, that he played fast and loose with women.'

William lived in a modern and luxurious flat at Chalfont Court, at the top of Baker Street, just below Regent's Park. It was only a few blocks from where Evelyn Hamilton had been found dead that February. That end of Baker Street hadn't suffered much from the bombs, but the shabbiness of the war was evident everywhere.

Raven's clothing business had been struggling during the war, as the needs of the army took precedence over civilian supplies. Civilian clothing had been rationed since 1941, and in 1942, adults could only use forty-eight points a year. A man's suit was between twenty-six and twenty-nine points, and a pair of shoes seven. So, when someone broke into Raven's flat and stole all his clothing and shoes, he was understandably upset.

On the afternoon of 15 October, wearing the only clothing he had left, a blue double-breasted pinstripe suit, he went to the company he owned, Horstman and Raven Ltd, at Imperial House, 80 Regent Street. He spoke to his manager, Wallace Steggle, asked him for £20 in £1 notes to spend on replacements and picked out some new clothing. He got a new fawn suit, two new shirts, six pairs of socks and two pairs of white cotton shorts, which Steggle packed into a brown paper parcel. He walked out the door, holding his package under his arm. Steggle would never see him alive again.

This was not the first robbery Raven had been subjected to. A month earlier, he had been out with friends when a soldier had overheard him ask the others back to his flat and had invited himself along. While the others were drinking, he went through their overcoat pockets, took all the money and ran off. Raven had seen the man later in Piccadilly and tried to chase him, but he had got away. A week after that, Raven accused a hotel porter named John Cooper, who had also been invited back to Raven's flat with a group of others, of stealing £3 from him.

Why was Raven a target for these robberies? He was well liked, according to the manager from the outfitting company: 'As far as I know, Raven had not an enemy in the world.'[31] He was a shrewd businessman, who worked hard and was generous to his friends. His one vulnerability was his sociability. His cousin told police: 'Mr. Raven was of the "hail fellow, well met" type, who, meeting someone who was down on his luck, might give him a shilling or two . . . If he met someone in the Services, who satisfied him as to his genuineness, he might be likely to extend hospitality to that person to the extent of bringing him to his flat and possibly, although less likely, of putting him up for the night.'

What Raven's family and colleagues were alluding to was openly acknowledged by his friends and lovers – Raven was a homosexual who enjoyed casual relationships with men, in particular men in the armed forces. Male homosexuality was illegal and discriminated against, and rarely publicly discussed except in trial reporting in the tabloid press.[32]

But behind the headlines, London did offer some potential for freedom. Harry Daley, an openly homosexual policeman stationed in Westminster and Hammersmith during the war, described London's vibrant queer subculture and the general tolerance of his colleagues and superiors.[33] Certain London pubs, clubs and cafés were meeting places for queer sociability and sexual encounters.[34]

Raven was an habitué of many of these pubs. He went to the Volunteer Pub in Baker Street, where Gordon Cummins had claimed to be drinking on the night Greta Heywood was attacked, every night for dinner. After that, he visited other West End pubs according to mood: the York Minster, also known as the 'French House', the Red Lion in Dean Street, the Standard in Coventry Street and the Fitzroy Tavern and the Marquis of Granby in Charlotte Street. Raven liked to drink with his friends and chat with strangers, and he often invited them, especially young men, back to his flat. The head porter of his flat, Frederick Rowen, told police that Raven had taken over the lease six months ago and had had many visitors: 'I would go so far as to say that I have seen men in the Army, Navy and Air Force knock on his door and be admitted by Mr. Raven. The men had chiefly been privates, sailors and aircraftsmen.'

At his house, Raven would serve drinks, and sometimes food, and invite men to stay over. Sometimes he propositioned them for sex. In a blacked-out city with so many anonymous men in uniform, it could be a dangerous thing to do. The man who had stolen his clothes, John Copeland, was a deserter who Raven had known for two years. They had had sex on several occasions in the previous few months, and Raven had taken him out afterwards and treated him to meals and drinks. When Copeland was short of money, he told three of his 'boys' that they should break into Raven's flat and described how they could get in. The four men took the trunk of clothes and shoes to Shepherd's Bush, sold them for £10 and shared the proceeds.

On the night of 15 October 1942, Raven was seen by an acquaintance, Stanley D'Arcy, in the Swiss Hotel Public House on Old Compton

Street, drinking with another civilian man and two Canadian soldiers. Raven's neighbour Henry Bueglin and his wife shared an elevator with him up to his flat at 10.30 pm. He was with two men in battle dress, who, contrary to the norms of military discipline, were unshaven and untidy looking. Later, at 1 a.m., Bueglin was woken by steps going down the fire escape.

The next day, another neighbour, Mrs Vogt, noticed that Raven's newspaper had not been taken in from the mailbox and that his bathroom window was open. She alerted the porter, Mr Rowen, who climbed into the flat through the open window. The disordered bedroom was dimly lit from the sunlight filtering through the blackout curtains. Drawers were open and clothes and boots discarded on the floor. The bed was unmade and had blood stains on one of the pillows. Mr Rowan walked two or three steps into the room and saw Raven lying face down on the far side of the bed. His head was covered in blood, and there were blood splashes 3 feet up the wall above him. As Rowen said later, 'The sight gave me a shock and I hurried from the room.' He and the building manager phoned the police. When the police arrived, they discovered that Raven was still alive. Raven was taken to St Mary's Hospital in Paddington and diagnosed with a fractured skull. He died at 6 p.m., without having regained consciousness.

In the corner, near an open and empty cupboard, police found dirty military shorts and pants, a pair of much-worn socks and military boots, a military forage cap minus badge, two khaki shirts and a metal match case with the crest of the Royal Army Service Corps. There were also some strands of blood-stained raffia, similar to that covering an empty bottle of rum in a cupboard. Of all the clothing Raven had picked up that afternoon from his office, only one pair of socks remained.

From the beginning of the investigation, police had to follow two parallel inquiries. Very little was known about the men seen with Raven on his last night, other than that they were soldiers and that they had left fingerprints in the flat. The dirty clothes found on the floor were issued by the Canadian Armed Forces, but over 370,000 Canadian soldiers were stationed in Britain prior to 1944.[35] The Metropolitan Police sent copies of the prints to the Royal Canadian Mounted Police Commissioner of the Fingerprint Section on 20 October. A month later they replied that they had no match but would keep the fingerprints on file.

Meanwhile, the police looked into Raven's life. Raven had joined the Metropolitan War Reserve in 1941 and been stationed at the West End Police Station. He had not been there very long when he quit to join the Ministry of War Transport, where he worked for a year until joining the Merchant Navy Supply Association. The police first traced his professional colleagues, his cousin and his sister, Mrs Lillian Agar of Leeds. They knew of his family and his professional life, but little of his social life in London. His sister told police: 'I know that my brother was a keen businessman, who, out of business hours, liked to be surrounded by friends, but apart from that, I cannot give any information about him.'

But the flat itself had clues to Raven's private life. In his desk, he had three address books full of the names and numbers of his friends and acquaintances. The police spent months tracing as many as they could find, interviewing people who saw him in clubs in Soho and creating a picture of a sociable, generous man and a vibrant, exciting wartime nightlife in Soho. But while police found some of Raven's friends and lovers, and even the man who stole his clothes, they didn't find anyone who wanted to hurt him.

Meanwhile, the Canadian Armed Forces decided to fingerprint any soldier who had been sentenced to a period of detention since 15 October. In July 1943, they sent a batch to Superintendent Cherrill for comparison. Cherrill matched a set belonging to Henry Smith to those found in Raven's flat. Chief Inspector Beveridge and Inspector Tansill went to Headly Down in Hampshire to interview Smith on 17 July 1943.

Smith seemed to be expecting them. He told the inspector he wanted to get it off his chest and tell him what happened. The previous September, he and his friend George Frederick Brimacombe had absented themselves from their unit. They had gone to stay with Smith's uncle in Ashington for twelve days, then had made their way to London, staying at the YMCA in Croydon for three or four days.

On the last night, they went to Soho, and went to a bar called the 'French House', aka the York Minster. It was very crowded, and a man beckoned them over. He said his name was Bill, and he was with a friend called George who had books under his arm. Bill bought them drinks, and they all drank together for three-quarters of an hour. Then they went to other pubs and had more drinks and something to eat. When the pubs closed at 11 p.m., Smith and Brimacombe said they were going back to Croydon, but Bill told them: 'I'll take the both of you up to my place where we'll get plenty of drink. I've got some Old Nick rum there, I call it Nelson's Blood.'

Smith and Brimacombe agreed and went to Bill's flat by Underground. They settled down in the sitting room, and Bill served them some more drinks. According to Smith, at about midnight, Bill told Brimacombe to come to bed with him, and said that Smith could sleep on a single bed in the lounge. After they had undressed and got into bed, Bill came out again and told Smith to come into the bedroom and have another drink. That's when, according to Smith, things started going wrong.

While they were sitting on the bed having a drink, Bill between the soldiers, Bill turned out the light and 'started messing about with our private parts . . . and asked us to put both our cocks in his mouth at the same time'. Brimacombe turned the light on again, but Bill turned it off and 'seemed determined to suck Brimacombe's cock off'.

Smith didn't react, but Brimacombe did: 'I next heard a thud, and the light was turned on again . . . I saw Bill lying in the centre of the bed, he was groaning and bleeding from the head, ears and nose.' Bill rolled off the bed and lay on the floor, groaning. Smith asked Brimacombe what he wanted to do that for, and he replied, 'Well, the bastard asked for it. Let's get out of here.'

While Bill lay on the floor, the men helped themselves to his things. Smith dressed himself in Bill's underclothes, shirt, suit and hat and wrapped up his own battle dress in a brown paper box. Brimacombe did the same, and although they didn't mention it in their statements, they must have taken the £20 in notes Bill had got that day to replace his stolen clothes. Raven's national identity registration card and his ration books were also missing.

After they had packed up everything they could, they tried to get out of the flat. They couldn't find the key, so they went out through the window and took a train back to Croydon. Smith claimed they gave the clothes away to men he couldn't remember, slept in a siding for a few days, then turned themselves in to their own unit as deserters. 'When I gave myself up, I was still wearing the shoes I had taken from Bill's flat. As soon as I was issued a new kit, I gave the shoes away to a fellow in the camp.'[36]

Henry Smith was Canadian, but born of British parents. His father had served in the First World War and had immigrated with his family to British Columbia in 1928 as a British soldier settler. The family farmed in Kinistino but had a poor local reputation because of the father's drinking and the mother's 'slovenly habits'. Henry's friend George Brimacombe was a private in the Royal Canadian Army Service Corps, 47th General Field Transport Company. Brimacombe was from a poor family in Montreal, the second oldest of ten children. His father had also fought in the First World War and lost a foot. The parents were 'constantly at loggerheads' and did not enforce discipline, and the home environment was not good. He joined the army at seventeen years old by lying about his age and came to Britain in February 1940. His older brother was also a private in the 45th Company. He had been a defaulter numerous times. Smith and Brimacombe had been absent from their unit from 29 September to 19 October 1942, when they handed themselves in at the Column Headquarters, at Forest Row in Sussex.

After the two men were committed for trial, the presiding judge from the Central Criminal Court, Mr Justice Singleton, asked the prosecuting counsel if there was any evidence that the men had entered the flat with the intention of committing a robbery. If there wasn't, he proposed that

Brimacombe should plead guilty to the lesser charge of manslaughter and that no evidence be offered against Smith. The two men appeared before the judge in September 1943, and Brimacombe pleaded not guilty to murder but guilty of manslaughter, and Smith pleaded not guilty. The prosecuting counsel then addressed the court, arguing that these pleas were appropriate since there was no intention to rob him, and 'the deceased was unquestionably a homo-sexual, and there was plain evidence that his conduct and actions were such as to provoke the two defendants – undoubtedly there was very strong provocation'.[37]

The police were outraged at the plea bargain, because all the 'evidence' of Raven's conduct came from the men accused of murdering him. The Deputy Assistant Commissioner of the CID, Ronald Howe, sent a protesting letter to the Director of Public Prosecutions, setting out his 'bitter opposition'. He pointed out that there was plenty of proof of criminal intent, including the fact that Raven was hit on the head with a bottle six times, hard enough to fracture his skull in several places: 'These men went to the flat needing money. They had been on the run for many months and surely the inference is that they went there to get money. Now, in spite of the robbery, one of them gets off Scot free of everything. We know Raven was a sodomite, but if he made advances to those soldiers, it is only their word. He is not there to give evidence, and I must say the feeling here is as they are very busy at the Old Bailey this is a compromise to save time and trouble.'

Despite Howe's anger, Smith was released, and Brimacombe was sentenced to only three years' penal servitude.[38] After the war, he returned to Canada. In 1953, he surfaces in the records as a resident of a Salvation Hotel in Vancouver, BC, hitchhiking across the American border to meet a casual acquaintance at the Seattle bus depot. From there he disappears without a trace.

Historian Emma Vicker described the joy that John Alcock, a queer man from Birmingham, felt when he first came to Leicester Square in 1945 and saw 'young Air Force boys wearing make-up'.[39] Wartime

London seemed to offer the possibility of new sexual freedoms for both men and women, but its blacked-out streets were not without danger, especially from men in uniform.

In April 1943, Maurice 'Jack' Horner was found in bed suffering from severe head injuries. He had been struck nine times with a chair, which lay broken in the kitchen, and his wallet and cigarette case were missing. In a brief period of consciousness before dying, he told his doctor he had been assaulted by a Canadian soldier who he had invited home for a meal in his flat in Finchley.[40] The police believed that Horner, like Raven, often picked up men in pubs, with his wife's acceptance, and that the soldier may have been offended. The cigarette case was found a few days later, wiped of prints. Although 100 Canadian soldiers were interviewed, and 250 statements taken, the crime was never solved.

The rhetoric of the war, with its emphasis on shared sacrifice and civilian cooperation, had the potential to create a new postwar era of autonomy for women and acceptance of homosexuality. But while prejudices were sometimes suspended for the sake of the war effort, after the war, attitudes hardened.[41] Women were expected to return to the home, and criminal prosecutions of homosexual men tripled.[42] Not until the 1960s would they gain the freedoms glimpsed so tantalisingly during the war.

CHAPTER 6

WASTE GROUND

I think it will be alright; the only thing that would be used would be an enema and soapy water. If it's not all right, I have left a letter.

Phyllis Newberry, 20 July 1942[1]

In the middle years of war, while soldiers were flocking to pubs and clubs in the capital, a different kind of violence was reaching its height. Unlike the anonymous desires for sex or money that motivated soldiers and deserters, infants, babies and pregnant women were vulnerable for more intimate reasons. In 1942, the body of Phyllis Newberry was found stripped and dumped in the forecourt of a youth hostel, left there by her abortionist, and in 1943, five months pregnant Irene Manton was discovered naked and tied in four sacks in the river at Luton, killed by her husband. Their killers tried to remove every identifying feature from the women, but clues in the bodies themselves (fingerprints and dental records), along with the laundry marks on clothing nearby, helped police to trace these bodies back to Phyllis's and Irene's lives. The infants who were found in London's parks, lavatories and phone boxes and in the river were sadly not so lucky – with no clue to tether them to their brief lives and deaths, they remain unknown.

Why were infants and pregnant women so vulnerable during the war, and in particular in the middle years of war? Because by 1942, it was much, much harder to raise a baby. By August of that year, almost all food was rationed, except for fresh vegetables, fruit and fish, which were all in short supply, and bread. Clothing, shoes, soap and fuel were also rationed, and had become more expensive.

The burden of childcare always fell on the mother. Millions of women, whether married or unmarried, were on their own, as, by 1942, 2.5 million men had been conscripted into the British Army, 1 million into the RAF, and another 1 million into the Royal Navy. With so many men serving overseas, it was more difficult to get married in cases of unplanned pregnancy, leaving women to struggle with the shame and stigma of unmarried motherhood. In an era of very few social welfare provisions for mothers, it was tough for women without strong social or community support to survive. In 1943, seven women killed themselves and their infants, up from a wartime average of one a year.[2] It was the bleakest time of the war, with no end in sight.

Women's deaths from illegal abortions are not generally counted among the war's violent crimes. In a sense, they are different, because the victims wanted the abortions and often tried to protect their abortionists from police prosecution if they became ill. Medicalised abortion had become legal in 1938 with the landmark acquittal of doctor Aleck Bourne for performing an abortion on a fourteen-year-old rape victim. If the abortion was performed by a medical professional of high repute, in a hospital, to 'preserve the life of the mother', it was protected by law.[3] But high fees and the difficulty in finding a sympathetic doctor meant that medical abortion was out of reach of most women. Despite knowing the risks, some pregnant women were desperate enough to either try to abort themselves, or pay someone to help them.

Women's lives were also more in danger from illegal abortions than from murder by strangers. Women's deaths from illegal abortions made up 18 per cent of the total recorded suspicious deaths between 1933 and 1953 (176 women), and in the years 1943 and 1944, the proportion rose to 37 per cent and 41 per cent: 46 women in two years.[4] The lack of accessible medical care for women was deadly. This was one reason why police investigated illegal abortions so seriously – not so much to punish pregnant women or women who helped their friends out of sympathy, but to stop 'professional' abortionists who exploited pregnant women and whose ministrations could end in death, from either infection or shock. Death could happen almost instantly in cases of reflex vagal inhibition from an object touching the cervix or from the effects of the fluid being too hot, too cold or too corrosive.[5] Syringing could also introduce air into the womb, creating an air embolism that led to collapse in seconds. This is what happened to Phyllis Newberry.

PHYLLIS NEWBERRY

Phyllis Newberry was a hard worker. On that, everyone seemed to agree. As a woman supporting herself, she took on a variety of jobs. Her former boss, Nevvar Hikmet, first employed Phyllis in his office in New Oxford Street, in which he ran a subletting agency, in 1938. After a few months, he sent her to manage his restaurant in Greek Street, at a salary of £3 a week. His brother Ibrahim worked there as a chef, and he and Phyllis did not get on, so she left at the end of 1938. In September 1939, she was working as a stenographer and living in Harringay.[6] She left London during the Blitz and worked as a telephone operator for Odeon Cinemas in Cookham, living in the Moor Hall hotel. But when the raids were over she wanted to come back to London. In April 1942, Phyllis asked Nevvar for another job. He hired her as assistant manager at a café at 7 Wardour Street, at £4 10s a week. She worked from March to May but then left because of the late hours, although she still came in to work on Saturday nights.

On 14 July 1942, Phyllis came to Nevvar to ask him for help. She needed £15 and would not tell him what the money was for. He may have been suspicious. He must have noticed that Phyllis seemed more tired than usual. But he lent it to her anyway. He already owed her £1 and thought he could get the money back in wages if she could not repay the cash. He reassured the police that there was never any personal association between them, and that he found her a 'good, honest, willing worker'.

Her current boss agreed. Edwin Bailey was the export manager at Booth's Distillery, 83–85 Turnmill Street in Clerkenwell, EC1, the oldest gin distillery in London. He hired Phyllis in June 1942 as an invoice typist, and 'she gave every satisfaction'. Bailey's secretary, Frances Heggerman, instructed Phyllis and the other clerks in their duties and had more chance to get to know her. Frances said she used to tease Phyllis about her beautiful long dark hair, which she parted in the middle and plaited around her head. Frances had also noticed her clothes: Phyllis wore horn-rimmed glasses at work and had a white blouse and a grey suit, and a camel-coloured coat. She also had black suede shoes with red piping and a flap over the front. Frances and Phyllis also had personal conversations. Phyllis told Frances that she was worried because she had not heard from her 'fellow' in seven weeks. His name was Jimmy, he was a lieutenant colonel, and he was on his way 'abroad'.

On 20 July, Phyllis went to speak to Edwin Bailey. She told him she was not really 'Miss' Newberry, but 'Mrs', a divorced woman with a child who had been evacuated to Saffron Walden, Essex. Her daughter, Mona Daphne, was twelve years old.[7] The woman who was hosting her daughter was expecting a baby, and Phyllis asked Bailey for permission to go and arrange to have her daughter's billet changed. She said that she was not sure how long she would be gone, and that she would let him know. He agreed, but when he didn't hear from her after five days, he sent a letter to the address on file, 71 Carrington Mews, terminating her employment.

The early morning of 22 July was clear, with a quarter moon shining its weak light over the city.[8] War Reserve Constable Frank Woods was walking his beat along Stockwell Road at 3 a.m. when he saw something which made him stop in his tracks. In the thin shafts of moonlight, he saw a woman propped against the wall of King George's House. She was fully dressed, sitting up with her legs spread and her head hanging down, leaning against a stack pipe in the right-hand side of the empty forecourt. The hostel had been established in 1937 to accommodate 200 boys, aged fourteen to eighteen, but it had been closed during the war as the boys were evacuated or working.[9] At first, the constable thought the woman might be asleep or passed out. He went to Stockwell Tube Station to phone an ambulance. At the telephone kiosk he met another officer, who went back with him to the woman. When they touched her, they found her cold and rigid. There were no external marks of injury and no suspicious circumstance, so she was taken to King's College Hospital, as a 'collapse in the street'. There, a doctor declared life extinct but could not find an obvious cause of death.

She was fully dressed in a white blouse, grey skirt, shoes, stockings and yellow cami-knickers: a one-piece bodysuit with a camisole top, and loose French knicker-style bottom. But she had no bag, no coat and nothing to identify her. When the pathologist took a closer look, he found that she was four months pregnant and had been dead for twelve hours. Since she had not been in front of the hostel at midnight, she must have died elsewhere and been moved. The pathologist notified the police.

The police first asked if any local women had been reported missing. None had. With no paper trail, the police turned to the body itself and what clues it could give to the woman's identity. They took her fingerprints and her photograph and asked Sir Bernard Spilsbury to do a second post-mortem. Fingerprints had only been collected by the Metropolitan Police since 1901, and only in certain arrests. But here the police got lucky. The fingerprints matched those of Phyllis Osbourne, a young woman who had been convicted of shoplifting at the Marlborough Street Police Court, 21 July 1928. Her address then was 7 Salisbury Road, Harringay. Police searched old electoral registers from that year and found Phyllis and her parents. Her father was Frederick Osbourne, a boot-shop manager, and her mother was Millicent Osbourne. By this time, the second examination by Spilsbury confirmed Phyllis had died from shock following an attempted abortion. There were also physical signs that she had already given birth to a child. The police therefore assumed Phyllis Osbourne would have changed her name by marriage.

It took four more days of tedious record-searching, but on 27 July, police were able to find Phyllis's old Ministry of Labour unemployment records from 1927, which were cross-referenced to her married name of Newberry. She had married William Newberry in 1929, but the marriage had only lasted two years. Her most recent employment record gave an address of 16 Fairbridge Road, Holloway. 'Discreet enquiries' on the part of police revealed that Phyllis's parents lived there. They had only the one child, and although Phyllis had not lived with them since her marriage, she often visited them. They had last seen her on 14 July, when she had come to dinner. 'She was then her usual self in quite good spirits. She did not appear to have any worries whatsoever.' But Phyllis's father went on to say that Phyllis never discussed her private life with them. They did not know where she lived, but knew she was working at Messrs Booth's Distillery in Turnmill Street.

Police immediately went to Booth's, where they spoke to Phyllis's supervisors. They identified the picture of the woman in the mortuary as Phyllis. Phyllis had given her address as 71 Carrington Mews Dwellings, Shepherd Street, a short street off White Horse Street in Mayfair, Westminster. When police went to number 71, they didn't know her. Police asked the local tradesmen and found out that two women, one who answered to Phyllis's description, lived at 7 Carrington Mews Dwellings. There they waited outside for somebody to come home.

At around 5 p.m., Violet Mortlock came home to the flat. She was also a divorced woman, forty-four years old, who worked as a cook.[10] She had been living at 7 Carrington Mews for two years. Soon after she had moved in, Phyllis had paid to rent a room from her and moved some boxes in from her room in Cookham. She had come and had tea with Violet several times but never actually lived in the flat, as the bombs were beginning to fall on London. After six weeks of intensifying raids and a high-explosive bomb falling onto Carrington Street, just south of the mews, Phyllis had decided to stay where she was and moved her boxes back out.

But in June 1942, Phyllis wrote to ask Violet if the room was still free and moved back in. She was out of work and told Violet she was run down and in need of a rest. The first week she moved in, she slept constantly. The next week, she got the job at the Booth's distillery, but she was still feeling poorly. One night, she called out to Violet to come and help her, as she had been sick after drinking rum and Epsom salts. She confessed to Violet that she was pregnant, about two months, but she could not be sure as she had been feeling ill for some time. Violet encouraged her to go to a doctor to be X-rayed to confirm the pregnancy. Phyllis did go to a doctor, but the doctor could not tell her if she was pregnant or not. She told Violet that her boyfriend Jimmy, a lieutenant colonel in the Army, was the father, and showed her his photograph. But Phyllis had not been able to get hold of him for weeks.

A few days later, Phyllis returned to the flat in a better mood. She told Violet that a local chemist, Bernard Fogelman, was going to introduce her to a nurse who would perform an abortion. It would cost £15, but she thought she could borrow the money. The Sunday before the operation, Phyllis was in her room alone and told Violet that she had met the nurse and 'she looked quite nice', and that she had arranged to go to an address at 2 p.m. on 21 July.

Violet asked her if she thought she would be all right and what they would do to her. She told her: 'I think it will be alright; the only thing that would be used would be an enema and soapy water.' She then said, 'in a joking manner', 'If it's not all right, I have left a letter,' pointing to a letter on the dresser. Violet looked over at it, and Phyllis told her to hide it: 'Don't leave it there.' Violet was concerned for her friend and asked her to give her an idea of where she was going. Phyllis described the house as having green railings in a dip with no other houses near it due to bombings, at Stockwell, two streets from the clock tower, near a bicycle shop.She said she would be staying in a bed with a girl of seventeen and would take two nightdresses to wear during her recuperation.

On the night before she died, Violet, Phyllis and their mutual friend RAF Flight Lieutenant Glossop went for a drink at the Chesterfield Pub, Shepherd Street (now the Chesterfield Arms). Glossop went back to the Tuscan Hotel and the two women went to bed. The next morning, Violet got up at her usual time and left without seeing Phyllis. She called out, 'Goodbye! I hope you will soon be feeling better!' And Phyllis answered, 'Bye bye!'

Phyllis did not come home that night, or the night after. By the weekend, Violet was very uneasy: 'I kept thinking over the weekend that I would come home from work on Monday and find her at the flat.' But instead, she found the police waiting for her.

At first, she told the police nothing. They took her to Brixton Police Station, where she was detained and the flat searched. Then she was subject to a 'severe interrogation'. She was shown the clothing that Phyllis had been found wearing, and, faced with the death of her friend, Violet finally admitted that she knew Phyllis was pregnant. She gave police the directions to the house that Phyllis had given her. Police immediately went to Stockwell but could not find the house. They then brought Violet, who 'could not or would not' identify the house.

It was only after this that Violet finally admitted, or remembered, that Phyllis had left a letter, which she had hidden in her wardrobe and that the police searches had failed to find. On the envelope was written, 'To be opened only if necessary, Phyllis Newberry, 21/7/42'. According to the police report, Phyllis 'must obviously have had a premonition of something going wrong'. In the letter, she wrote the names and addresses of her parents, of her daughter and of her boyfriend, Lieutenant Colonel William J. Feist of 96th Light Anti-Aircraft Regiment, Royal Artillery. He was married, with a fourteen-year-old son. She also drew a map of the precise position of the house she was going to, and included the name of Bernard Fogelman, manager to Gosling Chemist in Stockwell Road.[11] She added a final line, 'All my private letters to be burned unread.'

Armed with the map, the inspectors went to Burnley Road, a street of Victorian terraces. By this time, it was midnight, and the street was quiet. There they found 25 Burnley Road, which matched the description Phyllis had left. It was directly across the street from where the Special Operations Executive agent Violette Szabo, who was executed at Ravensbrück by the Germans in 1945, had grown up with her family. Number 25 was on the end of the terrace, and the rear entrance was down two flights of stairs. The basement flat was leased to a Mrs Edith Alice Gould, aged fifty-one. She had one conviction for larceny but no suspicions of being an abortionist. She was also known as Mrs Marsh.

Certain now that they had found the right place, police broke down the door and surprised Mrs Gould, who was in bed with a 'young girl' who was obviously pregnant. They were told to dress and taken into separate rooms to be questioned. At first, Mrs Gould said nothing, until the searchers came back with clothing – cami-knickers, corsets, a brassiere, two nightdresses and a mackintosh – with laundry marks that matched those of the clothing Phyllis Newberry had been found wearing, from Quality Laundry, around the corner in White Horse Street.

Then Mrs Gould admitted: 'That's right. I will tell you the truth. It has been worrying me. I was in the flat, but I did not touch her. I have got most of her things. I will fetch them.' She brought out a flowered dressing gown from the box room, then said, 'It's terrible. I haven't slept a wink. I will tell you everything. I'm glad to get it off my mind. It's been haunting me.'

Police also found Phyllis's handbag, a black Bakelite cigarette holder with a self-ejector and two books: *Koenigsmark*, a 1918 adventure novel by the French writer Pierre Benoît, and *The Seat of the Scornful*, a 1942 mystery novel by John Dickson Carr, from the Boots lending library.

All that was still missing was Phyllis's coat, and her yellow metal watch, which Violet told police she treasured and wore every day. It had been given to her by a friend.

Mrs Gould eventually described, at least in part, her role in a system of illegal abortions that had probably operated for years. Her job was to provide the flat and to take care of the women after 'Nurse Vi' aborted them. Mrs Victoria Alice Prior, or Vi, was a forty-eight-year-old house-wife from Blackheath, who used a syringe, soap flakes and Dettol to try to force a miscarriage. Mrs Gould told police that the fee was £10, and that she received £5 and Vi the other £5. She handed over to police what she said was Nurse Vi's share of the money, saying she had burnt hers. Phyllis, however, had told Violet that the fee was £15 and had borrowed that amount. Mrs Gould was leaving out the £5 that was probably paid to Bernard Fogelman, who acted as the 'tout', using his job at the chemist to introduce clients to Mrs Gould and Nurse Vi.

She also gave police £10 she had received from Miriam Glasel, the other woman who was in the flat. Although the police described her as young, in part because Phyllis had told Violet she would be sharing a bed with a seventeen-year-old girl, Miriam was in fact a twenty-six-year-old clerk, described by police as a 'very truculent type of individual'. At first, Miriam refused to talk, because she was friends with Mrs Gould and she admired her. She must also have felt grateful, since Mrs Gould was helping her. She said: 'I am not going to say anything to get Mrs. Marsh into trouble. She takes all the risks, and she is not too well paid for it.' She finally agreed to tell them part of the story but not to mention names. She lived with her parents in Islington, and had discovered she was pregnant. She had told her mother she was going on holiday to Maidstone, taken the train there and mailed her a postcard. Then she had come back to London, where she was staying with Mrs Gould, having paid her the £10 that police found in the flat. She told police she had been there only one day, but in fact she had been there all week.

Both women were arrested and taken to Brixton Police Station with Phyllis's clothing, leaving officers to arrest Mrs Gould's son Henry when he came home from his shift in a rubber factory in Willesden. Meanwhile, the inspectors went out to arrest Fogelman and Prior at their flats, waking them both up at 3 a.m. and bringing them to Brixton station.

When police went to Blackheath to interview Victoria Alice Prior and her husband, at first, she denied everything: having been to Stockwell, having been a nurse and knowing any of the people involved. After she was brought to the station, she was given Mrs Gould's statement to read. She then reluctantly agreed to make a statement herself, although she strenuously denied having anything to do with dumping the body: 'It's terrible, but I swear I had nothing to do with putting the body in the street. When I left the poor woman, she was in the flat. What shall I do, to think I have dragged my poor husband's name into all this trouble.'

Prior's first statement was mostly lies, but it showed a clear knowledge of the laws against abortion, or 'unlawfully using an instrument to procure a miscarriage', and was carefully calibrated to avoid any act that showed criminal intent. She denied arranging to meet Phyllis, taking any payment or inserting anything into her vagina. Prior claimed that she had dropped into Mrs Gould's house by chance to find Phyllis there. Phyllis had asked the two women for help as she was 'in a stew', and as they were sitting talking in the kitchen, Phyllis took a syringe out of her own bag. Mrs Gould boiled some Lux soap flakes and Dettol on the stove in the kitchen, and Phyllis tried to syringe herself while sitting in a chair but couldn't manage it. Prior decided to help her with the syringe, which was 'already in her person', as she said, 'out of sympathy'. This did not match with how Mrs Gould, or Phyllis herself, described the circumstances of their meeting.

But both Mrs Prior and Mrs Gould described what happened next with painful clarity. While she was being syringed, Phyllis suddenly said, 'I'm going to be sick.' Mrs Prior said not to worry, and to be sick in the basin, but Phyllis suddenly fell forward in a faint. The two women splashed water on her face and wrists, and Mrs Gould ran to the doctor's surgery, Dr Fenton's, but he was out. When she got back, it was clear that Phyllis was dead. According to Mrs Gould, 'Vi said, "Oh my God, why did I touch the girl?"'

By this time, Henry Gould had arrived home from work, to be greeted by policemen. He said, 'I'm glad it's all over . . . I had nothing to do with the death. What I did, I did to help my mother, who was in a terrible mess.' After asking after his mother, he took the gold watch off his wrist and handed it to the policeman, saying, 'That is the woman's watch.'

According to all three accounts, the women woke him up to help them carry Phyllis's body into the bedroom. Mrs Prior went home, and Miriam was sent with a message for Fogelman. As time passed, Henry was getting more and more worried: 'I knew in my own mind that we ought to send for a doctor and get one for he could have then certified the true cause of death which would no doubt hinge on the attempted abortion. The facts of the attempted abortion caused the panic in me to override my logical reasoning and my proper duty as by this time a considerable amount of time had elapsed. In my panic, and thinking mainly of my mother, I began to suggest concealment of the body.'

Meanwhile, Fogelman did not know there was anything wrong. When he received the message that he was wanted at Mrs Gould's, he went there at around 8 p.m., 'all smiles and carrying a bunch of flowers'.[12] When Mrs Gould and Mrs Prior told him Phyllis had died, he recalled, 'I just sat calmly and thought over matters. I now realise I had got myself into a devil of a mess . . . Eventually we decided to leave the body outside somewhere. I think the son suggested we leave the body in the opening outside the Burnley Road.'[13]

At about 1.30 a.m., Fogelman helped Henry put Phyllis's body over his shoulder. With Mrs Gould as lookout, Fogelman and Henry walked down the blacked-out street and across to King George's House where Henry dumped her in the yard.[14] Then the men went to a nearby coffee stall, the Plough in Clapham Common, where they had some food before going home. When Henry got back to Stockwell Road, he saw

Phyllis's coat in the street where it had dropped off. He took it inside, and at about 5.30 a.m. he took a Tube to Hyde Park and threw it in a bin. He hid Phyllis's belongings around the flat.

Fogelman eventually admitted his part in the affair, although he claimed he had no financial gain in the matter: 'I can see that I made a proper fool of myself, but I wish to be manly and face up to the matter. I do insist, however, that this is the only incident of this nature in which I have been involved.'

All five people were charged with conspiracy to procure abortion. Gould and Prior were originally charged with manslaughter, but these charges were dropped at trial, and they were found guilty of using an instrument. They were sentenced, along with Fogelman, to two years' imprisonment. Henry was bound over for two years for being an accessory after the fact, and Miriam was bound over for conspiracy to procure her own miscarriage.

Police believed that both women had been abortionists for many years, with a large West End clientele. Fogelman's role as a 'tout', and the high fee to be shared between them, suggests they were well organised. While newspaper reports were careful to say that there was no allegation that they had done this before – 'They were women of good character' – the physical evidence suggested otherwise.[15] In the kitchen, the police found a steel hospital bed and a rubber sheet, the essential tools of the professional abortionist.[16]

Phyllis's daughter, Mona, survived the war. In the early 1950s, she worked for the London department store Bourne & Hollingsworth and lived at Warwickshire House on Gower Street. In her thirties, she married, and she lived out the rest of her life in Surrey and Somerset. Phyllis's boyfriend, Lieutenant Colonel William J. Feist, moved with his regiment to East Africa in September 1942. His address was included in Phyllis's letter. Did Violet write to tell him Phyllis had died and why? Phyllis said she hadn't heard from him in seven weeks, which could have meant that he was on a troop ship on his way to Africa, or that he had lost interest in their relationship. Although he survived the war, he died soon afterwards. He relinquished his command on account of disability in May 1945 and died in 1947 at the age of fifty-five.

The story of Phyllis's life is remarkable in part because it tells us how hard women worked during the war. Phyllis worked as a stenographer, manager, waitress, typist and telephone switchboard operator, for about £4 a week. She contributed to her daughter's upkeep and spent the rest on life's necessities: she had no savings. It would have been difficult, if not impossible, to have a baby in her circumstances and to continue to work and provide for her daughter. With a married lover who was not answering her letters, she must have felt desperate. Desperate enough to be prepared to endanger her life.

What is also fascinating is the extent to which women wanted to protect each other in the case of something going wrong. Violet refused at first to tell the police anything about her flatmate. They probably threatened to charge her, which would put her reputation and job as a cook in jeopardy, before she would reveal Phyllis's secret. And Miriam Glasel, who had appealed to Mrs Marsh for help through Bernard Fogelman, admired her and wanted to protect her from prosecution, even after she had witnessed Phyllis's death.

Similar motives are apparent in the death of sixteen-year-old Anita Myerovitch, a shop assistant from Windsor. She was visiting London with her sisters on 9 February 1945 when she was found dead in Frederick Street in King's Cross, the same afternoon as a V-2 rocket raid. ARP worker Mrs Beatrice Macnab reported the death at the King's Cross Police Station two and a half hours after the raid, describing how the girl had collapsed in the street outside her house when the rocket exploded.[17] But Station Sergeant Martin was suspicious of the story because no one else had noticed the girl collapse during the raid, and death from bomb blast was almost always instantaneous.[18] The body was transferred from the ARP mortuary to the St Pancras Mortuary, and Coroner Bentley Purchase held an inquest.

Anita's sister, Mrs Ann Saunders, described her version of what happened that afternoon. She told the coroner they had been shopping in London when a bomb fell nearby: 'I'm afraid we panicked. Then my sister started running and I saw her change colour.' The sisters took refuge in a nearby house for two hours, and then Anita died. Coroner Bentley Purchase adjourned the inquest and said, 'I'm not entirely satisfied with the evidence of Mrs. Saunders. I try hard to believe it, but I find it difficult.'[19]

He was right to be suspicious. The post-mortem examination by Bernard Spilsbury showed Anita was six months pregnant and had died of shock from an attempted abortion. The ARP worker who reported the death was the person who had attempted the abortion. The sisters had brought Anita to Mrs Macnab because one of them had had a successful operation by her years before. The price was reasonable, only 3 guineas.

Mrs Macnab pleaded guilty to manslaughter and was sentenced by Mr Justice Humphreys to four years' penal servitude, as he told her: 'You are another professional abortionist, and you make your living by it.'[20] The severe sentence also reflected Anita's age, as well as the advanced stage of her pregnancy; like Phyllis, she must have been desperate in order to undergo such a risky operation. But she was one of many; as Mrs Macnab had told the sisters: 'I have done hundreds of cases, and this is the first one that has gone wrong.'[21]

IRENE MANTON

Pregnant women were not just vulnerable in wartime when they wanted to end their pregnancies. Adding a child to an existing family could add an enormous amount of stress to a relationship. Pregnant women were the victims of violence in several wartime murders. The most infamous case was that of Irene Manton in 1943. She was from Luton, an industrial town just north of London, with a population of 70,000, known for the manufacture of straw hats and Vauxhall cars.

On a foggy morning in November 1943, two sewer men employed by the Luton Corporation to check the level of the river saw something wrapped in sacks caught in some branches, floating in a few inches of water on the banks of the River Lea. It had not been there the day before, and only the bottom of the sacks was wet, so someone must have dumped it there during the night. When the workers opened the sacks, they were shocked and horrified to see that they contained the naked body of a middle-aged woman. Her legs had been tied into a fetal position and tied together above the ankles. She had terrible injuries to the head and face. There was a star-shaped wound that suggested to the police surgeon at first that she had been shot.

There were no usable clues: the woman had been stripped of all jewellery and clothing, there were no footprints as the footpath was churned up by workers coming to and from the nearby Vauxhall car factory each day, and the sacks were potato sacks in general use.

Luton Police asked for help from Scotland Yard, who sent Chief Inspector William Chapman and Detective Sergeant Judge to carry out the investigation. Pathologist Keith Simpson was called in by the Home Office to examine the body. The victim was a woman in her thirties, 5 foot 3, who was five and a half months pregnant. Her body had no extraordinary features that would help identify her, but there were identifying marks that could be compared to medical records: an old appendectomy scar, the roots of teeth in her jaw and lineae gravidae, or lines across the abdomen, which showed she had had at least one child. But thousands of women in London would have shared these features. Her blood group was taken (O), her fingerprints and hair samples were kept, and somewhat macabrely, her feet were preserved to match them to shoes at some point in the future.

The body was still in rigor mortis, meaning the death likely took place the night of 18–19 November. There was a mark at the front of the throat showing the grip of a right hand, revealing that there had been an attempt at strangulation. The grip showed in two places, showing that it had been released then reapplied. Bruising of the elbows, hips and spine showed that the woman had struggled violently and had been held against a hard surface such as the floor or a wall. Death was due to a violent, crushing blow on the left side of the head from a blunt object. This split the ear, broke the upper and lower jaw and loosened the skull bones on that side. A less severe injury on the right side of the head could have been from the same weapon, or from the woman having struck her head on a piece of furniture as she fell. Although she would have been immediately unconscious, she did not die until forty-five minutes later, when she was being tied into the sacks. She was alive when the string was tightened around her legs, but dead when the string was tightened around her body.

Several photographs of the woman were published a year later in the *Police Journal*. In the first one, she is still tied in the sacking at the edge of the river, with her face, bare shoulder, thigh and bound feet exposed. Another photograph shows the mortuary photograph circulated in hopes of identifying her. Her face is shown from the side, with a description and the caption: 'Murder: police are still anxious to establish the identity of this unfortunate woman. This is her picture.' A lantern slide of the image was shown in the local Luton cinemas and a poster displayed in shop windows.[22]

The woman's oldest daughter saw the poster in the cinema but didn't recognise it. Her sons saw it in a shop window and thought the woman looked like their mother. They went home and told their father, but he said it couldn't be her as she had stopped in a few days earlier to 'get some clothes'. Another neighbour thought he recognised her and wanted to go to the police but was told by his wife 'not to be a damn fool'.[23]

The police traced or excluded 404 missing women. Thirty-nine people came to view the body before it was buried, and nine mistaken identifications were made for four different women. Twenty-five lorry drivers who had made deliveries to the Vauxhall factory were interviewed, local rubbish dumps were searched and local dentists were canvassed for a patient who had only one molar remaining in her upper left jaw.[24] Information circulated to newspapers, the BBC and other local police forces. There was still no result.

By February, the police decided to go back and reexamine all the material they had collected, including household waste they had found on a local rubbish tip. Someone had found a piece of black cloth from what looked like a woman's coat. It was unusual for any clothing or cloth scrap to be thrown away, as cloth was strictly rationed by this time, so it was kept. This time, a dry-cleaning mark was found in the lining. The mark was traced to Mrs Irene Manton, who had handed the coat in for dyeing the previous November. That a coat good enough to be dyed would be torn up a few months later was suspicious, and enquiries showed Mrs Manton had not been seen in Luton since 18 November, the day before the body was found.

Inspector Chapman found a photograph of Irene Manton in life, and with the mortuary photograph he went to her house at 14 Regent Street, where she was registered as living with her husband and children: Ivy, seventeen, Ronald, fifteen, Roy, fourteen, and Sheila, ten. The older children were working, with only Sheila still at the local council school. The oldest daughter, Ivy, opened the door, looking almost identical to the photograph: with dark brown hair, bobbed and parted in the middle, brown eyes with thick brows and a straight, prominent nose. The inspector showed her the photographs, and this time she recognised both as her mother. But when her father got home, he swore the photograph of the woman in the mortuary was not his wife.

Irene's husband, Bertie Manton, was a short, broad-shouldered man. He had been an amateur boxer in his teens and still had the pugnacious stance. He was one of four sons from a family that had lived in Luton since the 1800s. Before the war, he had been a van driver, and in 1942 he worked for the National Fire Service and occasionally made extra money by working at the local pub, the Plume of Feathers.

Manton told police that Irene was still alive, and that she had left him after a series of arguments. Irene was from a large family of eight children and had been living with her mother, Minnie Bavister, for brief periods in the years before. Irene's mother had received four letters signed 'Irene' in December and January that had been posted from

North London. Bertie identified them as being in Irene's handwriting. In the letters, she told her mother she was living in 'Hamstead'. When the police asked Bertie to write the word 'Hampstead' for a handwriting sample, he made the same mistake. It seemed like the letters had come from Bertie himself.

There was little other evidence to connect Bertie to the crime. When the police searched the house on Regent Street, it had been so thoroughly cleaned that they only found a single fingerprint of Irene's: on a pickle jar in a cupboard. Irene's dentist, when shown a photograph of Irene in life as well as the diagram of her jaw, this time recognised her and the pattern of tooth root. Irene had lost all her teeth at the age of thirty-five but refused to have the roots extracted, and so the shrinkage of the gums was slight.

As with the case of Rachel Dobkin, police had enough evidence to show that the woman found in the river was Irene Manton. But unlike Harry Dobkin, who denied the crime to the end, Bertie Manton eventually confessed to killing his wife: 'I killed her, but it was only because I lost my temper. I didn't want to. If it hadn't been for the children, I think I would have given myself up. I had to study their happiness. I shan't worry about anything as long as they are looked after.'[25] He told police he had killed her with a wooden stool in a fit of rage after she had thrown a cup of hot tea on him during an argument over his association with a barmaid at the pub where he worked. Whether this was true or not is impossible to say.

Their relationship had certainly become rocky during the war. They had married in January 1926, when Irene was just seventeen years old. Six months later, Ivy was born, suggesting their marriage was one of necessity. Three more children followed in the next six years. Irene had never worked and had focused on her family. But in 1942, she got a job at a local tobacco factory in Melson Street. They offered good wages and a war bonus, a gratuity on each pay packet.[26] For the first time, she was earning her own money, and she had more independence and a life outside the home.

This led to conflict with Bertie. In November 1942, she left and went to live with her mother. Five months later, in March 1943, she came back, but in June she left again. But then her sister also had a fight with her husband and needed to live with her mother, so in August, Irene came back. According to Bertie, their fights were because of Irene's bad behaviour: 'Some time in 1942, my wife went out to work and I think she got into bad company. She drank more than usual, smoked heavily, went dancing, and stayed out late. When I asked her what she was doing she told me to mind my own business.' According to Bertie, after they had quarrelled, he had made them both a cup of tea, and she had thrown hers in his face. Enraged, he had picked up a stool and struck her on the head, once or twice. She fell to the floor, and he thought he had killed her.

Bertie stripped Irene and trussed her into four potato sacks. He claimed he did not realise she was still alive. He hid her body and cleaned up the blood in time for the children to come home. Later that night, he cleaned the house and burned her clothes and dentures. He lay her body over the handlebars of his bicycle and cycled over to the river, where he rolled the body down the bank. It was a foggy night and morning, which helped to hide what he was doing.

Irene Manton is still as unrecognisable to us in death as her police poster was to her children. All that remains of her in the public record is the forensic evidence from her body and the claims made by Bertie Manton about her, which are clearly meant to exonerate himself: 'I have always worked hard and been an honest man and I don't deserve the trouble my wife has brought on me.'

Yet Bertie lied to his children, the neighbours, the police and Irene's family. His story of what happened in their final fight was not borne out by the forensic evidence, as was shown at trial. Irene had been choked and released twice and held against a hard surface.[27] It was not the story of just one angry blow, but a longer attack, against which she, as a small and slight person against a former boxer, would have had little defence.

*12. Ronald and Roy Manton gather signatures for their father
Bertie Manton's reprieve, 1944.*

The jury was absent for two and a half hours, and when they returned
with the guilty verdict, one of the two women jurors was in tears.[28] But
tears for whom? Manton was sentenced to death, with no recommendation to mercy.

But his children stood by him. They helped to organise a petition for
mercy, and a poignant contemporary photograph of his sons Ronald
and Roy shows them collecting some of the 26,000 signatures.[29]
Manton's capital sentence was commuted, and he was transferred to the
Parkhill Prison on the Isle of Wight (next door to the Camp Hill Prison
from which James McCallum was about to be released).[30] He died three
years later, in 1947, and was buried in the prison cemetery.[31]

One of the reasons that so little is known about Irene is that the
records remain sealed. Although the newspaper reports of the trial and
Keith Simpson's article on the forensic investigation of Irene's body are

public, the secrets of Irene's family life are not. The police investigation files, and the court depositions and case files, are all closed until 2035. The Home Office file is closed for 100 years, until 2045.[32] Generally, criminal files are only kept closed for such long periods because the information in them could harm some living person, usually the children involved in the case.[33] While her body gave up the secrets of her death to the forensic investigators, Irene still keeps the secrets of her life.

Bertie dumped Irene in a collection of sacks into the River Lea, probably hoping she would float down the river away from where she was known. She was one of dozens of bodies found in the Thames each year: mostly suicides, some accidents and a few murders.[34] The river was also where the bodies of newborn infants were most likely to be washed up during the war, none of whom were identified. In 1943, seven mothers in London tried to kill themselves after killing their newborn infants.[35] It was a hard year to become a mother.

CHAPTER 7

FOOD STALLS AND CAFÉS

You B—— bastard, come into the street and have a fight!
Dutch seaman Jan Pureveen, to American GI Herman Robinson[1]

The war news was getting better at last. After years of heavy losses, 1943 had seen some hard-won victories in North Africa and in Italy. On 6 June 1944, after years of preparation, the Allied invasion of Northern France began. The war had shifted from defence to attack. The long years of waiting and tension seemed to be over, and eventual victory seemed inevitable.

But for Londoners, it was not over yet. Less than a week after the D-Day landings, London was attacked with a new type of weapon, the V-1 'flying bomb'. The V-1, or Vergeltungswaffe-1, 'Vengeance-weapon', was a relatively cheap, pilotless aircraft, like a flying torpedo, capable of carrying 1 ton of explosives. When its pulse-jet engine, which made a distinct buzzing sound, died, the bomb fell to earth, giving the people below a twelve-second gap to dive for cover. These bombs fell at all times of day and night, and with little warning. By 22 July 1944, 5,000 rockets had fallen on an exhausted London.

It would get worse. In September, the Germans unleashed a terrifying new weapon on Londoners: the German 'secret weapon' known as the V-2. The V-2 was an internally guided ballistic missile that could not be stopped by anti-aircraft guns and fighter planes. They travelled from their secret launching pads in Holland in four minutes, faster than the speed of sound. With no radar signal and no noise, Londoners hit by the V-2 died without ever hearing or seeing a thing.

Because the new wave of attacks was from pilotless weapons, it seemed pointless to keep the cities blacked out at night. In September 1944, the blackout was replaced by a 'dim-out', where lighting was allowed but only as bright as moonlight. For the first time since the beginning of the war, people in London could see each other's faces in the night streets.

People could see better at night, but they were even more afraid. The constant listening for a near-invisible attack created a feeling of help-lessness and dread, which is what the new weapons were intended to do. The V-ls and the V-2s had no conventional military purpose, because by 1944, Allied victory was certain. Even as the Allied armies advanced, the Germans moved the launching sites and continued the V-1 and V-2 attacks all winter. Only in March 1945 was the last site captured. The death toll was high: 5,864 people were killed in V-l attacks, with 17,197 seriously injured; and 2,754 people were killed by V-2s, with 6,523 seriously injured. The rockets also created an enor-mous amount of property damage, gouging out holes in streets and houses, particularly in South London.

RACIAL TENSIONS

The years 1944, 1945 and 1946 were also years of high racial tension in London. London had always had a sizable Black community. At least 15,000 and up to 40,0000 Black and mixed-race citizens of African, Caribbean, American and British heritage lived in Britain in 1939, with a community of 3,000 people in Canning Town and the Custom House area of East London's Docklands.[2] Jamaican-born doctor Harold Moody and other campaigners fought for greater civil rights for Black people in Britain. Moody founded the *League of Coloured Peoples* in 1931, which through its journal, *The Keys*, highlighted examples of racial discrimination and inequality in Britain in employment and housing, and in popular culture, such as the use of the N-word on BBC Radio.[3]

The war brought more people of colour to Britain. Black people from across the British Empire, including Trinidad, Jamaica, Guyana, Nigeria and Sierra Leone, worked in munitions, health care and civilian defence: as firewatchers, air-raid wardens, firemen, stretcher-bearers, first-aid workers and mobile canteen personnel. Jamaican Fernando Henriques worked for the National Fire Service for three years, E.I. Ekpenyon from Nigeria was an air-raid warden in Marylebone, and Lambeth-born Len Bradbrook worked on the Light Rescue team in Brixton. In a 1941 article, Henriques wrote that there was at least one 'representative of the coloured population of Britain' working in civil defence in each borough, with a particularly strong Black ARP section in St Pancras.[4]

The treatment of Black people in wartime London, particularly African American soldiers after 1942, ranged from admiration to hatred and everything in between. This 'short, sharp but transformative trans-atlantic encounter', in the words of historian Oliver Ayers, highlighted Britain's deep racial ambivalence and would have far-reaching implica-tions for the US civil rights movement, British domestic race relations and the decline of the British Empire.[5]

Despite the discrimination they faced, Black people in wartime London helped the war effort when they could. Ekpenyon wrote in his memoir about civilians' attempts to segregate the shelters: 'Some of the shelterers told others to go back to their own countries, and some tried to practise segregation. So, I told the people that though I am an air raid warden in London I am still an African. I said I would like to see a spirit of friendliness, cooperation and comradeship prevail at this very trying time in the history of Empire. I further warned my audience that if what I had said was not going to be practised, I would advise those who did not agree to seek shelter somewhere else.'[6] He didn't record any more disagreements.

The British Army and Royal Navy scrapped their colour bar in 1939, but the RAF kept theirs until 1940. When Henriques tried to volunteer at a recruiting centre, 'An RAF sergeant told me quite bluntly that "w——s", that is people of non-European descent, were not considered officer material. That of course was in 1939. A year later, as Britain became pressed, the situation became quite different. I cannot say that disgust invaded me totally at this rejection. It was rather like being confronted with hatred by someone you loved, and you thought loved you.'[7] In 1941, 250 Trinidadians were accepted into the RAF and made the journey to Britain, and more went to bolster the numbers in the British Army and Royal Navy. The RAF began actively recruiting in the Caribbean in September 1943. Approximately 6,500 volunteers from the Caribbean enlisted, and of these, around 5,500 came to Britain to serve during the war.[8]

Black servicemen from other countries increased the numbers in London even more. Over 370,000 Canadian soldiers were stationed in Britain prior to 1944. Since race was not listed on enlistment forms and there were no segregated battalions, there are no official statistics on how many Black men served. But since the 1941 Canadian census listed 4,691 Black men between the ages of fifteen and forty-four, we can assume that several hundreds, if not thousands, of Black men would have volunteered for overseas service.[9] And of the 1.5 million American troops stationed in Britain just before D-Day in June 1944, 150,000 were Black.[10]

Many of these soldiers stationed in England would have come to London on leave, looking for fun and a place to stay. The famous Red Cross Rainbow Corner for American servicemen was set up in November 1942 at the Piccadilly end of Shaftesbury Avenue. It was not officially segregated, but many white American soldiers resented sharing meals and rooms with Black personnel, so commanders gave out passes to Black and white soldiers for the club on different nights. The

American Red Cross eventually set up their own African American Red Cross clubs, including the Liberty Club, near Euston Station, and the Duchess Club, just north of Oxford Circus.

The increasing number of Black people in London made racist discrimination more visible. Trinidadian cricketer Learie Constantine, who was also a local welfare officer in Liverpool for West Indians serving in the RAF, was invited to London to captain the West Indian team against England at Lords in 1943. He made a reservation for himself, his wife and his daughter at the Imperial Hotel in Russell Square, but when they arrived, they were refused a room. Constantine asked his boss at the Ministry to come to the hotel and intercede on his behalf, but the manager told Watson: 'We won't have n——s staying in this hotel.' When Watson pointed out to her that Constantine was a civil servant and a British subject, she repeated: 'He is a n——.'[11]

Constantine sued the hotel for refusing accommodation for unjust cause in 1944 and won £5 5s. in damages. Justice Birkett, in awarding the damages, pointed out that the language and actions of the manager were 'grossly insulting . . . [she] used the word "n——" and was very offensive'.[12] He praised Constantine for his modesty and dignity in the face of 'the indignity and humiliation which he justifiably resented'. The case was widely reported in the press and commented on in Parliament, with support for Constantine, strong criticism of the 'colour-bar' and a recognition of the emotional impact of racially abusive insults.[13]

JAN PUREVEEN

Jan Barnabus Pureveen, a Dutch seaman, was an abusive, racist drunk.[14] In mid-January 1945, he was staying at the Osbourne Hotel in Endsleigh Street, and went out to the pubs each night, ending up at a coffee stall near Euston station, trying to pick fights. At 6 foot 2 and heavily built, he was a menacing presence. On 14 January 1945, he went out with another seaman at the hotel, Gerrit Bravenboer, to a public house near King's Cross. They had six drinks each, and with each drink, Pureveen became noisier and more argumentative. He tried to pick a fight with the barman before they left when the pubs closed at 10 p.m. The two men went to a nearby coffee stall and had steak and chips and coffee, then had another coffee with a group of Dutch sailors they met on the street, then returned to the hotel to listen to the news in Dutch at 11.45 p.m. on the wireless. But at midnight, Pureveen wanted cigarettes and asked Bravenboer to come out again and show him where to get some.[15]

They walked up to Walley's Snack Bar, a coffee stall at 137 Euston Road, a little after midnight. Fred White, a large ex-sailor who was the manager, had just served a white American soldier, US Private Jeremiah Sullivan, and a white civilian. Next in line were African American Herman Carter Robinson, a Private First Class in the Quarter Master Service Company, and the woman he had just met and invited to have a bite with him, Mrs Alice Shepherd.[16] They ordered two teas and two cakes. As White was ringing in their money, Pureveen and Bravenboer came and ordered two teas and two fish sandwiches. Pureveen asked for American cigarettes, but there weren't any, which made Pureveen even more argumentative. Bravenboer, fed up with his compatriot's complaining, stood back from the coffee stall.

Pureveen took out his anger on the nearest target, Robinson, who was standing drinking his tea with Mrs Shepherd. Robinson, who was stationed at Taunton, Somerset, was in London for the first time and did not know anybody at the stall. He had been out visiting pubs and had had five beers and five ciders but could clearly remember everything that happened next. Pureveen turned to him and said, 'You black bastard, you wouldn't be with a white girl in the States. I have been over there and know what they would do with you, you Mexican bastard.'

Robinson ignored him, but Pureveen shouted more racial abuse at him, including the N-word, and challenged him to a fight. Robinson, who was likely used to racist abuse, turned to walk away with Mrs Shepherd. When his back was turned, Pureveen knocked Robinson into the road and jumped on his back and started smashing his face into the ground. Robinson shook him off and got up, but Pureveen continued to attack him, and got him on the ground again with his hands around his throat. Robinson put his fingers into Pureveen's mouth so he could not breathe, and Pureveen loosened his grip. Coming out from behind his stall, White came to intervene. He pulled Pureveen back and told Mrs Shepherd to take Robinson to the Liberty Club, the Red Cross Hotel for African American soldiers at 12 Upper Woburn Place, only a four-minute walk away.

As they walked away, Pureveen ran down the street and attacked Robinson again. Mrs Shepherd stood by screaming as Pureveen again knocked Robinson into the road, and White again went to separate them. He was the only person that came to Robinson's defence, as Robinson later told police: 'I did not see any coloured male civilians and nobody intervened to take my side.' By this time, the manager of another coffee stall, Charles Mitchell, had come along to see what was wrong. White pushed Pureveen back up the Euston Road against the storefronts and stood in front of him to stop him following Robinson again. Pureveen was still enraged, shouting over and over, 'I'll kill you, you black bastard, I'll kill you!'[17] When Robinson got back to the hostel, he saw that Pureveen had ripped the medal ribbons off his uniform: green for overseas service and red for good conduct.

Four people still standing in the Euston Road saw what happened next. The white American soldier, Sullivan, had watched the whole fight, even moving down the road to see Pureveen attack Robinson again, while offering no help. In his statement to police, he referred to Robinson as 'the N——' and seemed to have enjoyed watching the attack. When asked at trial why he did not intervene to help a fellow countryman – 'Surely two American soldiers are good for one Dutchman?' – he replied, 'Well, that did not really bother me. Why should I butt in?'[18] Sullivan stood about 10 feet away from Pureveen, with Gerrit Bravenboer.

Charles Mitchell, who was standing closer, noticed a 'short, coloured man' walking up and down near Pureveen, coming closer and sticking his face towards him, then walking away, while Pureveen continued to shout racist abuse. Fred White didn't notice this new man until he came up beside him, and pushed him aside, saying 'Get out of my way.' White stumbled back against the kerb. The Black stranger stood about 2 feet away from Pureveen and pulled out a revolver. Pureveen was shouting, 'Black son of a bitch!' when the stranger shot him in the elbow and the wrist. Pureveen was still standing, and moved towards the stranger, saying, 'You couldn't kill me, buddy.' The stranger fired the revolver again into his shoulder and then chest, and Pureveen staggered back against the wall and called for help. Then he collapsed on his face into the street.

The white American soldier, Sullivan, cried out, 'Run', and Gerrit Bravenboer ran away, to the Merchant Navy Club in King's Cross, where he spent the night. White, recovering his balance, called out for Mitchell to phone the police, while he stood over Pureveen and made sure nobody came near.

Meanwhile, Alice Shepherd had left Robinson at the Liberty Club and was coming back along the Euston Road. She heard the shots, then a man in a dark overcoat and trilby hat ran past her into Eversholt Street. As the streetlights were on, although dimly, she got a good look at him as he passed. She recognised him as a man called 'Jesus', who had 'pestered me on previous occasions and was known to women I know who told me his name'. She knew he had recently been in prison for causing grievous bodily harm to a woman. With this information, the police traced his name: Philip Berry.

Philip Berry was a small, stocky man, only 5 foot 1. He was thirty-seven, an Igbo speaker from Nigeria in West Africa. At the time of his arrest, he was working as a stoker in the War Office and also sleeping there. He had been a seaman and had been torpedoed in July 1942. He had suffered severe frostbite on his right hand and had to find a new occupation. Since then, he had lived in London, working a variety of jobs.

In 1943 and 1944, Berry had been living with Mary Miller at 22 Torriano Avenue, Kentish Town. After a series of quarrels, she had turned him out of the house. Enraged, he threatened to kill her, and he frightened her so much she sought police protection. On 22 February 1944, he came back to the flat to get one of his bags, and they started fighting again. According to Berry, Mary got so afraid of him, she ran to the window and jumped out. But two nine-year old boys, playing in the street outside, heard Mary screaming and looked up to see her clinging to the window ledge, with a Black man behind her. They saw the man push her in the middle of her back, and Mary fall out headfirst onto the pavement. They said they saw the Black man come out of the house, look at the woman lying there, and then walk away down the street.

Mary Miller was badly injured: she had a fractured skull and was in hospital for three months. Berry was found and charged with attempted murder and grievous bodily harm and found guilty of the lesser charge of unlawfully wounding. He was sentenced to nine months' hard labour. He had been released from prison only two months before the attack on Pureveen.[19]

Police found and arrested Berry at the War Office. He denied having been at the coffee stall the night before, and said he had been in a pub in Charing Cross. Around midnight, he said, he had gone to the Coloured Colonial Club and played billiards with two men, Daniel and Branco. He had spent the night there, sleeping on two chairs in front of the fire, until the manager of the club, Ernest Marke, woke him up at 6 a.m. and sent him home.

Ernest Marke was a well-known man in Soho. He first came to Britain in 1917 as a stowaway aged fifteen on a ship from Sierra Leone. He worked as a seaman for ten years then settled in London's West End, where he ran several night clubs. Having himself experienced unprovoked violence from white GIs in 1943, he opened the Coloured Colonial Club at 5 Gerrard Street as a safe place for men of colour to socialise.[20] On Sundays, his Gerrard Street Club was reserved for political discussions. Two young African Nationalists who took part, Kwame Nkrumah and Jomo Kenyatta, would later become the presidents of

Ghana and Kenya. These Sunday discussions laid the foundation for the 5th Pan African Congress in Manchester, October 1945. Marke also organised the Coloured Workers Association.

When the police came to ask Marke about Berry, he did not recognise the name until shown a photograph of a man he called 'Creeping Jesus': 'He is a very little, stocky built fellow who wears glasses.' Berry was not a member of the club, and according to Marke, 'I wouldn't have made him one if he had cried his eyes out, simply because he had a creepy way about him that gave me the shivers.'[21] Berry had been banned from the club earlier that week after he was accused of stealing, but he had got back in somehow on the night of the shooting. According to Berry and three men who testified at his trial, he had walked into the billiards room around midnight and challenged the winner of the game. But according to Betty Williams, who was working the snack bar in the billiards room, he came in at 12.30 a.m.

Although he didn't like Berry, Marke admired his defence of a fellow Black man against a racist bully. In his memoir, he described the attack: '[Berry] tapped the big man on the back and told him to lay off the GI. Naturally when the big bully looked round and saw that it was another n—— and a little one at that, he lifted his hand to hit Berry – but that was the last thing he ever did.'[22] The newspapers carried only a cursory description of the attack, perhaps to avoid publicising racist attacks on American GIs, so Marke must have been repeating what he had heard at the time and at the trial.

Marke even visited Berry in Brixton Prison and brought another Igbo man, Mr Yallah from Nigeria, to speak to him in his own language. According to Marke, Berry told him, 'Mr. Marke, you can't do not'in fo' me, nobody can! T'ank you jus' same. If Ah get chance to do same t'ing again, Ah'll do it! Dat man him was no good!'[23] Marke fundraised some money, although it was 'a mere pittance', and added some money of his own, to help with Berry's legal defence.

The trial started on 12 March and ran for three days. Berry was defended by Mr Richard O'Sullivan KC and Koi Larbi, a Ghanaian lawyer who had just qualified in 1944. Larbi was the chairman of the Committee for the Defence of People of African Descent, which had just been formed to provide legal support to Black people. He went on to become a Supreme Court judge in Ghana.[24] Berry's legal defence was based on an alibi, and he took the stand and produced three witnesses who claimed he had been in the Coloured Colonial Club shortly after midnight and could not have done the shooting.

The prosecution called the witnesses that had identified him in the police lineup that night: Alice Shepherd, who had seen the man run by her on Euston Road, the coffee stall managers, Fred White and Charles Mitchell, US Private Jeremiah Sullivan and Betty Williams, who worked in the club. Berry's defence counsel, Mr O'Sullivan, called into question these identifications, pointing out that in each parade, no man was shorter than Berry, and that several witnesses looked at the policemen present before picking out Berry.

At trial, two of the witnesses did not definitely identify him. At the parade, Private Sullivan walked up and down the line of men without identifying anyone, then around the back of the line, facing police officers, before picking out Berry. When asked at trial if he was doubtful, he answered, 'Yes.' Betty Williams told the court that she could not identify the man in the dock without him having a hat on. She asked to be allowed to get out of the witness box to look at him more closely, but even after that she could not be sure. The police report on the case dismissed this uncertainty as collusion: 'Some of these witnesses at the Central Criminal Court did not come up to their original statements to police, possibly because they were living or working in negro circles.'[25]

Although Berry's defence was an alibi and not provocation, the issues of racism percolated through the trial. As part of the defence, Mr O'Sullivan asked the coffee stall managers if they were familiar with telling men of other races apart. Charles Mitchell told the court he had known men of other races at sea, and Fred White went even further. When he was asked, 'Are you familiar with coloured men?', he answered: 'Yes, very friendly with them too. I have always had a fair deal with them . . . They have always treated me with courtesy.' It is not surprising these words came from the only man who had stepped up to defend Herman Robinson.

The supposed difficulty in identifying men of colour was a factor in the earliest part of the case, when police did not realise the shooter was not the same man who had been the victim of Pureveen's attack. The police noted: 'This crime was a shooting at midnight, on a dark and stormy night by a negro who was not in any way involved in a quarrel which preceded the murder, and it did not look too hopeful at the beginning.' Even twenty years later, in Robert Jackson's biography of coroner Bentley Purchase, he identifies the shooter as Robinson, referred to as 'the Negro' who 'grinned in a deprecating way and sensibly refused a challenge to fight', but then returned with a revolver to do the shooting.[26] This was despite the fact that Berry was a foot shorter than Robinson.

Other than eyewitnesses identifying Berry as the shooter, the other part of the prosecution's case was based on remarks that Berry supposedly made to PC Cecil Isdell and Sergeant Stoneham in the car on the way back to Brixton prison after an identification parade. According to them, Berry seemed to be talking to himself. They heard him say, 'No men are born n———. They are born coloured. I am a man, not a child.'[27] At trial, these words were used by the prosecution to suggest that Berry had been there at the stall and heard Pureveen's insults. Berry's rebuttal at trial was that the policemen had been questioning him, and that his words were a response to them trying to entrap him: 'I said, "Don't think I am a child." I said, "I am a man," I say, "You want to find something from me to go against me in court".'[28]

In his summing up, Judge Macnaghten directed the jury that they should believe the evidence of Sergeant Stoneham because it would be a grave offence for him as a police officer to lie. He did not tell the jury that if the officers had been questioning Berry in the car, as Berry claimed, any statement he would have made would be inadmissible. This was one of the main points of Berry's appeal.

But to the modern reader, there are two glaring omissions from the prosecution's case, which had nothing to do with race. The first was the issue of the gun. The defence asked PC Vennel if Berry had a certificate to own a gun, which he did not. The police never found a gun, or even anyone who had seen Berry with a gun. The closest they could get was a statement from Mary Miller that he had threatened to shoot her, and that she had once felt something hard in his pocket. Yet this uncertainty was not used by the defence. How could a man two months out of prison and so poor he had to sleep at work afford a gun?

The second factor was Berry's right hand. Not only was Berry distinctively short, so much so that there were no shorter men found to go in the identification parade, but he had been disfigured by frostbite injuries to his hands and to his left foot. At trial, his defence lawyer asked Berry to hold up his hands while he was in the witness stand. He asked Berry, 'Is your right hand permanently in that condition?' to which Berry answered, 'Yes.' Although the court transcript doesn't describe what was seen, the reporter for the *Daily News* described him as a 'stockily built West African, with hands deformed by frostbite caused when he was torpedoed in a merchant ship.'[29]

Berry's hand was in such bad condition that in his trial for assault against Mary Miller, he is described as being unable to write because the fingers of his right hand were permanently contracted. Instead, he made his mark on his statement with his left hand. How could a man with such a badly damaged hand fire a gun?

Such questions were not raised at trial. Instead, the focus lay on the reliability of the eyewitnesses who identified Berry, and Berry's remarks in the police car. The judge told the jury in his summing up that the case could not be considered manslaughter by reason of provocation, since legally provocation could only be caused by actions or threats rather than words, and 'in this case I can see no evidence that the Prisoner was provoked, except, of course, that he may well have heard the Dutch sailor using offensive words about n——'. Although several witnesses testified that Pureveen had also abused and threatened Berry, the judge told the jury that there was only evidence for the abuse of Robinson, and that one man abusing another did not count as provocation for a third. The jury agreed and, after being out of the court for an hour, returned with a guilty verdict. Berry was sentenced to hang. He showed no emotion at the verdict.[30]

Berry's appeal in April 1945, on the grounds that the judge misdirected the jury on the nature of provocation, was dismissed. And yet, despite there being no recommendation of mercy from the jury, Berry was reprieved on 27 April. The Home Office index summary reads: 'Berry, Phillip (1945) West African. Shot a man who was attacking and abusing a coloured US soldier. Suffered from effects of wartime torpedoing. Respited.'

According to historians Lizzie Seal and Alexa Neale, Berry was reprieved not because of the psychological effects of being torpedoed, which were never mentioned at trial, but because it was now understood that the racial prejudice Berry was subjected to had a specific emotional impact that could provoke lethal violence – what they call 'provocative prejudice'.[31] Learie Constantine's successful civil case, among others, had highlighted the negative emotional effects of racial abuse, and in particular of the N-word. From this point, the Home Office was more likely to consider racist or prejudiced comments by victims as part of provocation in capital cases.[32] The social and legal landscape for people of colour changed during the war. That Berry would come to the defence of an American soldier he had never met shows a strong solidarity in London, formed in part by the shared experience of racism, and fostered by clubs like Marke's.[33]

The aftermath of the trial was the profound unhappiness of at least three women. On the day of the verdict, the *Daily Mirror* reported that Adel Akitoye, a student from Bristol University whose uncle was a police chief in Lagos, was there at court and telegraphed the news of Berry's sentence to his wife.[34] This was the only mention of her. A week later, the police received a note from a Miss L. Brooks, in Southport, Lancashire. It read: 'Dear Inspector Black, After reading the Daily

Express on March 15th of a column about "the Creeper", I have been very worried.' She enclosed a photo and asked if he could tell her if Pureveen was the same man, who is 'a very dear friend'. Her friend only visited her once a year, and never wrote to her because his English was too poor.[35] It was him. Her yearly visitor would come no more.

Mary Miller, who had moved back to her flat in Kentish Town after leaving hospital, was also unhappy. She had seen Berry twice since his first release from prison. When he first came out in November, he had come looking for her in the Chinese Café, in New Compton Street, asking for money for food and help to find a place to stay. He had come a second time and had threatened to shoot her.[36] The police interviewed her during the murder investigation and, somehow, discovered she had been bigamously married in 1941. Mary had married William Hanks in Birmingham in 1935. Hanks left to go into the army in 1939, and in October 1940, she received a letter from the paymaster that her husband had stopped her allowance. A few months later, another soldier told her Hanks was dead, and because she hoped it were true, she did not follow up with his family. She married Robert Miller, a sergeant in the Royal Electrical and Mechanical Engineers, in 1941, and received a separation allowance from him. But by 1943, that marriage also broke down, and she started living with Berry.

In 1946, Mary Miller was charged with bigamy and fraudulently receiving a separation allowance of £2 13s. in April 1943. Her sister, Annie Hunter in Scotland, wrote a letter to be given to Mary Miller's legal representative, but Mary could not afford one. She handed it to the investigating police detective. In it, the sister says that Mary's legal husband had been charged three times for cruelty and imprisoned for it during the marriage, and that this should be considered in her case. Her sister also asked to be told which prison Mary would go to, presumably so she could write to her. Mary pleaded guilty and was sentenced to six months' imprisonment in Holloway. Berry had only served nine for fracturing her skull.

What became of Philip Berry? He was released after eight years in prison. Walking along Soho Square on his way to the Jungle Club in

Frith Street one evening in 1954, Ernest Marke came across Berry and gave him a couple of bob. Less than half an hour later, someone came into the club to tell Marke that Berry had died of a heart attack at a bus stop, just a few moments after seeing him.[37]

THE WAR ENDS

As Philip Berry's trial and appeal were winding their way through the courts, the war was entering its final phase. After a slow winter, in February 1945, the Western Allies resumed their offensive against Germany, advancing across Italy, France and Austria. By the end of March, they passed Germany's borders, and by April, Berlin was surrounded. Realising at last that Germany had lost the war, Hitler committed suicide in his underground bunker near the Reich Chancellery on 30 April. His successor, Admiral Dönitz, announced an unconditional German surrender on 7 May, to take effect the following day.

After six long years, the war in Europe was over. Celebrations began all over Britain, and 8 and 9 May were declared holidays. In Churchill's official broadcast at 3 p.m., he told Britons that 'we may allow ourselves a brief period of rejoicing but let us not forget for a moment the toils and efforts that lie ahead'.

And the rejoicing was fierce. Lights blazed out again over the capital. Buckingham Palace, the Tower of London and other iconic buildings were floodlit for the crowds and the cameras, with spotlights making a 'V' for victory behind St Paul's Cathedral. Tens of thousands of people crowded around Trafalgar Square, Buckingham Palace and Whitehall, singing and dancing in the streets. The Royal Family came out to wave to the crowd on the balcony of the palace over and over, to rapturous cheers. Churchill twice appeared on the balcony of the Ministry of Health and addressed the huge crowd in Whitehall. He told them, 'This is your victory!' Many in the crowd shouted back, 'No, yours!' On his second appearance, made just after 10.30 p.m., he led the crowd in singing 'Land of Hope and Glory'.[38]

THE LIGHTS OF LONDON: FAMOUS BUILDINGS FLOODLIT ON VICTORY NIGHT.

THE FLOODLIT FAÇADE OF BUCKINGHAM PALACE, WITH PART OF THE DENSE CROWD WHICH GREETED THE KING AND QUEEN.

TRIUMPHANT AMID THE RUINS, ST. PAUL'S CATHEDRAL FROM THE EAST, FLOODLIT, WITH THE BALL AND CROSS SPOT-LIGHTED BY SEARCHLIGHTS.

THE DETAIL OF THE PEDIMENT AND FLUTED CORINTHIAN COLUMNS OF THE MANSION HOUSE REVEALED BY VICTORY FLOODLIGHTING.

HORSE GUARDS PARADE—THE WELL-KNOWN SCENE OF THE CHANGING OF THE GUARD—SEEN FROM WHITEHALL IN A GLOW OF LIGHT.

THE TOWER OF LONDON, TRANSFORMED BY THE FLOODLIGHTS OF VICTORY INTO A PANORAMA TO ILLUSTRATE A FAIRY-TALE.

As at the outbreak of war one of the most poignant phrases was "The lights are going out all over Europe," so it was most fitting that the lights of London should blaze out to celebrate Victory in Europe; and Victory Night was celebrated with lights of every form, colour and source. Not only were the pyrotechnics of war—searchlights, flares, rockets and bonfires—turned to the celebration of peace; but that peculiarly modern art of peace—floodlighting—was used to illuminate and to illustrate all the main buildings of the metropolis. Our pictures show some of the chief landmarks of London, glowing in the unaccustomed light; and among other notable buildings floodlit were the Admiralty Arch, the Royal Exchange, Nelson's Column and the Houses of Parliament.

13. 'The Lights of London', Illustrated London News, 1945.

Three months later, when Japan surrendered and the war was truly over, Londoners celebrated again. On V-J Day, 'London went wild', according to British Pathé News's *Peace on Earth*.[39] The newsreel pans across the celebrating crowds outside Buckingham Palace and in Trafalgar Square. It also shows smaller celebrations in a West End nightclub and in Charlie Brown's pub in Limehouse, where 'all nations rejoiced'. Black pub-goers, possibly members of London's East End community of seafarers and dockworkers, were filmed dancing arm in arm with a multiracial mix of patrons, and a mixed-sex interracial couple are briefly shown dancing together.[40] The film suggested a peaceful future of cross-class and cross-race harmony. But off-screen, things were not so peaceful.

That same night, a fight broke out outside Marke's Colonial Club between West Indian and African American and white American personnel. When rumours started to spread that someone had been stabbed, according to newspapers, a mob of white service personnel reportedly 'dashed down Gerrard Street' and 'seized two Negroes', who were 'brutally pummeled'.[41]

Marke, working in his office upstairs, heard a crowd of white GIs shouting outside, and when he rushed downstairs to 'see what it was all about . . . a brick whizzed an inch wide of my head and landed on the stairway'.[42] He barricaded the doors against the angry white crowd and organised the twenty Black men, soldiers and civilians, inside. He and his croupier, Ola Dusumo, gave out orders and tried to stem the panic. One man tried to escape by jumping out the window but was caught by a group of GIs in Shaftesbury Avenue: 'They nearly murdered him.'[43]

Having no weapons in the club, they filled up empty glass bottles with water and lined up along the front door. On a signal, Ola suddenly unlocked it: 'As the door flew open, those who fell in were immediately dealt with, while the rest of us rushed out and started lashing at the others . . . We battered the hell out of those we handled. Within one minute we were back in with the door closed, getting ready for the next assault.'[44] Just then a shot was fired in the air by an American military policeman, and, with civilian policemen, they managed to restore order.

They eventually arrested twenty-three Black troops, two white soldiers and three women.[45] For the next month, Gerrard Street was patrolled by civil and military police and out of bounds to all American servicemen, and, in this atmosphere of safety, the Colonial Club attracted many new members. Marke gleefully recalled: 'Never have I made so much money in such a short time. Black faces were coming to the Colonial Club to play the illegal games of dice and poker, lawfully, under the watchful eyes of the two greatest authorities in the West. This is not likely to happen again in my or anybody else's lifetime.'[46]

POSTWAR LONDON

Marke's joy in the moment of triumph, along with that of many others, was short-lived. Despite the big celebrations and nationalist fanfare, victory was in many ways anti-climactic. The end of the war was, as historian Alan Allport wrote, 'an experience both intense and often sharply double-edged – a national moment rich in joy and relief, certainly, sanguine and self-confident for many, but also one of doubts, frustrations, sadnesses and private defeats'.[47] London had lost 43,000 civilians and had over 50,000 seriously injured.[48] Around 1.5 million Londoners were now homeless and approximately 9 million square feet of office space had been destroyed.[49] Bombsites and ruins peppered central London, and large areas in the East and the South were devastated. It would take years to clear the rubble and decades to rebuild and ease the postwar housing crisis. Over 8 million people, or 40 per cent of London's population, had moved from their neighbourhood for some part of the war, and many would never return. The old London was gone.

The end of hostilities did mean no more German air attacks and threatened invasions. But in many ways, wartime conditions carried on, and even worsened. Rationing continued for longer in peacetime than war and got even stricter. Bread was rationed for the first time between 1946 and 1948, and the last foods didn't come off the ration until 1953.[50]

The end of hostilities in 1945 also meant that most of Britain's 2 million armed forces serving overseas would be coming home.[51] But the pace of demobilisation was glacial. In the early months, only 3,000 men a day were being released from service; in 1919 the discharge centers had processed ten times as many. By the beginning of 1946, 80 per cent of servicemen were still not home. Full demobilisation would not be complete until 1947.[52]

Frustrated at being unable to join their families or get back to their pre-war lives, many soldiers just walked away. In 1947, it was estimated that there were 20,000 British deserters, not including the American, Canadian and other Allied deserters, many of whom were trying to scrape a living in London without ration cards and avoiding the police.[53] Faced with the choice of returning to their units, serving a period of detention and another period in the forces or continuing their 'illegal' existences, most chose the latter. As the Deserter's Amnesty Campaign wrote in a letter to *The Times* in March 1947, deserters were in danger of drifting 'into becoming full-time criminals by pressure of circumstances'.[54]

These end-of-war anxieties and disappointments contributed to growing racial tensions in London. African American journalists reported to their home audiences that, ever since V-J Day violence, 'interracial relations, [which were] never very good, have markedly degenerated, so much so that Africans, West Indians and other dark-skinned Britishers are forced to walk in groups after nightfall for their mutual protection'.[55] As African American journalist Ollie Stewart wrote in September 1945: 'The British want us to go home and make no bones about it.'[56] Aloysius Abbott, a young Jamaican airman, would soon find this out.

ALOYSIUS ABBOTT

On Christmas Eve, 1946, twenty-year-old Aloysius Abbott was happy. After five years of service as an RAF aircraftsman, he was being demobilised home to Jamaica in January.[57] He was going back to marry his sweetheart, and he had a letter in his breast pocket, telling him she had found somewhere for them to live. First, he was having one last leave in London with his friends and his older brother Victor, who were stationed with him at RAF Little Rissington, near Cheltenham in Gloucestershire. 'Little Rissi' accommodated No. 6 Service Flying Training School and No. 8 Maintenance Unit RAF and was one of the prettiest RAF airfields, built partly in local Cotswold stone. But it could not compare to the bright lights of London, now fully ablaze.

Aloysius Joseph Abbott was born in 1926 in the parish of St Andrew, in Kingston, Jamaica. He was the fifth child of Herbert and Berna Abbott. Kingston had prospered as a busy port and commercial centre in the nineteenth century, but a series of agricultural crises, economic depressions and cyclones and a hurricane which almost destroyed the island in 1930 had made conditions there increasingly difficult. More and more people poured into the city from the hard-hit rural areas: the population of Kingston nearly doubled in thirty years, from 59,674 in 1911 to 110,083 in 1943.[58] This rapid urbanisation widened the gap between rich and poor in Kingston: 'uptown, the Jamaica of the rich minority, mostly white and mixed, living in wealthy neighborhoods such as Mona or Liguanea, and downtown, the Jamaica of the poor, Afro-Jamaicans rotting in overcrowded inner-city areas of Kingston such as Back O' Wall and Trench Town'. Cross Roads was the boundary between these two worlds, and it was the home of the Abbott family.[59]

When the RAF came recruiting in Jamaica, they found thousands of willing volunteers. More than 6,000 Black Caribbean men joined up: 5,500 as ground staff and some 450 as aircrew. Another 100 women joined the Women's Auxiliary Air Force (WAAF). The largest Caribbean contingent came from Jamaica, and by February 1945 there were over 3,700 Jamaicans in the RAF, almost all of whom served overseas. Many of them liked Britain so much they stayed or returned to Britain after the war.[60]

Aloysius and his older brother Victor joined the RAF in 1941: Victor was eighteen, but Aloysius was only fifteen. He must have looked convincingly older, for he was accepted into service. The brothers stuck together throughout the war, and on this last leave, they came to London together.

The brothers found rooms at the YMCA Hostel at the Westminster Services Club behind Westminster Abbey and, together with thirteen comrades from the RAF, set out to explore the city one last time. After a few watered-down drinks, they went to the Paramount Dance Hall, in Tottenham Court Road. The wall of sandbags that had protected the entrance during the war years had now gone, and the sign outside was now as brightly lit as the colourful, mirrored interior. For only a few shillings' admission, they were guaranteed a fun few hours of entertainment. The Paramount was known as a place where men of colour were welcomed, and where there were lots of willing partners. The conventions of dancing allowed for easy introductions and conversations between strangers, as much as the fast jitterbugging and other popular wartime dances would allow.

The men enjoyed themselves hugely, as Aloysius's brother Victor told police: 'He was with some other boys from Jamaica, and we had all be together for a few hours.'[61] Victor was tired, so after they left the dance hall at around 9 p.m., he went back to the YMCA club with his friend Herbert Allen.

The other men, famished, went out to find something to eat. Food was harder to find than fun in postwar London. With even more shortages and stricter rationing in 1946, meat, cheese, fats and sugar were scarce. Food stalls had sandwiches and buns, and cheap cafés served potatoes, vegetables, a little meat and a lot of eggs.[62] That autumn, a small café in Marylebone was caught selling 'Filleted Steaks' at 4 shillings and sixpence, which were actually horseflesh.[63] The café was fined £15 and 5 guineas for costs, and the manager £5.

The RAF men found a café closer to them, Esther's restaurant at 140 New Cavendish Street.[64] It was a small, narrow café, which seated thirty people. The men sat with two Black women friends at the tables at the front. They ordered meals, mostly omelettes, and sat down to chat about their night.

14. Esther's restaurant, 140 New Cavendish Street, 1946.

Laughter and chatter were echoing in the room when, after the public houses had shut, two white men entered with a young blonde woman. Stella Violet Mooney was a twenty-three-year-old maid at Osbourne Hotel in Russell Square. She was married, but her husband had abandoned her the year before, taking a troop ship to Australia and deserting his unit there. She was four months pregnant at the time. She now had eleven-month-old twins, who were being cared for at St Margaret's Nursery, Kentish Town, a residential nursery for seventy babies run by the London County Council.

Stella had nowhere to live and, on this Christmas Eve, nowhere to stay. She had known one of the men, Albert Westlake, for a few weeks, because they went to the same pub, the George and Dragon in Cleveland

Street, W1 (still operating). That night she had seen him in the pub around 8 p.m.: 'He came over and bought me a drink. I told him that I had no where to stay the night. He told me that he might be able to fix me up.' He went to the other end of the bar, and after a few minutes came back with 'Fred', Frederick Westbrook, who was staying at the Royal Hotel. Fred told her she could probably stay with him. The three of them drank until closing time at 11.30 p.m., then went to Esther's to have a meal. They sat at the only empty table, near the back of the room and the food counter. They ordered three omelettes, and the café worker put down cutlery in front of them.

There was only one waitress: Mrs Diana Bendter. According to the *Daily Mirror*, Diana was the thirty-four-year-old wife of a Black US Army staff sergeant stationed in Germany, who was waiting for permission to join him in the States. American soldiers had to be granted leave to marry by their commanding officer, and it was almost unheard of for African American men to be given permission to marry white English women.[65] Because of this, the 2,000 'brown babies' born to English women were almost all illegitimate. If Mrs Bendter did go the States, she did not stay long – electoral records show her in London from 1949 into the 1960s.

As Mrs Bendter told the *Mirror* journalist, one of the white men at the table was impatient and angry: 'One the men asked me to serve him first because he was in a hurry, but I said I must serve everyone in order.' She asked him if she could take his cutlery for another customer whose meal had arrived, but he did not answer. She took them anyway and put them in front of a Black man at the next table. This enraged the impatient white man: 'Then he jumped up and pushed me and punched me in the face.'

The café erupted in shouts, and half of the men jumped up to defend Mrs Bendter. Hoping to avert a riot, Sergeant Oswald McDonald, a Jamaican wireless operator, and a student named Lloyd Emmanuel Williams came to the table and grabbed the white man's arms, ready to escort him to the door. According to the police report, 'These two

Jamaicans apparently assist in the welfare of other Jamaicans in London and neither wanted to see the younger members start trouble. They were all annoyed at Westbrook for striking a woman.'[66]

But Mrs Bendter was not done with Westbrook: 'I found my nose was bleeding –and that made me mad. The man was being held by coloured airmen. I slapped his face – twice – hard, and then I picked up a plate and smashed it on his face. The coloured boys escorted him to the door.'[67] Behind them trailed Abbott and a couple of other men, ready to lend a hand.

At the doorway of the restaurant, the Jamaican men pushed Westbrook out and told him to be on his way. When he struggled and tried to get back in, Williams slapped his face. In his later account, Westbrook claimed that the men surrounded him and beat him, and that he had to push through their legs to escape, while they chased him up the street. But in reality, no one chased him. Westbrook ran away from the men and ran up the street about 25 yards towards Hansen Street. Back in the café, Diana Bendter had asked Westbrook's companions to leave, and they were walking towards the door.

In the street, Westbrook turned around, and pulled out a gun, a 9mm Browning automatic pistol. He shot towards the café three times. Aloysius, who was just turning to go back inside, was shot through the left side of his chest. The bullet went through the letter from his sweetheart in the left breast pocket of his tunic, and then through both of his lungs. The other two shots hit the front of the café.[68]

Aloysius fell in the doorway, head and shoulders inside, feet on the pavement. Stella Mooney, walking out with Albert Westlake, saw him fall: 'We were then near the door, and I saw a Royal Air Force chap lying at my feet.'[69]

Stella and Albert stepped over Aloysius in the doorway and stood on the street, as Fred Westbrook ran back towards the café. Sergeant McDonald pulled Aloysius inside and kicked the door shut, as patrons scattered down into the basement and Diana called the police and an ambulance. Westbrook, his gun jammed, turned away and ran up the street, with Stella in tow, who still needed a place to sleep. Albert went home.

As Westbrook was running away, Diana came to the front to see if she could help Aloysius: 'I did not know him, but I had served him a meal.' But it was too late. Aloysius had died within moments of being shot.

Freda Dempsey, a mixed-race woman who had been in the café with the Jamaican men, recognised one of the white men as Albert Westlake. Police traced him that night, asleep in bed, and he told them the names of his two friends, and that he had not been involved in the violence.

Frederick Westbrook and Stella Mooney spent Christmas Day and Boxing Day holed up at the Royal Hotel, under the name of Mr and Mrs French. What a strange day it must have been for Stella, her twins' first Christmas, no home, in hiding with a man she knew had a gun and who had shot someone right in front of her. Westbrook continued to show off his gun, bragging to her that he would have fired more shots into the café if it had not jammed, and firing shots into the hotel bed. Surprisingly, this did not seem to arouse any concern from the hotel staff.

Westbrook had no happy family to go to either. The only son of a widowed charwoman from Holborn, he had been an uncontrollable child. He had been sent to an approved school, a type of boarding school for wayward youth, at eight years old, from which he easily escaped. He spent his childhood going back and forth between foster parents, the school and his mother. After stealing a bicycle at fourteen years old, he was sent to a tougher borstal, a juvenile prison. Whenever he was released, he would continue stealing. Despite his criminal record, he joined the South Wales Borderers in 1939. He was a frequent deserter, and he was convicted of thefts in 1941, 1942, 1943 and 1945. His most recent sentence was twenty-one months in prison for theft, from which he had been released in October 1946. The police file has no details of his military record, so it's unclear why he had not been discharged after so many convictions and stints in prison.

Fred and Stella spent Boxing Day in cafés and at the pictures, waiting for the holiday to be over. They agreed not to go to pubs except for a quick drink in case they were recognised. When the first post-holiday newspapers came out on 27 December, the headlines read: 'Police Hunt Killer after Café Quarrel.'[70] The shot had been deadly, and Westbrook was wanted for murder: 'Divisional Detective Inspector R. Higgins, of West End Central, and his officers, were searching throughout Christmas Day and yesterday for a tall, slim-built, hatless man, aged about 30, who, it is believed, fired the shots, and for other men who disappeared after the shooting.'[71] Fred and Stella decided to split up. Fred gave Stella three pounds to find a place to stay and a suitcase with some stolen ration books, clothing and bacon, and he promised to meet up with her later.

They left the hotel in the morning and were heading towards Russell Square Tube Station. Westbrook had his gun in his pocket, and he told Stella, 'I won't be caught alive. I'll shoot it out.'[72] Two police constables in the street stopped them and asked Westbrook for his identity card. Westbrook shoved his gun in PC Strange's stomach and said, 'Don't come another inch, or I'll ram your guts in.'

After he turned and ran away, the policemen followed him. One jumped into a taxi, the other into an army vehicle, as Westbrook weaved in and out of streets and alleyways across to Grays Inn Road, shooting back at the taxi. He ran back west along Tavistock Place, before diving into a dairy near Cartwright Gardens. He managed to get up onto the roof, dodging the chimney pots and parapets, followed by the policemen and other bystanders who had joined in the chase. Over the next hour and twenty minutes, reinforcements poured in, and eventually nearly a hundred policemen were concentrated in the area round Cartwright Gardens, Tavistock Place and Marchmont Street. They were stationed in groups of three at three-yard intervals.

Richard Gloyne, who was driving a horse-drawn luggage cart, joined in the chase at Cartwright Gardens. Abandoning his cart, he followed the officers up to the roof of the Cambria Hotel. He heard Westbrook fire shots at PC Strange, one of which went through his sleeve, and heard someone say, 'He's got no more left.' A moment later, Westbrook took aim at PC Rowswell and shot. He missed, but the bullet ricocheted and struck Rowswell in the eye, and he cried out and fell.[73]

Westbrook dropped through a skylight in the roof and into an empty hotel room. Realising he was surrounded, he tried to hide the gun and waited in a chair for the police. After a few minutes, policemen burst into the room. He was hustled, struggling, down the hotel steps into a waiting police van and to the Bow Street Police Station.

The chase among the chimney pots was watched from below by hundreds of people, and the bravery and tenacity of the officers who led the chase at great personal risk was widely commended.[74] Rowswell lost his eye and was in hospital for weeks. Both officers were eventually awarded £15 from the Bow Street Reward fund.

In the back of the fireside chair in the hotel room, police found a 9mm Browning automatic pistol, and in one of Westbrook's waistcoat pockets, they found a round of 9mm ammunition. The pistol had been made in Canada, but the police could not trace its origin: 'Just another of those service weapons that went astray in the war.'[75] Murders involving guns were relatively rare in London before the war, but with returning servicemen and deserters in the capital, gun crime surged. Guns were involved in ten London murders in 1946 and seven in 1947, a twenty-year high. Along with the ammunition, Westbrook also had £27 in his pocket.[76]

Westbrook was arrested and charged with the murder of Aloysius Abbott and unlawfully shooting at police constables Norman Strange and Bertie Rowswell with intent to resist arrest. At the magistrate's court hearing on 28 December, an unnamed 'Jamaican lawyer' was present, who said he represented Abbott's family. He sat next to two flight lieutenants, one of whom was most likely Victor Abbott. The police brought Abbott's bloodstained RAF battledress and two overcoats into court: evidence designed to have a profound emotional impact on the spectators and magistrate.[77]

Westbrook's statement in his own defence was that he had never intended to shoot anybody. He had fired into the café in a heat of passion, to frighten 'a so-called gang of coloured men who were attacking him'.[78] Westbrook tried to recast the Jamaican soldiers as criminals by appealing to racial stereotypes. But no one was fooled. The police report observed: 'It was not fear of the coloured men that caused this, but absolute rage at having been ejected from the restaurant following his assault on the waitress.'[79]

The jury gave Westbrook the benefit of the doubt when he said he never aimed the gun at Abbott, and he was found guilty of manslaughter instead of murder. Mr Justice Atkinson, passing sentence, told him, 'The jury have given you the benefit of a very slender doubt. I have examined your career and can find no reason for extending leniency. Borstal was made a farce. If ever a criminal had a chance given to him who did not deserve it, you were he. You have proved you are a deter- mined criminal.' He was sentenced to eleven years' penal servitude for manslaughter and malicious shooting.[80]

Aloysius was buried at Brookwood Military Cemetery, in Surrey. His headstone reads: 'A darling son and brother. Till memory fades and life depart. You will live on in our hearts.'[81] He never made it back to his sweetheart and family in Jamaica, but stayed in England, a victim of racial aggression and rage.

Violent attacks on people of colour reflected the increased racial tension in public spaces during wartime. The deaths of Pureveen and Abbott give us a glimpse into the gap between Londoners who respected and protected people of colour, and those who insulted and attacked them. The questioning of witnesses at trial also reveals contemporary attitudes and assumptions about race.

These attitudes signalled some of the challenges London would face in the years after the war. Britain had been an imperial power with its colonial subjects largely located elsewhere. But all this would change during the war. Facing the Germans alone after 1940, Britain called on its colonial citizens to help with the war effort. Facing labour shortages after the war, British companies again recruited for workers in the Caribbean.

The SS *Ormonde* was an ex-troop ship that arrived in Britain in 1947 with 241 Caribbean migrants, including carpenters, engineers and plumbers. Next was the *Almanzora*, bringing 200 Caribbean passengers, many of whom were former wartime RAF service personnel. And then, famously, came the *Empire Windrush* on 21 June 1948, carrying 802 passengers from the Caribbean.[82] Many of them had paid £28 (about £1,000 today) to travel to Britain in response to job advertisements in their local newspapers.

While their labour was welcomed, they faced social discrimination and overt racism. Finding safe and affordable housing was especially difficult in London. Over 70,000 homes had been destroyed in war, and another 1.7 million were damaged. Many landlords refused to rent to people of colour, and neighbours could be hostile. Many of the Windrush migrants would first find accommodation in the deep air-raid shelters underneath Clapham South Underground station, now open as a museum.

In 1951, Beresford Brown and his family, immigrants from the West Indies, moved into the top-floor flat at 10 Rillington Place, Kensington, much to the horror of downstairs neighbours Reg and Ethel Christie. The Christies sent a stream of complaining letters to Kensington Council, accusing their new neighbours of being dirty and loud. After the Christies left the flat, the landlord let Brown use the downstairs kitchen. While putting up a shelf for a radio, Beresford peeled off the wallpaper and discovered the alcove where Reg Christie had hidden the bodies of the three women he had murdered in 1953.

Christie's defence at his trial was insanity, brought on by the persecution of his Jamaican neighbours and the terrible pressures of trying to maintain his and his wife's respectability and standard of living. His defence counsel even insinuated to Franklin Stewart, one of the new Jamaican tenants, that the reason that Christie sprinkled disinfectant in the hallway was not to cover the smell of the corpses in his flat, but because of the 'filthy habits' of tenants like himself.[83] The racial hatred of some white Notting Hill residents would eventually erupt in the violent Notting Hill riots of 1958, in which hundreds of white residents attacked the homes and businesses of their West Indian neighbours for seven nights in a row.

The racial prejudice that led to violence in the murders of Jan Pureveen and Aloysius Abbott was a taste of the tensions and violence that were to come. What was striking about these cases was not that racial prejudice existed and was increased by the war, but the solidarity and help given to Black men who were attacked.

CHAPTER 8

AFTERMATH

Every Christmas I think of Beryl singing, and it brings tears to my eyes. Lovely as Beryl was, she sang out of tune, and I remember my dad putting his hands over his ears. Even worse, she couldn't whistle, but tried to impersonate Bing Crosby nonetheless. Beryl's attempts sounded like one of those old kettles howling on the stove. We loved her just the same.

Peter Thorley, Beryl Evans's brother[1]

Aloysius Abbott never made it home to Jamaica. But in the years after the war, hundreds of thousands of Londoners serving in the armed forces did come home. Only home had changed. The old London was gone: the neighbourhoods, the social networks, the squares and railings. In 1945, 56,000 children were still evacuated. When evacuation officers visited their London addresses, they found that 19,000 of them had no home to return to. Their parents had died, disappeared or didn't want them back.[2]

London had changed in other ways too. As the base for an international and imperial war effort, the city became more diverse. The Irish were still the largest immigrant group, but Poles, Greek Cypriots, Indians and German and Austrian refugees created their own London communities after the war. In 1946, West Indians began to arrive and settled in Brixton, Notting Hill and North Kensington.[3] The 1948 Nationality Act made Britons and all colonial subjects equal citizens with free right of entry to the UK, which led to even more Commonwealth migration in the 1950s.

People themselves had changed too.

Londoners had dealt with the hardships of war, the breakup of families, the enemy bombing and the fear and anxiety, but they had also enjoyed the freedoms. More women had entered the workforce, and they had been well paid. Hundreds of thousands of women also had had to get along without their husbands. Children had grown up. Grandparents had died. Demobilised soldiers had to come home to families that had struggled on without them, and had to try to find their way back in. Thousands could not.

KATHLEEN PATMORE

Cyril Patmore was one who could not. He was a soldier in the Royal Scots Fusiliers, serving in India. In July 1945, he received letters from two women: his wife Kathleen and her oldest sister. Because of what the letters said, the Welfare Officer granted him twenty-eight days' compassionate leave to return home and see her, despite the battalion's preparation for a seaborne landing on the west coast of Malaya (Operation Zipper).

We don't know what Kathleen Patmore looked like, if she was tall or short, dark or fair. But we do know one detail of her appearance in July 1945, which defined the crisis that she and her family were in. Kathleen was eight months pregnant, with a visible belly stretching out her clothes. And her husband hadn't been home in over a year.

Kathleen Patmore was born Kathleen Margaret Jennings in 1907 in Wallingford, Berkshire. She was eighth in a family of ten children, and her father and brother worked as labourers in an ironstone quarry near Banbury. Kathleen left home as soon as she could: at seventeen she married Alfred Shaw, and they had a son, Reginald. But then Kathleen met Cyril Patmore, and they ran away together to Oxford. They had a daughter, Christine, in 1933, and Shaw divorced Kathleen, citing Cyril as the co-respondent. Kathleen and Cyril married in 1937 and moved to London in 1938 to start a new life.

At the outbreak of war, they were living in a small flat in St John's Wood. Cyril was working as a restaurant waiter at the Embassy Hotel, and Kathleen was about to have another baby, Terence, born in 1939.[4] In 1941, they moved to Maida Vale and lodged with Frank Tobin, in 63A Randolph Avenue. Tobin, who was friendly with the family, said they were very happy and seemed to get along, and they had another daughter, Noreen, in 1941. But according to Kathleen's sister, Cyril joined the army in 1942 after a fight with his wife. After that, Kathleen lived in the flat with the children, getting occasional visits from Cyril on leave. Another daughter, Kathleen, was born in 1942.

In June or July of 1944, Kathleen left London with her children and went to live with her sister May Canning in Woodend Cottages, Farmoor, Botley, Oxford. May was fourteen years older. Her first husband had been killed in 1915, and she had married again in 1917. In 1932, she was convicted of bigamy for marrying a third time and served three months. In 1941, she was convicted of bigamy again for marrying a fourth time, to John Seale in 1936, and drawing his army pension. She served another four months' imprisonment.[5] In 1944, May did not have a steady male companion. She lived with her two youngest daughters and three lorry-driving male lodgers who would stay over occasionally. With Kathleen's four children, it must have been a full house. Their brother, Horace, who lived 8 miles away in Thrupp, often came to visit them.

The house was a sociable place, and Kathleen and May enjoyed themselves with the men around them. According to her sister, brother and her daughter Christine who shared her room, Kathleen had affairs with two of the lodgers, Gordon Grey, a lorry driver, and another man, called Bill. They all frequented the local pub, the Seacourt Bridge Hotel in Botley. But according to the pub landlord, the behaviour of the sisters and another, unnamed, woman was so bad that they were barred.

Both Kathleen and May were friendly with the four Italian prisoners of war who were billeted on the farm where they rented a cottage. The prisoners were from Hostel Headington, a satellite of 43 Camp which housed about 500 men. Most of the men lived in barracks and worked in surrounding farms and were allowed within a 5-mile radius of the camp. Horace Jennings described seeing both sisters go out into the woods with Italian men and return home at 7 a.m. Neighbours also saw Italian men and American soldiers going into the cottage to visit the women, as well as the three lodgers. People were talking.

The owner of the farm, George Podbery, was so appalled by the number of women and children in the cottage, and the stream of male visitors, that he complained. When their behaviour did not improve, he gave them notice to leave at the end of May. He wanted them out so badly, he didn't ask for any of the rent they owed. Evicted, they went to live with their brother, Horace, in his cottage in Thrupp.

The sisters must have had a colossal falling out around this time, possibly to do with their friendships with the Italian prisoners of war. May Canning wrote two letters, one to the camp commandant complaining of her sister's relationship with Antonio Frunzo, and one to her own special friend Mario Saviello. As a result, the men were transferred to 144 Labour Battalion at Kew, in London. She also wrote a letter to Cyril in India, telling him Kathleen had been sleeping with a stream of men and was pregnant. Kathleen also wrote to Cyril, pleading letters telling him she was sorry and begging for reconciliation and for him to accept the child as his.

Kathleen didn't stay long in Thrupp. By 28 May, she left her children behind and went to London, seven months pregnant. She rented a furnished room in Harlesden, at 12 Greenhill Road. It was only 5 miles from Kew, but there is no record of her seeing Frunzo again. The building was owned by undertaker Edward Treeves, who let out the eight rooms for £1 a week, with a shared kitchen and scullery. Treeves met her a few times when visiting the house, and on 30 July, she joked to him: 'He [Cyril]'ll be walking in any day. I don't know what he'll do but he threatened to strangle me.'[6]

Cyril was already in London. He arrived at St Pancras station on 29 July and started looking for a place to stay. He went to his old landlord Frank Tobin's house, but there was no room, so he left some of his kit and went off again. He went to another former landlady, Beatrice Martin, who the couple had lived with before the war. He confided his domestic troubles to her and stayed the night with her.

He went down to Thrupp in Oxford on 31 July 1945, to see his children and to find out what had been happening. They were living in Lower Farm Cottages, with Kathleen's brother Horace Jennings and sister. He asked them about Kathleen's association with other men, and they told him what they had seen. May Canning even provided him a written list of names of all the men Kathleen had supposedly slept with. His daughter also told him she had seen her mother in bed with Bill.

After hearing all the stories, Cyril started questioning Kathleen's faithfulness even before he had gone abroad. Kathleen's niece told him of seeing a letter from Kathleen to their landlord Frank Tobin, signed, 'Love from your little Noreen', with 'your' underlined several times. Cyril looked at his youngest daughters, Kathleen and Noreen, shook his head, and said to Horace Jennings, 'I can't make this out. They look just like the bastard,' meaning Tobin. Jennings asked Cyril if Noreen was his, and he said, 'I do not think so. I can't make out why she did this to me. I have played straight since I went abroad.' Leaving the house, he said, 'I will do her in and I will hang for it.'[7] He took the train back to London.

Instead of being angry at Tobin, Cyril went back to him for advice and comfort. On Thursday 2 August, Cyril went to Tobin's to collect his things, and he broke down in tears. He told him, 'I've been to see the children. They're in rags. They're hungry. It broke my heart. After all I've done in the war and all the time I've spent in the jungle just thinking of my wife and family.' Tobin told him to forget about

Kathleen and to try and get the children settled. Cyril seemed to calm down and accept this advice and said he would tell Kathleen what he thought of her when he saw her. He went back to Beatrice Martin's, told her of the terrible conditions the children were living in and told her, 'She's done a terrible thing to me. She must be punished for doing this to me.'

On Thursday afternoon, Cyril knocked on the door at Greenhill Road. Kathleen was sitting in the kitchen with fellow lodger Ernest Thwaites and got up to answer it. She popped her head back in to say, 'It's my husband. I'm taking him upstairs; he's had something to drink.' The other people in the house heard shouting and arguing all afternoon, and Cyril left that evening. Kathleen appeared again with bruises on her face and told Thwaites: 'It's worse than I thought. He's been given a list of names and addresses, most of which I know nothing about. I tried to pacify him, but I couldn't manage it. He said he would have forgiven me if I hadn't let the house go and had the boy with me.'[8] Another lodger, Marg Ellis, spoke to Kathleen on Thursday, and said she had a bruised mouth and seemed frightened.

On Friday, Cyril put a note through the letter box to ask Kathleen to bring him his belongings, and she went to Paddington to collect them. She met up with Cyril at 10 a.m., but according to him, when he saw her, he felt sorry for her, forgot about his belongings and took her to the pictures. They spent the day together, and he went to a Church Army Hostel to sleep.

On Saturday morning, Kathleen got up and dressed in a print frock, blue ankle socks and brown shoes. She had tea and was chatting with her neighbour Marg Ellis in the doorway of her room. When she heard the knock, according to Marg, she said, 'I expect that's my husband,' and started to tremble. She said, 'I'm frightened. I don't know whether to open the door. I'll let him knock again. Perhaps he'll put a letter through and go away.' But then another knock came, and Kathleen walked downstairs. A few minutes later, Mrs Ellis heard Kathleen calling her, 'Marg! Marg!', and then groaning. She ran down the stairs.

According to Cyril, he went back to Kathleen's flat that morning with every intention of forgiving her and overlooking her behaviour. He came to the door and asked her to come upstairs and talk: 'She stood there, cool and defiant and said, "Wait a minute and see my friends."' When he said he didn't want to, she said, 'Since you've been back you've got me a bag of nerves, asking questions.' He asked her again if she wanted to come upstairs as he was leaving, and she said, 'You know everything, I've told you everything, do what the hell you like.' Because of these remarks, he told police, 'I knew I was finished then. That's all. I only meant to scar her so nobody else could have her but me. She struggled and I stabbed her in the wrong place.'

Cyril pulled out a knife and grabbed Kathleen. He slashed her across her forehead, then inflicted a fierce downward stab into her neck.

As Marg Ellis got near the kitchen, she saw Cyril coming out into the passage, with a knife in his hand and with blood on his trousers. She looked into the kitchen and saw Kathleen on a kitchen chair, bending forward, moaning. She called for Ernest Thwaites, who came to the kitchen and tried to speak to Kathleen. She didn't answer, so he went outside to get help.

At 9 a.m., Frederick Keeling, a taxi driver, was waiting for a fare at 16 Greenhill Road, when he saw a soldier covered in blood and holding a knife come into the street. He hailed the driver and said, 'Get the police, I've just done my missus.' The driver immediately drove to the station, then back to the flat with the detectives. A police car on its way to the flat stopped Cyril walking down the street. He confessed again and was taken in the car to the station. On the way, he repeatedly said, 'To think it was a Wop she was going with.' He had five letters in his pocket, four from Kathleen asking for forgiveness, and one from May with the list of names.

When the first police officer, Detective Sergeant Gibbs, arrived at the flat on Greenhill Road, he saw Kathleen on the floor, face down in the kitchen. He saw her body move and quickly turned her over to see if he could help. But Kathleen was already dead. It was the unborn child still moving for a few minutes more.

Back at the police station, Cyril confessed everything, telling officers how much he loved his wife and how he hoped his children would be cared for. The investigating officers interviewed all the lodgers, Frank Tobin and Beatrice Martin and travelled to Oxford to interview Kathleen's family and neighbours there. They all told the same story: Cyril had threatened his wife, he had planned to kill her, and she had been frightened. And yet, Cyril was a serving soldier in a situation 'all the men in Burma were worried about'.[9] The police notes state that there is 'ample evidence for pre-meditation', but that 'The motive for the crime is most apparent and it cannot be disputed that the moral character of the deceased woman was of the lowest.'[10]

At his trial, Cyril played on these sympathies when he took the stand. He recalled the speech he had made to her the night they had gone to the cinema: 'How can you expect me to come and sleep with you, when you've been with another man. For years I've waited for this moment to return and have you for my own again and I was robbed of everything.'[11]

According to the newspapers, the jury was moved to tears by the testimony, and by Cyril's weeping on the witness stand. The judge, Mr Justice Charles, gauging their mood, told them before they went to deliberate on the verdict: 'I am bound to tell you that if a man comes back, finds his wife unfaithful, and enters into a conversation with her as to whether or not he will forgive her and yet he stabs her and she dies, he is guilty of stark murder. It would be the law of the jungle, if a man, finding his wife had been unfaithful once or even twenty times, is entitled in law to kill her and then say, "Look at the provocation I have received: you only ought to find a verdict of manslaughter against me."'[12]

But after only a short recess, the jury came back with a guilty verdict on the reduced charge of manslaughter.[13] The judge expressed disapproval: 'The jury have taken a certain view of your case, but I want to make it perfectly clear that it was their view and not mine,' he told Cyril. 'If manslaughter it be – and I am bound by the jury's verdict – then it is a bad case of manslaughter, although, as your counsel has said, you were a sorely tried man. If you had not been so sorely tried, I would have been bound to give you a very, very heavy sentence.'[14] He sentenced Cyril to five years' imprisonment. A five-year sentence was the average for husbands killing their unfaithful wives in wartime London, although Constantine Savva, who found his wife in bed with another man, was only sentenced to eighteen months' imprisonment.[15] Women who killed their unfaithful partners were not seen as having suffered the same provocation under the law. In 1944, dressmaker Marie Scherz shot her lover, airman Francis Turner, out of jealousy and was sentenced to ten years, although her German nationality may have counted against her. Florence Crisp was acquitted of murdering her husband after discovering him with his mistress of fourteen years, but only because he had physically abused her for years and was in the process of attacking her when she stabbed him.[16]

Cyril lived another thirty-four years; he died in 1999. His will left everything to his son, Terence, with three small extra bequests: one to Kathleen's son Reginald and his wife, one to Christine Fox and her husband, who might be his eldest daughter, and one to Deborah Fox. No mention is made of his youngest two daughters.

Kathleen Patmore's death is compelling not just because it happened, but because it was not inevitable. When the doorbell rang on Saturday morning, 4 August 1945, it was a moment when anything was possible. Kathleen was frightened, but as she told her neighbour, she didn't know what to expect: Cyril may have been forgiving, or he may have left a letter again and gone away. She and Cyril could have reconciled, or could have separated, and violence could have been averted. Wartime reunions were complex, and returning soldiers had to adapt to changed family relationships, new friends and new living patterns.

GERALDINE AND BERYL EVANS

Even years after the war, it was very difficult to set up home in London. One of the things that Kathleen's husband Cyril blamed her for most was leaving the children in Oxford, where they were neglected, and coming back to London to take a room on her own. Setting up a family home in London was not only emotionally complicated, but it was also practically difficult. The war had damaged and destroyed millions of homes, and the continued rationing and the scarcity of materials made it a challenge to find basic furniture, pots and pans and bedding.

One of the young couples struggling to make a home for themselves in postwar London was Beryl and Timothy Evans. With a baby on the way, the young newlyweds needed a place of their own. In the spring of 1948, they found a dilapidated flat on the top floor of a run-down house in Rillington Place, in a run-down area of Notting Hill. Despite the downstairs tenants, Reg and Ethel Christie, denying them the use of the back garden, it was the best they could do, and close to both of their families in Notting Hill. Timothy was a food delivery driver, earning £7 pounds a week with overtime. Their rent for the two rooms was 10 shillings a week, and the hire-purchase payment on the furniture was £7 a week. Despite the shabby surroundings and their stretched finances, they were excited to start a new life on their own.

Beryl Evans was born Beryl Thorley in Lewisham in 1929. Her mother, Lizzie Simmonds, was one of ten children born to a Jewish family in Stepney. Lizzie's father, a rag sorter, died when her mother was pregnant with their tenth living child. Lizzie worked as a tailoress until she married William 'Bill' Thorley, a petrol filler attendant for the London General Omnibus Company, when she was only nineteen. William was a Christian, and they married in the St John the Divine Church in Kennington. Bill had been a sniper in the First World War and had been gassed three times. According to his son Peter, the trauma of his wartime experiences kept him distant and disengaged towards his family for the rest of his life.[17]

The Thorley family struggled financially, along with many others in the 1930s, and they moved from address to address in south London. Beryl was their first child, and they had three more: Basil, born in 1931, Isabella Patricia, known as Pat, in 1933, and Peter in 1934. In 1939, William got a better job working night shift on buses for the London

211

Transport Board, and the family moved to North London. When war broke out in 1939, the children were evacuated to the village of Brockham in Surrey. Over the next three and a half years, the children saw their parents only twice. Beryl was lucky enough to be billeted with the family who ran the local sweet shop at one end of the green, Pat was sent to Mrs Blunden and Basil and Peter to a Mrs Smith, where they slept in the kitchen cupboards under the stairs. Brockham was safer than London but still suffered several raids because it was only 10 miles from the airfields of RAF Kenley.[18]

In 1943, during a lull between bombings, Beryl and her siblings returned home to their parents in the top-floor flat at 112 Cambridge Gardens in Ladbroke Grove, just off St Mark's Road. For the children, now used to the Surrey countryside, London looked like the face of the moon, covered in craters and debris. They had a year of relative family happiness, although their father worked nights and their mother was seriously ill with bronchial asthma and pleurisy. That Christmas, Beryl was obsessed with the song 'White Christmas' from the hit Bing Crosby film *Holiday Inn*. Her brother Peter remembered: 'All over the house, wherever she was, she would sing it. "For Christ's sake, Beryl, shut up!" we'd all say.'[19]

In the summer of 1944, when the V-1 raids began, the younger children were sent away again. Pat went to Margate, and Basil and Peter lived with a family in Aberystwyth, Wales. Beryl had left school and wanted to learn shorthand and typing, so she stayed in London to work. She had part-time jobs to pay for her tuition, one selling posh hats at a ladieswear shop at the top of Cambridge Gardens.

Beryl was a small woman, only 5 foot 2 and 7½ stone (105 pounds). She had dark hair, a prominent chin and a big smile. She had a sense of fun and liked to be social. Her brother Peter described her as 'petite, pretty and highly intelligent. She had always been on the shy side when it came to men. Beryl would rather meet up with her pals and go to the cinema.'[20] Beryl's friends were very important to her. Her best friend from school days, Joan Vincent, remained close to her for the rest of her life.

The Thorleys were reunited at the end of the war in 1945, but not for long. Beryl's mother, Lizzie, whose health had been worsening for years, died on 2 March 1947. The children were devastated. Without their mother, they felt lost, especially with a distant father who worked nights. Beryl was now working as a clerical telephonist at Grosvenor House Hotel in Park Lane, Mayfair. She became friendly with Lucy Endicott, who was a few years younger than her but more worldly.

Lucy introduced Beryl to Timothy Evans in January 1947. Beryl was only seventeen and had never dated before. Tim was twenty-four, a small and handsome Welshman with dark hair and a confident swagger. He had moved to London with his mother, stepfather and two sisters from Merthyr Tydfil in 1936 to find work. Although he had trouble reading, after a sickly childhood, he had steady work as a lorry driver. He was also sociable and fun, with a vivid imagination and a reputation as a liar.

After her mother's death, Beryl needed a new sense of family, away from her oppressive home. With three younger siblings and a father she didn't get on with, she wanted to escape. The easiest way to do that, for a young woman, was to get married.

On 20 September 1947, one day after Beryl turned eighteen, she and Tim married at Kensington Registry Office. The only guests were the groom's mother, Thomasina, her husband, Penry Probert, Evans's older sister, Eileen, his half-sister, Maureen, Beryl's father and her three siblings. Beryl wore a light-coloured dress with her hair in a pageboy style. There were no photographs or cars: the family walked to and from the registry office and had sandwiches and cakes at Mrs Probert's house in St Mark's Road afterwards.

The young couple lived with the Proberts for six months, until Beryl became pregnant. There wasn't enough room for six people and a baby in the flat. Beryl and Tim had to find somewhere of their own. Meanwhile, Bill Thorley had decided to leave London to follow a new love. Leaving Basil behind in London, he moved to Brighton, taking Beryl's younger brother, Peter, and sister, Pat, with him. Beryl was on her own.

Rillington Place was just around the corner from St Mark's Road. It was a cul-de-sac with no trees or greenery, with stained, yellow-brick terraced houses on each side. The houses had been built in the 1860s for middle-class families. But economic downturn meant that they had been subdivided for poor and working-class families. In 1871, Charlie Chaplin lived at number 15 with his father and three siblings. At the end of the street was a wall behind which the Victorian chimneys of Bartle Iron Works still jutted. In front of the crumbling houses, with their subsiding foundations, children played, and women chatted in the warmer months.

Number 10 was at the end of the left-hand side. On the ground floor lived Reg and Ethel Christie, a middle-aged, childless couple who commanded a certain respect for their genteel manners. Their flat opened to the street and the rear garden, and anyone using the stairs had to go by their rooms. On the first floor lived Charles Kitchener, who had been a tenant since 1918. His health was not good, and he was frequently in hospital for eye operations. He disliked both Evans and Christie and was convinced they stole from him: 'I was always missing little things.'[21] All the flats shared a toilet and a wash house at the back. A broken wooden gate led to the garden, rough patches of grass and lumps of dirt surrounded by a brick wall. On the second floor was a small flat of two rooms: a kitchen on the left, with a window overlooking the garden, and across the landing the sitting and bedroom overlooking Rillington Place.

On 14 October 1948, in the Queen Charlotte Hospital, Geraldine Evans was born. She was very loved by her parents and her paternal grandparents. Thomasina babysat every Wednesday night while Tim and Beryl went to the cinema. Peter Thorley, who took the train from Brighton to visit whenever he could, described Geraldine as a 'chunky, happy little soul, jumping up and down there in her pink romper suit with a cheeky smile on her face'.[22] Beryl's brother Basil and Tim's sisters also visited the family often.

The Christies downstairs were also kind to Beryl and the baby. They looked after Geraldine occasionally and let Beryl park her pram in their

15. Beryl and Geraldine Evans, 1948.

hallway to avoid bringing it up the stairs. Beryl and Tim liked the Christies, as did Beryl's brother Peter. Christie let him play with his dog and sometimes gave him tea and sticky buns. The Christies were always neatly dressed and polite and were very old-fashioned. Beryl often came to them for advice, and with the thin walls and open hallway, the Christies were privy to intimate details of the Evanses' increasingly fraught marriage.

Beryl and Tim's marriage erupted in row after row. They were both jealous. In July 1949, Beryl was working part time at a local newsagent's shop. She teased her husband about flirting with another man and he stormed into the shop and slapped her face, making such a scene that she was sacked. Evans himself had an affair with Beryl's friend Lucy

Endicott: on 27 August they spent the night together on the kitchen floor. The next day, Beryl confronted Lucy in front of Tim and his mother, and Lucy slapped her. The fight got so loud and violent that Inspector Percy Parks was called to the house. Beryl told him: 'She has been carrying on with my husband and last night went to the pictures and slept in the kitchen with him.' Lucy denied it, and said, 'There is nothing wrong. I will have a medical examination.' Beryl went to the magistrate's court the next day to get advice on a separation, but Lucy went back to her mother and the brief affair ended.

They also fought about Beryl's housekeeping skills. Because of the disruptions of the war, Beryl hadn't been at home to learn how to cook, clean and manage a household, all skills that were expected of a wife at the time. Tim's mother complained that their flat was untidy: 'She got no hot meal for him, except one day a week. She did not do the washing-up, but left heaps of dishes unwashed.'[23]

But what the couple fought about most was money. Tim and Beryl were in mounting debt. By the summer of 1949, their hire-purchase payments on the furniture were in arrears by £39 13s. and their rent by £12 1s. Lucy Endicott told police that the couple were 'continually squabbling . . . I know they used to have a lot of arguments about money, and he used to lie to her a lot . . . Tim used to say that he gave Beryl £5 a week for housekeeping, but she used to say she never received £5. He also used to say he was going to work and on some occasions, we found out he didn't. He would also make up excuses about not having received his money from Mr. Adler [his employer].' When Beryl complained, Evans would hit her. One night, Lucy was there when Tim 'set about her [Beryl], and began hitting her with his hand across her face and body. He was in a furious temper. [He said:] "I'll put you through the bloody window." '[24]

In October, things came to a head. Beryl realised she was pregnant again. She decided, with her marriage on the rocks and in mounting debt, she didn't want the baby. She tried to perform an abortion herself by taking pills and syringing herself with glycerine and carbolic soap. Everyone in her close circle knew about these attempts: her husband, her brother and mother-in-law, her friends and her neighbours, in particular, the Christies. The Christies later told police how they had advised Beryl to stop trying to end her pregnancy: 'Mrs. Evans did tell the wife and I what she was doing about six weeks ago, and I said to her, in my wife's presence, that she was looking a physical wreck and advised her to stop it. We warned her of the consequences, and she promised both of us that she would stop taking the stuff. The next day, Evans came down and said that any pills or similar things he had found about the place he had destroyed.'[25] Beryl was desperate.

On 2 November, her brother Peter came to visit her for the last time. His father, anxious to start a new life with his new wife, had bought him a one-way ticket to New Zealand in a child emigration scheme. In his 2020 memoir, Peter described his last visit to the flat, and seeing a fearful and sad Beryl, who had no money to feed Geraldine. According to him, she was desperate to escape an unhappy marriage and her violent husband. But Basil, who was friends with Evans, visited her on 4 November and saw nothing wrong. He said, 'She seemed to be in good spirits and said that she would be going away for a holiday with her daughter.' In 1965, he recalled: 'I think Timothy and Beryl were fond of each other and Timothy was definitely very fond of Geraldine. They had their tiffs, just like me and the wife and any other married couple, but I never thought there was anything serious in it.'[26] Beryl's father also visited her around this time and saw no reason for concern, although he later testified: 'I do not believe they were happily married.'[27]

During this week, workers had come to make some repairs at 10 Rillington Place, after the Christies complained to the council about blocked drains and rising damp. On 8 November, a worker saw two young women, Beryl and her friend Joan Vincent, come down the stairs with a baby and put the baby in the pram outside. He warned them about the ladder he was going to lay on the stairs, and one of the women said, 'I'll get by that all right.' Ethel and Reg Christie both claim to have seen Beryl leaving the house that afternoon with Geraldine. No one saw her come home.

According to Joan, that was the day she had visited the flat but not seen Beryl. They had had a tiff, and Joan had come to make up. She walked up the stairs: 'I called her name and tried to turn the handle of the door, and I felt that someone was pressing the door and holding it against me. I then remember thinking it must have been Beryl herself at the time, that perhaps she didn't want me in the flat at the moment, and I said, "Well if you don't want me to come in I'll go." But I had a nervous and uneasy feeling and felt very frightened at the time and hurried away from the house. I didn't meet anyone else at the flat that day.' The next day she went back and saw Geraldine's pram in the hall. Christie stopped her from going upstairs and seemed 'aggressive and rude'. He told her that Beryl had gone away, and that she should not come back.[28]

Beryl was never seen again. What exactly happened to her will never now be known. But around 8 November, she was punched in the face and strangled with a rope. She also had a small bruise on her vaginal wall. It could have been the result of a sexual assault. But the pathologist, Donald Teare, argued it was probably from a failed attempt to self-induce a miscarriage. The sixteen-week-old male foetus was still intact.[29]

Her body was wrapped in a blanket and a green tablecloth and tied with cord. It was likely hidden in Mr Kitchener's flat, as he was at the hospital at the time. The workers were in 10 Rillington Place until Saturday 12 November and swore they saw nothing. Sometime in the next two days, Geraldine was also strangled with a necktie. It was left around her neck, and she was wrapped in a blanket and hidden with her mother.

Evans spent one more week in the flat, telling people that Beryl had gone to Brighton or Bristol, including his family and her brother, Basil Thorley. Basil found this odd, as Beryl didn't get on with her father. Basil phoned his father, who told him that Beryl was not there. But neither man followed it up.

After selling the furniture, but keeping Geraldine's rattle, Evans took a train to Merthyr Tydfil, to stay with his aunt and uncle. By

29 November, the Evans family was worried. Evans's mother, Thomasina, wrote to her sister: 'I have not seen Beryl or the Baby for a month . . . [T]here is some mirstry [*sic*] about him . . . I never want to see him as long as I live . . . everywhere I go people asking for him for money he owes them I am ashamed to say he is my Son.' Mrs Lynch read the letter to Evans over breakfast, who denied the accusations but was visibly shaken.

A few hours later, Timothy Evans walked into a police station in Merthyr Tydfil and told the DC there, 'I have disposed of my wife . . . I put her down the drain.'[30] He claimed that Beryl had wanted to end her pregnancy, and that he had met a man in a transport café who had given him some abortion pills, but that they had killed Beryl. He had put her body in a drain in the street. He told the police he had given Geraldine to Mr Christie to be adopted.

The Welsh police contacted Scotland Yard, who connected them to the Notting Hill police station. Officers were sent to Rillington Place but found nothing in the manhole. After this was relayed back to Merthyr Tydfil, Evans admitted he had lied and made a second statement. This time he said that Christie had offered to help Beryl end her pregnancy, and that she had been keen, although he had been against it. On 8 November, Beryl told him to tell Mr Christie, 'Everything is alright.' When he came home from work, Christie met him at the foot of the stairs and told him that the operation had failed, and that Beryl had died. He said Christie had put the body in Mr Kitchener's kitchen and told him he would put it down the drains. He promised Evans that he would get someone to look after the baby, and that a couple from East Acton wanted to adopt her.

Notting Hill police went back to 10 Rillington Place, searched the drains and garden again, but found nothing. They missed the femur of Muriel Eady, propping up a fence in the backyard. Reg Christie was taken in for questioning and held all night. He claimed to know nothing about Beryl and Geraldine's disappearance. Not until a second search on 2 December did police find the bodies of Beryl and Geraldine, hidden under a sink in the wash house in the backyard.

When shown Beryl's and Geraldine's clothing and told they had both been strangled, Timothy Evans, now in Notting Hill, confessed to their murders. He told police that he had been angry and had hit Beryl, and that then, in an uncontrollable fit of temper, he had strangled her. Two days later, he strangled his daughter, then hid the bodies in the wash house. But he quickly recanted. When his mother visited him in prison, he said: 'I did not touch her, mum, Christie did it. I didn't even know the baby was dead until the Police brought me to Notting Hill. Christie told me the baby was at East Acton.'[31]

Beryl and Geraldine's bodies were identified by William Thorley, Beryl's father. But he didn't pay for a funeral. Instead, he left them to be buried at public expense in a grave shared by a stranger in the Catholic section of Gunnersbury Cemetery. He didn't write to his son Peter in New Zealand until January, and even then, he asked his foster parents in New Zealand to break the news of Beryl and Geraldine's deaths.[32]

On 6 December, Reg Christie's dog, Judy, had been digging in the garden and uncovered the skull of Muriel Eady. After dark, Christie hid the skull under his raincoat and put it in a bombed-out house on 133 St Mark's Road: 'There was a corrugated iron covering some bay windows and I dropped the skull through the window where the iron had been bent back. I heard it drop with a dull thud as though there were no floorboards.'[33] The skull was found the next day, immediately, and the police identified it as that of a woman. Police at the Harrow Road station made local enquiries, but there was no woman victim of air raids unaccounted for in the area. No connection was made to the discovery of Beryl and Geraldine just around the corner.

Timothy Evans was tried for the murder of Geraldine on 11 January 1950 at the Old Bailey. Mr Christmas Humphries was the prosecutor, and he wanted to avoid the defence motive of provocation. With Geraldine, there could be no such motive. In the short, three-day trial, Christie was the key witness for the prosecution. He gave vivid descriptions of the quarrels between the couple: 'Mrs. Evans has told my wife and I on more than one occasion that he [Timothy] has assaulted her and grabbed hold of her throat. She said he had a violent temper, and one time would do her in.'

Evans's case was taken by Freeborough, Slack, and Company. Evans withdrew his final confession and stuck to his second statement to the police, that Christie was the murderer. Evans's defending counsel, Malcolm Morris, accused Christie in court of being responsible for the death of Mrs Evans and Geraldine, but Christie denied knowing anything.[34] Morris had also brought out Christie's criminal record of theft and violence. But despite this, the jury believed Christie, and Timothy was found guilty.

As the death sentence against Evans was read out, Christie wept loud, hypocritical tears in the packed courtroom. Outside the court-room, Evans's mother confronted Christie and called him a murderer. On the following day, Christie went to the *Kensington Post* to try to sell them photographs he had taken of Evans. They refused.[35]

Evans was hanged on 9 March 1950, still protesting his innocence.

In 1953, the bodies of three more women were found in Christie's flat at 10 Rillington Place: Kathleen Maloney, Rita Nelson and Hectorina MacLennan. Maloney was a homeless woman from the Ladbroke Grove

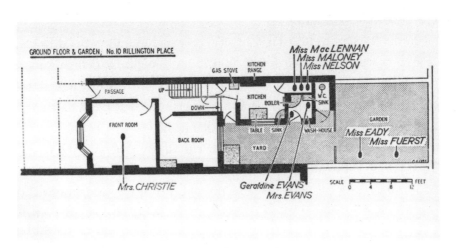

16. Plan of 10 Rillington Place, 1953.

area, who was four months pregnant. Nelson had come from Belfast a few months earlier to visit her sister in Ladbroke Grove; she was six months pregnant when she died. Christie first met Hectorina MacLennan with her boyfriend, Alex Baker. They had nowhere to live, and he let them stay at his flat for a few nights. When Christie managed to meet MacLennan on her own, he murdered her. All three women had been poisoned with carbon monoxide gas and strangled.

The body of Ethel Christie, killed four months earlier, was found under the floorboards in the parlour. And looking out into the garden, police officers finally noticed the femur against the fence that the detectives investigating Beryl and Geraldine's murders three years earlier had missed. More bones were uncovered in the back garden, with cloth fragments and a newspaper from 1942. Ruth Fuerst and Muriel Eady were found at last.

The discovery of the six women entombed in 10 Rillington Place made headlines all over the world. Journalists and curious onlookers gathered in the street day after day as teams of policemen and forensic experts literally took the flat and garden apart looking for clues. People were fascinated and horrified by the fate of the six women, and by what their deaths suggested about the murders of Beryl and Geraldine Evans. Had Timothy Evans been another of Christie's victims, hanged for a crime he didn't commit?

In the lead-up to his trial, Christie confessed to killing Beryl Evans, as well as the six women found in 1953, although he denied killing Geraldine. He gave several different versions of her death. In a statement made to police on 5 June 1953, he claimed that Beryl had asked him to help her commit suicide, and that he had twice tried to sexually assault her, and eventually strangled her to death: 'She said she would do anything if I would help her. I think she was referring to letting me be intimate with her. She brought the quilt from the front room and put it down in front of the fireplace . . . She lay down on the quilt. I turned the gas tap on and as near as I can make out, I held it close to her face. When she became unconscious, I turned the tap off. I was going to try again to have intercourse with her, but it was impossible, I couldn't bend over. I think that's when I strangled her.'[36] When Evans came home, according to Christie, he told him that Beryl had gassed herself, and that the police would think that Evans had done it. Together they came up with a plan to hide her body.

The problem for the courts, and for historians ever since, is untangling the knot of lies surrounding Beryl and Geraldine's deaths. At trial, Evans said only his second confession was true, in which he helped Christie dispose of Beryl's body and trusted him to have Geraldine adopted. His confessions to the murder, he claimed at the trial, were born out of fear of the police. Christie's testimony at Evans's trial was believed by the judge and jury, and yet in 1953 he confessed to killing Beryl himself. How could he be trustworthy in one instance, and yet lying in the second?

In 1953, most people could not accept that the British legal system could have allowed an innocent man to be hanged. It was too macabre to think that Christie's loud sobs in the courtroom as Evans was sentenced to death were tears of relief. So, Christie's defence at trial set out to show that Christie's confession to Beryl's murder was a lie, by exhuming her body to disprove Christie's version of events. The coffin plate for mother and daughter, misspelled 'Jeraldine', was taken by the police and is now held at the Crime Museum – formerly the Black Museum – at New Scotland Yard. Francis Camps, the pathologist who led the forensic investigation into the Christie murders, examined Beryl's body and agreed with Teare that there was no evidence of coal-gas poisoning.[37] It was this small shred of evidence that Christie's defence counsel, Mr Derek Curtis-Bennett QC, used to bolster his insanity defence, to spare him from the gallows and save the notion of British justice.

The tactic did not work to save Christie. In June 1953, he was tried only for the murder of his wife, Ethel. It was the same court in which he had testified against Evans just three years earlier. Christie pleaded insanity and claimed to have a poor memory of the events. After deliberating for only eighty-five minutes, the jury found Christie guilty. Christie did not appeal against his conviction.

Public calls for an investigation into the safety of Evans's conviction were met by a rushed and secretive inquiry after Christie's trial, led by Scott Henderson QC. Henderson's conclusions, although not the evidence, were published on the day Christie was hanged. Henderson wrote that the evidence for Timothy Evans killing both Geraldine and Beryl was 'overwhelming'.[38] And yet the public was not convinced. Why should Evans's confession to killing Beryl be believed, and Christie's not?

Campaigns led by former lawyer Michael Eddowes and journalist Harold Evans fought for a pardon for Evans. In 1955, Eddowes – whose interest in the affair had driven him to purchase 10 Rillington Place – published *The Man on Your Conscience*, in which he argued that Evans had been gulled by Christie. His book and prolonged crusade convinced many of Evans's innocence. Among them was Ludovic Kennedy, who wrote the 1961 book *Ten Rillington Place*, made into a film in 1971.

In June 1965, another inquiry into the case was held, led by High Court judge Sir Daniel Brabin. For thirty days, the original witnesses and new expert witnesses were cross-examined about all aspects of the case. Brabin concluded it was 'more likely than not' that Evans had not murdered his baby, for which he had been hanged, but that he probably had killed his wife, for which he had not been tried. This bizarre conclusion was contrary to the evidence and the original case for the prosecution that both crimes had been committed by the same person. But by ruling that Evans did not kill Geraldine, the way was opened for Evans's partial historical rehabilitation. On 18 October 1966, Timothy Evans was granted a royal pardon and was reburied away from Pentonville Prison, in a Roman Catholic churchyard.

Even as the public increasingly accepted that it was not Timothy Evans but rather Reg Christie who had murdered Beryl Evans, her siblings continued to believe in his guilt. They all struggled in the years after her death. Pat became a single mother in 1953, aged only sixteen. She later married and had three more children and became a Jehovah's

Witness. Peter joined the army, and Basil, back from New Zealand, got married in the 1960s. Basil Thorley told John Eddowes in the 1990s that he believed Evans had killed his sister and niece, as reported in *The Two Killers of Rillington Place* (1995). Peter Thorley's 2020 memoir, *Inside Rillington Place*, told of the violence Peter had witnessed between Tim and Beryl, and his unshaken belief that both Tim Evans and Reg Christie were killers.

But the courts did eventually rule that Evans was innocent. In 2003, the Home Office awarded Evans's half-sister, Mary Westlake, and his sister, Eileen Ashby, six-figure payments as compensation for the miscarriage of justice in Evans's trial. The independent assessor, Lord Brennan QC, accepted that 'There is no evidence to implicate Timothy Evans in the murder of his wife. She was most probably murdered by Christie.'[39]

The legacy of Beryl's death has long outlived her. Her husband's execution was a major factor in the abolition of capital punishment in Britain in 1969.[40] Beryl is remembered and missed by her family, and her name and photograph live on in the many retellings of the crimes of 10 Rillington Place. For a few weeks, she and Geraldine lay only a few feet from the graves of Ruth Fuerst and Muriel Eady. These women shared not only a common grave in death, but common experiences in life. Their lives were disrupted and dislocated by war. And they were all women who sought and ultimately failed to find a happy home for themselves. The dangers of war and of postwar deprivations made them vulnerable to a predator who looked for rootless women in London, pregnant or ill, who were searching for a help and reassurance. They did not find it at 10 Rillington Place.

On 3 September 1939, the lights went out in London. A reporter from the *Daily Herald* described how the city was transformed into an eerie landscape:

> A walk along Piccadilly in the black-out is one of the many queer experiences of this war. The once brilliant centre of London's night

life is now as dark as any forest, and indeed, like a forest, the darkness is full of rustlings and whisperings, of half-seen shapes, and of a sinister feeling of eager, but invisible, life. Although there are no shop windows to look at, the crowds still circulate with apparent aimlessness round the Circus. If one can judge in the dark, it would seem that this crowd is almost as big as in peace time. What these people do and why they do it night after night, no one knows.[41]

The article was titled 'Blackout Crime', and it went on to explain that some of 'what these people' did involved violent crimes. This book aimed to illustrate why.

During the war, people lost their families, their neighbourhoods, their moorings. The war made people vulnerable in new ways: it uprooted people from their neighbourhoods and cast them adrift, and it took away the scrutiny of neighbours and families. At the same time, the blackout offered a cover for the aggressive impulses of desperate people. The result was a new character of murder, one that was more reckless, brutal and often random.

When the war ended in 1945 and the lights came back on, they lit up a city and people that were forever changed. For those who had had a good war, who had been energised by the excitement, sociability and sense of purpose, going back to peacetime life felt flat and gray. For those who had suffered and had lost loved ones, rebuilding their lives was painful. Families struggled to live together again: there were seven times more divorces in 1947 than in 1939.[42]

Wartime restrictions had also, according to postwar Police Commissioner Harold Scott, eroded a sense of personal duty, ironically: 'A war to the death like the last one, in which the State perforce made great inroads on the liberties of the subject and the rights of property, was hardly the school in which one could expect respect for the law and the rights of others to flourish.'[43] The result was a postwar surge of gang violence and juvenile delinquency in London that would persist into the 1960s.

But the effects of war on postwar crime and violence went even deeper. Britain's war to the death had been won, and London had escaped the complete devastation prophesied in 1939. But other countries were not so lucky: Hamburg was firebombed in 1943, and Tokyo and Dresden in 1945. Hiroshima and Nagasaki were destroyed by atomic bombs whose devastating effects lasted for years. These mass civilian deaths, and the horrors revealed by Allied soldiers liberating Nazi death camps, changed attitudes to violence forever. The horrors of modern war, once seen, could not be unseen.

The discovery of Ruth Fuerst, Muriel Eady and five more women's bodies at 10 Rillington Place in 1953 was a media sensation, in the words of executioner Albert Pierrepoint, because the public was 'greedy for details of death and dealers of death'.[44] The stories of the vulnerable lives of Christie's victims were overshadowed by the grisly circumstances of their deaths. The spirit of the sinister forest of blacked-out London, alive with eager rustlings, lived on.

NOTES

INTRODUCTION

1. Clive Emsley, *Hard Men: The English and Violence since 1750* (London: Hambledon, 2005), 9.
2. See Richard Titmuss, *Problems of Social Policy* (London: HMSO, 1950), A.J.P. Taylor, *English History 1914–1945* (Oxford: Oxford University Press, 1965) and, more recently, Robert Mackay, *Half the Battle: Civilian Morale in Britain during the Second World War* (Manchester: Manchester University Press, 2003).
3. See Angus Calder, *The Myth of the Blitz* (London: Pimlico, 1992) and Sonya O. Rose, *Which People's War? National Identity and Citizenship in Britain, 1939–1945* (Oxford: Oxford University Press, 2003).
4. Lucy Noakes, *Dying for the Nation: Death, Grief and Bereavement in Second World War Britain* (Manchester: Manchester University Press, 2020).
5. Quentin Reynolds, *A London Diary* (New York: Random House, 1941), 220–1.
6. Robert Jackson, *Coroner: The Biography of Bentley Purchase* (London: George Harrap, 1963), 122.
7. Thomas Grant, *Court Number One: The Trials and Scandals that Shocked Modern Britain* (London: John Murray, 2019).
8. Shani D'Cruze, 'Murder and Fatality: The Changing Face of Homicide', in Anne-Marie Kilday and David Nash (eds), *Histories of Crime: Britain 1600–2000* (Basingstoke: Palgrave Macmillan, 2010), 108. See Ian Burney and Neil Pemberton, *Murder and the Making of the English CSI* (Baltimore: Johns Hopkins University Press, 2016) and Ian Burney and Neil Pemberton, 'Bruised Witness: Bernard Spilsbury and the Performance of Early Twentieth-Century English Forensic Pathology', *Medical History*, 55, no. 1 (2011), 41–60.
9. Frederick Arthur Mackenzie, *The Mystery of the Daily Mail, 1896–1921* (London: Associated Newspapers, 1921) and Adrian Bingham and Martin Conboy, *Tabloid*

228

Century: The Popular Press in Britain, 1896 to the Present (Oxford: Peter Lang, 2015).

10. Andy Croll, 'Street Disorder, Surveillance and Shame: Regulating Behaviour in the Public Spaces of the Late Victorian British Town', *Social History*, 24, no. 3 (1999), 250–68.

11. Home Office, 'A summary of recorded crime data from 1898 to 2001/02' (2016), https://www.gov.uk/government/statistics/historical-crime-data, accessed 30 August 2022.

12. The identification of the remains has been challenged by mitochondrial DNA analysis of a surviving laboratory slide of skin from the torso, which suggests the body was of no genetic relation to Cora Crippen and was in fact male. See David Foran, et al., 'The Conviction of Dr. Crippen: New Forensic Findings in a Century-Old Murder', *Journal of Forensic Sciences*, 56 (2011), 233–40.

13. Rex v. Smith, 11 Cr. App. R. 229, 84 L.j.k.b. 2153 (1915) set a legal precedent for introducing evidence from other crimes to prove a 'system of murder'.

14. Imperial War Museum (IWM), Department of Documents, Mrs M. Morris, 80/39/1. Diary, 9 May 1941.

15. Peter Thorley, *Inside 10 Rillington Place: John Christie and Me, the Untold Truth* (London: Mirror Books, 2020), 40.

16. Elizabeth Bowen, *The Heat of the Day* (London: Jonathan Cape, 1948).

17. Julie Summers, *Dressed for War: The Story of Audrey Withers, Vogue Editor Extraordinaire from the Blitz to the Swinging Sixties* (London: Simon & Schuster, 2020).

18. Dan Lewis, 'The Sound of World War Two Planes', 2 April 2018, Now I Know, https://nowiknow.com/the-sound-of-world-war-ii-planes/.

19. IWM, Miss V. Bawtree, 91/511/. Diary, 8 September 1940.

20. IWM, Miss V. Hall, Documents 3989. Diary, 20 September 1940.

21. Rachel Pistol, 'Refugees from National Socialism Arriving in Great Britain 1933–1945', *Refugees, Relief and Resettlement* (Farmington Hills, MI: Gale, 2020).

22. Tony Kushner, 'Asylum or Servitude? Refugee Domestics in Britain, 1933–1945', *Bulletin of the Society for the Study of Labour History*, 53 (1988), 19–27.

23. She was registered as Certificate 856822.

24. The National Archives (TNA), MEPO 2/9535; Jonathan Oates, *John Christie of 10 Rillington Place* (Barnsley: Wharncliffe True Crime, 2017), 34.

25. 1939 England and Wales Register, ancestry.co.uk.

26. Joanna Mack and Steve Humphries, *London at War: The Making of Modern London 1939–45* (London: Sidgwick & Jackson, 1985), 26; Philip Ziegler, *London at War* (London: Sinclair-Stevenson, 1995), 94.

27. Ziegler, *London at War*, 96.

28. Peter and Leni Gillman, *'Collar the Lot!': How Britain Interned and Expelled its Wartime Refugees* (London: Quartet Books, 1980), 134.

29. TNA, HO 396/253: *Aliens Department: Internees Index, 1939–1947, Germans Interned in the UK, Fre–Fu*, Findmypast.co.uk, HO 396/173: German Internees Released in the UK.

30. Oates, *John Christie*, 34.

31. Oates, *John Christie*, 34. TNA, MEPO 2/9535.

32. Oates, *John Christie*, 34.

33. John Christie, 'My First Victim', *Sunday Mirror*, 5 July 1953, 1.

34. Oates, *John Christie*, 33.
35. TNA, CAB 143/14/1.
36. Christie, 'My First Victim', 1.
37. Oates, *John Christie*, 37.
38. 'Sack Murder: Manton to Die', *Beds and Herts Sunday Telegraph*, 20 May 1944, 1.
39. Memoirs published about the investigation and trials of wartime murders include the biography of Keith Simpson's secretary, Molly Lefebure, *Evidence for the Crown: Experiences of a Pathologist's Secretary* (London: W. Heinemann, 1955), Douglas Browne and E.B. Tullet, *Bernard Spilsbury: His Life and Cases* (London: George G. Harrap, 1952), Jackson, *Coroner* and, the latest and most popular, Keith Simpson, *Forty Years of Murder* (London: W.H. Allen, 1978).
40. Barbara Kelly (West End Central, late 1940s) and Shirley Beck (CID, 1945) were the first female detective constables in the Metropolitan Police. Kelly rose to become the first female superintendent in the CID in 1972. 'British Police Are Facing Female Chauvinism', *Sarasota Herald-Tribune*, 5 July 1974, 17, https://news.google.com/newspapers?id=uv8jAAAAIBAJ&sjid=4GYEAAAAIBAJ&pg=6963,1730260&dq=barbara-kelley+police&hl=en, accessed 10 September 2022.
41. Malcolm M. Feeley and Deborah L. Little, 'The Vanishing Female: The Decline of Women in the Criminal Process, 1687–1912', *Law & Society Review*, 25, no. 4 (1991), 719–58. See Ginger Frost, ' "Such a Poor Finish": Illegitimacy, Murder, and War Veterans in England, 1918–1923', *Historical Reflections/Réflexions Historiques*, 42, no. 3 (2016), 91–111, Annette Ballinger, 'Masculinity in the Dock: Legal Responses to Male Violence and Female Retaliation in England and Wales, 1900–1965', *Social & Legal Studies*, 16, no. 4 (2007), 459–81 and Anne-Marie Kilday, *A History of Infanticide in Britain, c. 1600 to the Present* (Basingstoke: Palgrave Macmillan, 2013).
42. Jury riders or recommendations are one of the only clues to how juries weighed evidence and perceived culpability. See Mark Coen and Niamh Howlin, 'The Jury Speaks: Jury Riders in the Nineteenth and Twentieth Centuries', *American Journal of Legal History*, 58, no. 4 (2018), 505–34.
43. 'Sack Murder: Manton to Die', *Beds and Herts Sunday Telegraph*, 20 May 1944, 1.
44. Other works that focus on the lives of victims are Hallie Rubenhold's *The Five* (London: Doubleday, 2019), which tells the stories of the five women killed in the Whitechapel murders in 1888–91 and Julia Laite's *The Disappearance of Lydia Harvey* (London: Profile, 2021), which traces the history of a victim of sex trafficking who testified against her abductors in 1910.
45. TNA, MEPO 4/306, 1940–1944.
46. TNA, MEPO 1/1399.
47. 'Soldier on Bridge Murder Charge', *Daily News*, 21 April 1942, 3.
48. 'Cleared of Murder Charge', *Daily News*, 23 April 1942, 3.
49. TNA, MEPO 20/3 and MEPO 20/4.
50. Coroners' court records for this period were seen as the coroner's personal property, and most records were destroyed. Surviving London records are deposited in a 10 per cent sample at the London Metropolitan Archive (LMA), though Coroners' Rule 57 restricts access to inquest records to 'properly interested persons', generally confined to family members, insurance companies and inquest witnesses.

51. Jackson, *Coroner*. This biography was based on numerous private conversations with Purchase and his colleagues. For more on coroners' inquests during the war, see TNA, MEPO 3/3066 and MEPO 30/41/68.
52. James Sharpe, *A Fiery and Furious People* (London: Random House, 2016), 27.
53. No national statistics were collected in 1939. The Metropolitan Police gathered statistical data on murders in several formats: the Registry of Suspicious Deaths, the Metropolitan Police Commissioner's Report, the Judicial Statistics for England and Wales and the Criminal Statistics for England and Wales, presented annually to Parliament. Statistics from *A summary of recorded crime data from 1898 to 2001/02* (Home Office, 2016), https://www.gov.uk/government/statistics/historical-crime-data, accessed 22 July 2022.
54. TNA, MEPO 20/3 and 20/4.
55. Edward Smithies, *Crime in Wartime* (London: George Allen & Unwin, 1982), 152.
56. See TNA, MEPO 4/306, 'Unidentified casualty lists'; Tom Fallon, *River Police: The Story of Scotland Yard's Little Ships* (London: Frederick Muller Ltd, 1956), 233.
57. See Amy Bell, *London was Ours* (London: I.B. Tauris, 2002), J.D. Caswell, *Only Five Were Hanged* (London: Corgi, 1964), Robert Fabian, *Fabian of the Yard* (London: Naldrett Press, 1950), Robert Fabian, *London After Dark* (London: Naldrett Press, 1954), Edward Greeno, *War on the Underworld* (London: Digit, 1959) and Ernest Marke, *In Troubled Waters: Memoirs of my Seventy Years in England* (London: Karia, 1986).
58. 'Notorious Killer Executed Today', *Evening Despatch*, Thursday 25 June 1942, 3. I am indebted to Ben Cutmore for this point. Ben Cutmore, 'Gordon Cummins: The Blackout Ripper', Dark Histories Podcast, Season 5, Episode 5, https://www.amazon.com/Ben-Cutmore/e/B09DT6BT5J%3Fref=dbs_a_mng_rwt_scns_share.
59. 'Blackout Ripper Hunt', *Daily Mirror*, 28 December 1939, 2.

1 LONDON AT WAR

1. TNA, CRIM 1/1175.
2. See diary excerpts in Mass Observation, *War Begins at Home* (London: Chatto & Windus, 1940).
3. Ziegler, *London at War*, 30.
4. Donald Thomas, *An Underworld at War: Spivs, Deserters, Racketeers and Civilians in the Second World War* (London: John Murray, 2003), 347.
5. Winston Churchill, 'Their Finest Hour', 18 June 1940, House of Commons, https://winstonchurchill.org/resources/speeches/1940-the-finest-hour/their-finest-hour/.
6. See Amy Helen Bell, 'Landscapes of Fear: Wartime London 1939–45', *Journal of British Studies*, 48, no. 1 (2009), 153–75.
7. Edward Glover, *The Psychology of Fear and Courage* (Harmondsworth: Penguin Books, 1940), 21–2.
8. Ian Burney, 'War on Fear: Solly Zuckerman and Civilian Nerve in the Second World War', *History of the Human Sciences*, 25, no. 5 (2012), 49–72.

9. Mass Observation, *War Begins at Home*, 187.
10. Mass Observation, *War Begins at Home*, 216.
11. For more on the transformation of London during and after the war, see Angus Calder, *The People's War* (London: Jonathan Cape, 1969), Mack and Humphries, *London at War* and Ziegler, *London at War*.
12. Niko Gartner, 'Administering "Operation Pied Piper" – How the London County Council Prepared for the Evacuation of its Schoolchildren 1938–1939', *Journal of Educational Administration & History*, 42 (2010), 17–32. See also Titmuss, *Problems of Social Policy*.
13. The Register was used for National Registration until 1952, and by the National Health Service until 1991. It records name changes, usually by marriage, up to that time. https://www.nationalarchives.gov.uk/help-with-your-research/research-guides/1939-register/.
14. 1939 England and Wales Register, ancestry.co.uk.
15. 1939 England and Wales Register, ancestry.co.uk.
16. Their half-uncle Souren attended Ramsgate College in the 1920s, which was shut down on the outbreak of war. 'Souren Allelamdjian', *New York Times* Archives, 5 December 1976, 53, https://www.nytimes.com/1976/12/05/archives/souren-m-allalemdjian.html.
17. *Old Bailey Proceedings Online* (www.oldbaileyonline.org, version 8.0, 22 August 2022), March 1874, trial of PAUL BAYARD (51) (t18740302-188).
18. Record for Leon Valeriani, *UK, Royal Navy Registers of Seamen's Services, 1848–1939*, ancestry.com.
19. 'Leon Valeriani: Dr Jameson's Despatch Rider', *Bexhill-on-Sea Observer*, 2 February 1901, 5.
20. 'Leon Valeriani: Dr Jameson's Despatch Rider'.
21. 'Epaminondas Leonidas Pelopidas Valeriani', England & Wales, National Probate Calendar (Index of Wills and Administrations), 1858–1995, ancestry.co.uk.
22. 'Opening of the Shelter Hall Rooms', *Bexhill-on-Sea Observer*, 18 June 1904, 9.
23. 'Another Chance', *Walthamstow and Leyton Guardian*, 5 February 1909, 3.
24. Daniel J.R. Grey, 'Murder, Mental Illness, and the Question of Nursing "Character" in Early Twentieth Century England', *History Workshop Journal*, 80 (2015), 183–200.
25. 'Claudina Valeriani', *Majestic*, New York City Passenger Lists, 1820–1957, United States, Passenger and Crew Lists, findmypast.co.uk.
26. 'Nurse and Child Dead in Gas-Filled Room', *Marylebone Mercury*, 9 December 1939, 3.
27. 'Grave Charge against Tooting Father', *South Western Star*, 14 November 1924, 8.
28. He often travelled across the Atlantic, and she may have met him on a voyage.
29. 'Nurse and Child Dead in Gas-Filled Room', 3.
30. 'Elbis A. Shoales, M.D.', *Rochester Democrat and Chronicle*, 16 February 2014, https://www.legacy.com/us/obituaries/democratandchronicle/name/elbis-shoales-obituary?id=23545627.
31. 'Araxi Prevot: Obituary', *Caledonian Record*, 2 May 2015', https://www.caledonianrecord.com/community/araxi-prevot---obituary/article_2358c827-69b4-508e-9604-db01238d54b3.html.
32. Interview with Roger Prevot, 30 August 2022.

33. 'Araxi Prevot, Class of 1946', 16:02–16:36, Alumnae Oral Histories (2011), Smith College Libraries, https://media.smith.edu/departments/archives/alumoh/playlists/1940s.html, accessed 25 August 2022.
34. TNA, CRIM 1/1175.
35. TNA, CRIM 1/1175.
36. 'Woman on Murder Charge was in Dread of German Terror', *Evening Despatch*, 4 April 1940, 7.
37. TNA, CRIM 1/1175.
38. 1939 England and Wales Register, ancestry.co.uk.
39. TNA, CRIM 1/1175.
40. The duo type of meter took either a penny or a shilling, which would supply 13 or 156 cubic feet. The gas meter was empty. TNA, CRIM 1/1175.
41. 'Mother is Charged with Murder', *North London Observer*, 23 February 1940, 1.
42. Catherine Cox and Hilary Marland, *Disorder Contained: Mental Breakdown and the Modern Prison in England and Ireland, 1840–1900* (Cambridge: Cambridge University Press, 2002).
43. TNA, CRIM 1/1175.
44. TNA, CRIM 1/1175.
45. 'Woman on Murder Charge was in Dread of German Terror', 1.
46. LMA, 'The Evacuation of Children from the County of London During the Second World War 1939–1945' (London, 1997).
47. 'Woman on Murder Charge was in Dread of German Terror', 7.
48. Bell, 'Landscapes of Fear'.
49. United Kingdom House of Lords Decisions, M'Naghten's case [1843] UKHL J16 (19 June 1843), http://www.bailii.org/uk/cases/UKHL/1843/J16.html.
50. Jonathan Andrews, 'The Boundaries of Her Majesty's Pleasure: Discharging Child-Murderers from Broadmoor and Perth Criminal Lunatic Department, c. 1860–1920', in Mark Jackson (ed.), *Infanticide: Historical Perspectives on Child Concealment and Murder* (Aldershot: Ashgate, 2002), 216–48.
51. England & Wales, Civil Registration Marriage Index, 1916–2005, 'Lily Wright and Robert Moule', registered Oct 1966, Haringey, Greater London, Volume 5b, p. 1858, via ancestry.co.uk; England & Wales, Civil Registration Death Index, 1916–2007, 'Lily Mary Moule', registered Mar 1984, Thanet, Kent, Volume 16, p. 2055, via ancestry.com.
52. TNA, CRIM 1/1175.
53. 'Briefly', *Daily News*, 19 February 1940, 7; 'Woman on Murder Charge', *Daily Mirror*, 22 February 1940, 20.
54. 'Mother is Charged with Murder', *North London Observer*, 23 February 1940, 1.
55. 'Where did Pamela Wright Die?', *North London Observer*, 8 March 1940, 7. See also 'Devoted Mother on Murder Charge', *North London Observer*, 13 March 1940, 3.
56. *North London Observer*, 5 April 1940, 1.
57. TNA, CRIM 1/1175.
58. This centre did pioneering postwar work with former prisoners of war. See J.M. Tanner and Maxwell Jones, 'The Psychological Symptoms and the Physiological Responses to Exercise of Repatriated Prisoners of War with Neurosis', *Journal of Neurology, Neurosurgery & Psychiatry*, 11 (1948), 61–71.

59. Edward Glover, 'Notes on the Psychological Effects of War Conditions on the Civilian Population', *International Journal of Psycho-Analysis*, 23 (1942), 17–37 and Edward Glover, *War, Sadism and Pacifism: Further Essays on Group Psychology and War* (London: G. Allen and Unwin, 1946).
60. TNA, MEPO 20/3.

2 BOMBSITES AND SHELTERS

1. TNA, MEPO 3/2235.
2. Richard Overy, *The Bombing War: Europe 1939–45* (London: Allen Lane, 2013).
3. IWM, Private Papers of F.W. Hurd, Documents.4833.
4. See Steve Hunnisett's photographs and blog at http://blitzwalkers.blogspot.com/2013/05/footprints-of-london-blitz-1.html.
5. TNA, Metropolitan Police War Diary, MEPO 3/3066.
6. TNA, CAB 75/3.
7. TNA, MEPO 3/3067.
8. 'Special Squad of 40 Policewomen will Patrol London where Incidents Reported', *Montreal Gazette*, 1 January 1941, 10; Thomas, *An Underworld at War*, 72.
9. 'Raid Shelter as "Casino": £50 Fine', *Shields Daily News*, 30 March 1940, 1.
10. 'Stole Handbag in Air Raid Shelter', *Westminster & Pimlico News*, 18 October 1940, 4.
11. 'Six Months for Persistent Thief', *Kensington Post*, 15 February 1941, 1.
12. See Beryl Pong, *British Literature and Culture in Second World Wartime: For the Duration* (Oxford: Oxford University Press, 2020) and Leo Mellor, *Reading the Ruins: Modernism, Bombsites and British Culture* (Cambridge, Cambridge University Press, 2011).
13. The block of houses was gone in the 1951 Ordnance Survey. National Grid Maps.
14. Jackson, *Coroner*, 119.
15. Jackson, *Coroner*, 117.
16. 'Monocled Man detained by Yard Detective', *Weekly Dispatch (London)*, 19 October 1941, 8.
17. Jackon, *Coroner*, 118.
18. 'Attacked Woman in the Blackout', *Marylebone Mercury*, 6 April 1940, 1; 'Screams Stop Train in Blackout', *Holloway Press*, 4 February 1944, 1; 'Glass Attack in Shelter', *Chelsea News and General Advertiser*, 14 July 1944, 1.
19. TNA, MEPO 3/2193 and 'Park Hunt for Clue in Murder', *The Daily Mirror*, 28 October 1941, 16.
20. TNA, HO 144/21854.
21. Phyllis Lassner and Mia Spiro, 'A Tale of Two Cities: Virginia Woolf's Imagined Jewish Spaces and London's East End Jewish Culture', *Woolf Studies Annual*, 19 (2013), 58–82.
22. Geoffrey Alderman, *London Jewry and London Politics, 1889–1986* (London: Routledge, 1986).
23. 'Murder Seen by Seer', *Daily Mail*, 24 November 1942, 1.
24. Molly Lefebure, *Evidence for the Crown: Experiences of a Pathologist's Secretary* (London: W. Heinemann, 1955).

25. TNA, MEPO 3/2235.
26. This chapel is sometimes referred to as the Vauxhall Baptist Chapel, as is the Baptist chapel further east on Cottington Street, just off Kennington Lane. The Cottington chapel survived the war and is now called Centenary Hall.
27. Walter Besant, *London – South of the Thames* (London: Adam & Charles Black, 1912).
28. Lefebure, *Evidence*, 55.
29. C.E. Bechhofer Roberts, *The Trial of Harry Dobkin* (London: Jarrolds, 1944), 66.
30. Lefebure, *Evidence*, 56.
31. Keith Simpson, 'R. v. Dobkin: The Baptist Church Cellar Murder', *Police Journal: Theory, Practice and Principles*, 16, no. 4 (1943), 270–80, https://doi.org/10.1177/0032258X4301600405.
32. Simpson, *Forty Years*, 58.
33. Amy Bell, 'The Development of Forensic Pathology in London, England: Keith Simpson and the Dobkin Case, 1942', *Canadian Bulletin of Medical History*, 29, no. 2 (2012), 265–82.
34. Simpson, *Forty Years*, 64.
35. The Guy's Hospital archives also hold less gruesome photographs that she took in these years, of friends, nurses, garden parties and prize givings at the hospital. LMA, Guy's Hospital. H09/GY/PH/12/014, packet of photographs taken by Mary Newman, a nurse at Guy's (later Mrs J.K. Hogg), 1924–43.
36. John Glaister and James Brash, *The Medico-Legal Aspects of the Ruxton Case* (Edinburgh: Livingstone, 1937).
37. Simpson, *Forty Years*, 62. See also '24 Points to Prove Identity of Dead Woman', *Evening Standard*, 19 November 1942, 1 and 'Woman's Body in Chapel Cellar', *The Times*, 24 November 1942, 2.
38. 'Began a Fire to Hide a Murder', *Daily Herald*, 24 November 1942, 1.
39. TNA, HO 144/21854.
40. Lefebure, *Evidence*, 81.
41. 'Air Cadet to Die for Ghoulish Murder', *Nottingham Journal*, 29 April 1942, 4.
42. TNA, MEPO 3/2235.
43. John Carter Wood, 'Press, Politics and the "Police and Public" Debates in Late 1920s Britain', *Crime, Histoire & Sociétés/Crime, History & Societies*, 16, no. 1 (2012), 75–98.
44. Simpson, *Forty Years*, 70.
45. TNA, MEPO 20/4.

3 PUBS AND CLUBS

1. 'Beloved Daddy Stabbed to Death', *Holloway Press*, 9 May 1941, 1.
2. IWM, Private Papers of Miss V. Hall, Documents 3989.
3. James Nott, *Going to the Palais: A Social and Cultural History of Dancing and Dance Halls in Britain, 1918–1960* (Oxford University Press, 2015), 70.
4. Juliet Gardiner, *Wartime: Britain 1939–1945* (London: Headline, 2004), 170.
5. Donald Thomas, *An Underworld at War* (London: John Murray, 2003), 251.
6. Ziegler, *London at War*, 53.

7. The Theatre Royal would be restored and reopened in 1965. https://theatreroyal. org/about-us/our-history/.

8. Heather Creaton, *Sources for the History of London 1939–45: A Guide and Bibliography* (London: British Records Association, 1998), 122–4.

9. Quoted in Creaton, *Sources for the History of London*, 124.

10. US Census 1910, ancestry.co.uk.

11. TNA, WO 329, via ancestry.co.uk.

12. British War Medal and Victory Medal, UK, World War I Service Medal and Award Rolls, 1914–1920, ancestry.co.uk.

13. Voter records, ancestry.co.uk.

14. He married Joy Lawrence in 1948 and they had two children, Jane and Harriet. They lived for some twenty years after the war in Wales, after moving from Battersea, running a retail business. They later moved to England, finally settling in Haddenham. http://gallery.commandoveterans.org/cdoGallery/v/units/12/manns/.

15. Parker House Hostel is still run by the Camden Council as a homeless shelter and assessment shelter with fourteen beds. https://cindex.camden.gov.uk/kb5/camden/cd/service.page?id=unwuwDFwvwo.

16. G.D. Sheffield, *The Redcaps: A History of the Royal Military Police and its Antecedents from the Middle Ages to the Gulf War* (London: Brassey's, 1994), 145.

17. Clive Emsley, *The Great British Bobby* (London: Quercus, 2009); TNA, MEPO 3/3067.

18. Beaver Club and Vincent Massey, 'Introduction', in *Six Years and a Day: The Story of the Beaver Club, 1940–1946* (London: Kelly and Kelly, 1946); Canadian YMCA, 'The Canadian Soldier's Leave Guide for London', revised 2nd edition (n.d.) [Pamphlet].

19. 'Canadian Accused of Shooting Barman had Complained of Pains in the Head', *Morning Advertiser*, 14 February 1941, in TNA, PCOM 9/893.

20. See Robin Neillands, *The Dieppe Raid: The Story of the Disastrous 1942 Expedition* (London: Aurum, 2005).

21. TNA, PCOM 9/893.

22. TNA, PCOM 9/893. Library and Archives Canada (LAC), Release from prison in the U.K. of J.D. McCallum, 1945/08/07-1946/01/10, RG25-A-3-b, Volume number: 3780, File number: 7998-40, Item ID number: 1803831.

23. Katelyn Verstraten, 'John McCallum, Former Ryerson Journalism Professor, was "Larger than Life"', *The Star*, 19 July 2014, https://www.thestar.com/news/gta/2014/07/19/john_mccallum_former_ryerson_journalism_professor_was_larger_than_life.html.

24. TNA, MEPO 20/3 and CRIM 1/1366.

25. 'Shooting Affair in London Streets: Soldier Charged with Three Murders', *The Times*, 4 December 1941, 8.

26. Anna Cottrell, *London Writing of the 1930s* (Edinburgh: Edinburgh University Press, 2017).

27. Judith Walkowitz, *Nights Out: Life in Cosmopolitan London* (New Haven and London: Yale University Press, 2012).

28. James Morton, *Gangland Soho* (London: Piatkus, 2008).

29. Stefan Slater, 'Prostitutes and Popular History: Notes on the "Underworld", 1918–1939', *Crime, Histoire & Sociétés*, 13, no. 1 (2009), 25–48.

30. Walkowitz, *Nights Out*, 12.
31. Walkowitz, *Nights Out*, 140.
32. 'Italian's Premises are Smashed up in Riots', *Daily Herald*, 11 June 1940, 1.
33. 'Big Round-Up', *The Scotsman*, 12 June 1940, 5.
34. Walkowitz, *Nights Out*, 133.
35. 'London's Murder Land', *John Bull*, 23 May 1936, 32.
36. Heather Shore, *London's Criminal Underworlds, 1720–1930* (London: Palgrave Macmillan, 2015), 178.
37. 'London's Murder Land'.
38. As late as 1947, Metropolitan Police detective superintendents told a press conference: 'It is the view of the crime chiefs that underworld crooks generally hate the use of firearms.' They appealed for the underworld's help in solving a recent shooting: 'Some of them know the identity of the gunmen who yesterday murdered Alec de Antiquis as he tried to stop them getting away from an armed hold-up of a jeweller's shop in Tottenham Street.' 'Four Gun Gangs Roam London', *Lancashire Evening Post*, 30 April 1947, 1.
39. Billy Hill, *Boss of Britain's Underworld* (London: Naldrett Press, 1955), 27–8.
40. Wensley Clarkson, *Billy Hill: Godfather of London* (London: Pennant Books, 2008).
41. Arthur Tietjen, *Soho: London's Vicious Circle* (London: Alan Wingate, 1956), 36.
42. Heather Shore, 'Undiscovered Country: Towards a History of the Criminal Underworld', *Law, Crime and History*, 1, no. 1 (2007), 41–68.
43. Shore, *London's Criminal Underworlds*, 177; James Morton, *Gangland: London's Underworld* (London: Warner, 1992), 33.
44. 'Yard Hunt Woman Gang Leader', *Daily Mirror*, 13 December 1945, 1.
45. Hill, *Boss of Britain's Underworld*, 73.
46. Tietjen, *Soho*, 66.
47. 'Gaoled', *Weekly Dispatch*, 16 October 1938, 9.
48. 'Difficult to Catch', *Gloucester Citizen*, 3 July 1935, 8.
49. 'Gaoled'.
50. 'Found in "Tube" Phone Box', *Weekly Dispatch*, 26 May 1940, 3.
51. 1939 England and Wales Register, ancestry.co.uk.
52. Vicky Iglikowski-Broad, 'The Shim Sham Club: "London's miniature Harlem"', TNA Blog, Wednesday 5 February 2020, https://blog.nationalarchives.gov.uk/the-shim-sham-club-queer-black-london-londons-miniature-harlem/.
53. Iglikowski-Broad, 'The Shim Sham Club'.
54. See Records of the Public Morality Council, A/PMC, LMA.
55. 'A Soho Bottle Party', *Fulham Chronicle*, 12 January 1940, 3; 'Baronet in Club Scene', *Daily Mirror*, 18 January 1940, 6; 'Bottle Party Dance Hostess of Seventeen', *Daily News*, 5 February 1940, 5.
56. UK, Calendar of Prisoners, 1868–1929 for Harry Distleman, ancestry.co.uk.
57. 'Three Constables Injured by Rival Gangsters', *Illustrated Police News*, 3 November 1927, 7.
58. Arthur Thorp, *Calling Scotland Yard* (London: Allan Wingate, 1954), 111–13.
59. London City Directory, 1930, ancestry.co.uk.
60. 'Jew and Blackshirt', *Sunday Mirror*, 10 September 1933, 4.
61. 'Jews to Appeal against Jail Sentence', *Daily Herald*, 9 May 1933, 7.
62. Morton, *Gangland Soho*, 1236.

63. Sid Colin, *And the Band Played On: An Informal History of British Dance Bands* (London: David and Charles, 1977). The Nest closed during the war and opened in 1944 as the Florida Club.

64. Morton, *Gangland London*, 35.

65. 'Murdered Man had Fourteen Previous Convictions, Six for Assault', *Holloway Press*, 6 June 1941, 3.

66. Thorp, *Calling Scotland Yard*, 111.

67. 'Murdered Man had Fourteen Previous Convictions, Six for Assault'.

68. Jackson, *Coroner*, 111.

69. Thorp, *Calling Scotland Yard*, 112.

70. Jackson, *Coroner*, 111.

71. 'Beloved Daddy Stabbed to Death', *Holloway Press*, 9 May 1941, 1.

72. 'Caterer on Murder Charge', *Shields Daily News*, 6 May 1941, 4.

73. 'Dagger in Club Fracas', *Nottingham Evening Post*, 16 May 1941, 6.

74. 'Stabbing Crime in Night Club', *Daily Mirror*, 24 September 1924, 2.

75. 'Catering Manager Sentenced to Die', *Dundee Evening Telegraph*, 5 July 1941, 5.

76. 'Somers Town Man's Murderer to Hang', *Holloway Press*, 11 July 1941, 5.

77. 'Soho Murder Charge', *Belfast Telegraph*, 4 July 1941, 7.

78. Thorp, *Calling Scotland Yard*, 113.

79. 'Beloved Daddy Stabbed to Death'.

80. *Holloway Press*, 6 June 1941, 3.

81. 'Death for Soho Gang Crime', *Daily Herald*, 5 July 1941, 3.

82. Tietjen, *Soho*, 67.

83. Mancini v DPP, Law Reports, England & Wales, House of Lords. Judges the Lord Chancellor, Viscount Sankey, Lord Russell of Killowen, Lord Wright, Lord Porter. 16 October 1941. Judgment citation (vLex) [1941] UKHL J1016-1, https://vlex.co.uk/vid/mancini-v-dpp-792977201.

84. 'House of Lords Decision', *Liverpool Evening Express*, 16 October 1941, 4.

85. 'Lords Discuss Mancini, while Wife Listens', *Daily News,* 3 October 1941, 3.

86. 'Mrs. Mancini Knew Appeal Had Failed', *Daily Mirror,* 17 October 1941, 3.

87. James Wills, 'Britain's Most Famous Executioner', *Daily Star*, 11 June 2021, https://www.dailystar.co.uk/news/britains-most-famous-executioner-killed-2429 2012.

88. 'Mancini, Hanged for Murder, Leaves £101', *Weekly Dispatch*, 21 December 1941, 3.

89. Morton, *Gangland London*, 37.

90. 'Man Wounded in London Club', *Shepton Mallet Journal*, 25 July 1941, 2.

91. 'Persuaded to Help', *East End News and London Shipping Chronicle*, 25 July 1947, 2.

92. Thorp, *Calling Scotland Yard*, 114.

93. Marthe Watts, *The Men in My Life* (London: Christopher Johnson, 1961); Stefan Slater, 'Pimps, Police and Filles de Joie: Foreign Prostitution in Interwar London', *The London Journal,* 32, no. 1 (2007), 53–74.

94. Rhoda Lee Finmore, *Immoral Earnings, or Mr. Martin's Profession: An Account of the Trial of Alfredo Messina* (London: M.H. Publications, 1951); Stefan Slater, 'Prostitutes and Popular History: Notes on the "Underworld", 1918–1939', *Crime History & Societies*, 13, no. 1 (2009), 25–48.

95. Sonya O. Rose, 'Temperate Heroes: Concepts of Masculinity in Second World War Britain', in Stefan Dudink, Karen Hagemann and John Tosh (eds), *Masculinities in Politics and War: Gendering Modern History* (Manchester: Manchester University Press, 2004).

4 HOME

1. TNA, HO 144/21533.
2. TNA, HO 144/21533.
3. See the police and trial files at TNA MEPO 3/2186 and CRIM 1/1337.
4. The area was hit by eighteen HE bombs, bombsight.org.
5. TNA, HO 144/21533.
6. TNA, HO 144/21533.
7. TNA, HO 144/21533.
8. 'Poisoner to Die', *The Morning Advertiser*, 19 September 1941, 1, in TNA HO 144/21533.
9. 'Ration Book Traps Poisoner', *Daily Mail*, 19 September 1941, 1.
10. 'Dug Grave for Bigamous Wife and Child', *News of the World*, 21 September 1941.
11. See Alana Harris and Timothy Willem Jones (eds), *Love and Romance in Britain 1918–1970* (Basingstoke: Palgrave Macmillan, 2015), Marcus Collins, *Modern Love: An Intimate History of Men and Women in Twentieth-Century Britain* (London: Atlantic Books, 2003), Simon Szreter and Kate Fisher, *Sex Before the Sexual Revolution: Intimate Life in England 1918–1963* (Cambridge: Cambridge University Press, 2010) and Kate Fisher, *Birth Control, Sex, and Marriage in Britain 1918–1960* (Oxford: Oxford University Press, 2006).
12. Lizzie Seal and Alexa Neale, '"In His Passionate Way": Emotion, Race and Gender in Cases of Partner Murder in England and Wales, 1900–39', *The British Journal of Criminology*, 60, no. 4 (2020), 811–29.
13. 'Run Over and Bombed-Out Refugee who Committed Suicide', *Hampstead and St. John's Wood News and Golders Green Gazette*, 1 May 1941, 3.
14. Heidrun Hannusch, *Todesstrafe für die Selbstmörderin* [Death Sentence for the Suicide Victim] (Berlin: Ch. Links, 2011), 45.
15. Irene Messinger, 'Marriages of Convenience as a Strategy to Escape to the UK', in Charmian Brinson, Jana Barbora Buresova and Andrea Hammel (eds), in *Exile and Gender II: Politics, Education and the Arts* (Leiden: Brill, 2017), 81–95, statistics from 84.
16. Jennifer Craig-Norton, 'Refugees at the Margins: Jewish Domestics in Britain 1938–1945', *Shofar*, 37, no. 3 (2019), 295–330, personal accounts from 320.
17. TNA, MEPO, 3/1092, 'Foreign born women holding British passports: marriages of convenience, general file'.
18. Angela Davis, 'Belonging and "Unbelonging": Jewish Refugee and Survivor Women in 1950s Britain', *Women's History Review*, 26, no. 1 (2017), 130–46.
19. Hannusch, *Death Sentence*, 48.
20. TNA MEPO 3/2196.
21. Henry Srebnik, 'The British Communist Party's National Jewish Committee and the Fight Against Anti-Semitism During the Second World War', in Tony Kushner and Kenneth Lunn (eds), *The Politics of Marginality* (London: Routledge,

1990); Aaron Goldman, 'The Resurgence of Antisemitism in Britain during World War II', *Jewish Social Studies*, 46, no. 1 (1984), 37–50.
22. TNA, MEPO 20/3 and MEPO 3/2196.
23. Hannusch, *Death Sentence*, 24.
24. Hannusch, *Death Sentence*, 71.
25. TNA, MEPO 3/2196.
26. TNA, MEPO 3/2196.
27. Hannusch, *Death Sentence*, 29.
28. Ella Sbaraini, 'The Materiality of English Suicide Letters, c.1700–c.1850', *The Historical Journal* (2021), 1–28.
29. Jacob Frederickson, ' "No Future to Look Forward to", Suicide Pacts, Intimacy and Society in 1920s and 1930s Britain', *Twentieth Century British History*, 34, no. 4 (2023), 657–80. See also Olive Anderson, *Suicide in Victorian and Edwardian England* (Oxford: Clarendon Press, 1987) and Victor Bailey, *'This Rash Act': Suicide Across the Life Cycle in the Victorian City* (Stanford, CA: Stanford University Press, 1998).
30. TNA, MEPO 20/3.
31. Hannusch, *Death Sentence*, 150.
32. Hannusch, *Death Sentence*, 158.
33. Hannusch, *Death Sentence*, 162.
34. 'Irene Coffee nee Brann', Remember.org: Holocaust history and stories, http://remember.org/irene1.htm.
35. The envelope is saved at ancestry.co.uk.
36. 'Otto Stern, 1876' and 'Irma Salomon Stern, 1885', Yad Vashem – the Holocaust Heroes' and Martyrs' Remembrance Authority, http://www.yadvashem.org.

5 DARK STREETS

1. TNA, MEPO 3/2206.
2. See Sonya O. Rose, 'Girls and GIs: Race, Sex, and Diplomacy in Second World War Britain', *The International History Review*, 19, no. 1 (1997), 146–60; Stephanie Makowski, 'For the Duration Only: Interracial Relationships in World War II Britain', *Journal of the History of Sexuality*, 29, no. 2 (2020), 222–52; Wendy Webster, ' "Fit to Fight, Fit to Mix": Sexual Patriotism in Second World War Britain', *Women's History Review*, 22, no. 4 (2013), 607–24; Annette Tim, 'The Challenges of Including Sexual Violence and Transgressive Love in Historical Writing on World War II and the Holocaust', *Journal of the History of Sexuality*, 26, no. 3 (2017), 351–65.
3. See G.R. Osborn, 'Pulmonary Concussion ("Blast")', *BMJ* (5 April 1941), 506–10 and J.V. Wilson, 'The Pathology of Closed Injuries of the Chest', *BMJ* (17 April 1943), 470–74.
4. Cuthbert Lindsay Dunn, *The History of the Second World War: United Kingdom Medical Series: The Emergency Medical Services* (London: Her Majesty's Stationery Office, 1952). See also TNA, CAB/68/2/13, War Cabinet Civil Defense Report, 15 October 1939.
5. W. McAdam Eccles and A.T. Densham, 'Clearance of Casualties from First Aid Posts', *BMJ* (7 September 1940), 332–3.

6. Anonymous, 'Hospitals and Air Raids: Organization of a City Casualty Hospital', *BMJ* (19 July 1941), 98–100.
7. Anonymous, 'Hospitals and Air Raids', 99.
8. TNA, MEPO 4/306, 'Unidentified Casualties', in Metropolitan Police Files. See also Lambeth Archives Department, 'Unidentified dead from mortuary', A,B,C, MBL/TC/CD/3/1/5, 1940–44 and 'Civilian war dead files', MBL/TC/CD/3/1 [n.d.], and Hackney Archives Department, 'Correspondence concerning unidentified civilian war dead', SN/A/32, 1940–42.
9. TNA, MEPO 4/306.
10. Elizabeth Bowen, *The Heat of the Day* (London: Jonathan Cape, 1948), 90.
11. 'Murdered Woman in Shelter', *West London Observer*, 13 February 1942, 4.
12. TNA, MEPO 20/3 and MEPO 3/2206.
13. 'Three Women Murdered in Two Days', *Daily Mirror*, 11 February 1942, 8.
14. 'University Woman Strangled', *Daily Herald*, 11 February 1942, 3.
15. TNA, MEPO 3/2206.
16. 'Three Women Murdered in Two Days'.
17. 'Former Keighley Girl Murdered', *Bradford Observer*, 11 February 1942, 4.
18. TNA, MEPO 3/2206.
19. 'Strangled in Shelter', *West London Observer*, 10 April 1942, 5.
20. Mike Hutton, *The Story of Soho: The Windmill Years 1932–1964* (Stroud: Amberley, 2012). The *People* did refer to him as London's modern Jack the Ripper, 15 February 1942, 5.
21. Judith Walkowitz, *Prostitution and Victorian Society: Women, Class, and the State* (Cambridge: Cambridge University Press, 1982).
22. Hallie Rubenhold, *The Five: The Untold Lives of Women Killed by Jack the Ripper* (Houghton Mifflin Harcourt, 2019).
23. F.D. Sharpe, *Sharpe of the Flying Squad* (London: John Long, 1938), 106–7.
24. Their estimate is based on the assumption that arrests before the court represented approximately one fifth of the total number. London School of Economics and Political Science, *The New Survey of London Life and Labour, Volume IX: Life and Leisure* (London: P.S. King and Son, 1935), 298.
25. Smithies, *Crime in Wartime*, 137; Quentin Crisp, *The Naked Civil Servant* (London, Jonathan Cape, 1968), 154.
26. TNA, MEPO 2/7078.
27. See David Reynolds, *Rich Relations: The American Occupation of Britain, 1942–1945* (London: Harper Collins, 1995) and Juliet Gardiner, *'Over Here': The GIs in Wartime Britain* (London: Collins & Brown, 1992).
28. Robert Lilly, *Taken by Force: Rape and American GIs in Europe during WWII* (Basingstoke: Palgrave Macmillan, 2007). See also Mary Louise Roberts, 'The Leroy Henry Case: Sexual Violence and Allied Relations in Great Britain, 1944', *Journal of the History of Sexuality*, 26, no. 3 (2017), 402–23, Miriam Gebhardt, trans. Nick Somers, *Crimes Unspoken: The Rape of German Women at the End of the Second World War* (Cambridge: Polity Press, 2016) and Thomas J. Kehoe and James E. Kehoe, 'Crimes Committed by U.S. Soldiers in Europe, 1945–1946', *The Journal of Interdisciplinary History*, 47, no. 1 (2017), 53–84.
29. 'Two Hunted in Wave of Theft and Murder', *The Daily Mirror*, 23 December 1942.
30. Muriel Raven, 73 Fitz Road, Cockermouth, Cumberland. TNA, MEPO 3/2238.

31. Wallace Steggle. TNA, MEPO 3/2238.
32. Chris Waters, 'The Homosexual as a Social Being in Britain, 1945–1968', *Journal of British Studies*, 51, no. 3 (2012), 685–710.
33. Harry Daley, *This Small Cloud: A Personal Memoir* (London: Weidenfeld, 1987).
34. See Matt Houlbrook, *Queer London: Perils and Pleasures in the Sexual Metropolis, 1918–1957* (Chicago: University of Chicago Press, 2005).
35. See C.P. Stacey, *The Canadian Army, 1939–1945: An Official Historical Summary* (Ottawa: King's Printer, 1948).
36. TNA, MEPO 3/2238.
37. TNA, MEPO 3/2238.
38. TNA, MEPO 20/3 and CRIM 1/1540.
39. Emma Vickers, 'Queer Sex in the Metropolis? Place, Subjectivity and the Second World War', *Feminist Review*, 96 (2010), 58–73.
40. TNA, MEPO 3/2250.
41. Emma Vickers, *Queen and Country: Same-Sex Desire in the British Armed Forces* (Manchester: Manchester University Press, 2013).
42. Harold Scott, *Your Obedient Servant* (London: Andre Deutsch, 1954), 61.

6 WASTE GROUND

1. TNA, MEPO 3/2227.
2. TNA, MEPO 3/2227.
3. See Amy Helen Bell, 'Abortion Crime Scene Photography in Metropolitan London 1950–1968', *Social History of Medicine*, 30, no. 3 (2017), 661–84, Barbara Brookes and Paul Roth, 'Rex v. Bourne and the Medicalization of Abortion', in Michael Clark and Catherine Crawford (eds), *Legal Medicine in History* (Cambridge: Cambridge University Press, 1994), 314–43, Stephen Brooke, ' "A New World for Women"? Abortion Law Reform in Britain during the 1930s', *American Historical Review*, 106 (2001), 431–59 and Emma Jones, 'Representations of Illegal Abortionists in England, 1900–1967', in Andrew Mangham and Greta Depledge (eds), *The Female Body in Medicine and Literature* (Liverpool: Liverpool University Press, 2011), 196–215.
4. TNA, MEPO 20/3, 20/4.
5. See Keith Simpson, *Forensic Medicine* (London: Edward Arnold, 1947, 1951 ed.).
6. 1939 England and Wales Register, 51 Pemberton Road, N4, ancestry.co.uk.
7. Mona Daphne was born 29 April 1929 and evacuated to Mrs Costown, 44 Summerhill Road, in Saffron Walden, Essex. Ancestry.co.uk.
8. 'Daily Weather Report 1942', Met Office Digital Library and Archive, https://digital.nmla.metoffice.gov.uk/IO_3d7bd818-99fa-4805-8e03-a1141bb76e98/.
9. 42 Stockwell Road. It later became a YMCA and now houses homeless young people.
10. 1939 England and Wales Register, 40 Hertford Street, City of Westminster, as housemaid and cook, ancestry.co.uk.
11. TNA, MEPO 3/2227.
12. 'Woman's Body Found in Alley', *South Western Star*, 2 October 1942, 6.
13. 'Woman's Body Found in Alley', 6.
14. TNA, MEPO 3/2227.

15. 'Sentences of Two Years', *Streatham News*, 25 September 1942, 8.
16. TNA, MEPO 3/2227.
17. TNA, MEPO 20/4.
18. Jackson, *Coroner*, 91.
19. 'Girl Among V-Bomb Dead is found to be the Victim of a Crime', *Daily Mirror*, 13 February 1945, 3.
20. TNA, CRIM 1/1664.
21. 'Girl's Fatal Visit', *Holloway Press*, 30 March, 1945, 1.
22. '"Sack" Murder Mystery: Dead Woman still Unidentified', *Dunstable Borough Gazette*, 10 December 1943, 1.
23. Keith Simpson, 'The Luton Sack Murder: R. v. Manton', *Police Journal: Theory, Practice and Principles*, 18, no. 4 (1945), 265.
24. 'Seventh Molar May Provide Clue: Dentists' Help Sought in Murder Riddle', *Dunstable Borough Gazette*, 26 November 1943, 1.
25. 'The Luton Murder', *Biggleswade Chronicle*, 31 March 1944, 1.
26. 'Fifteen Tobacco Co', *Liverpool Daily Post*, 27 January 1941, 6.
27. Simpson, 'The Luton Sack Murder', 271.
28. 'Sack Murder: Manton to Die'.
29. Photograph dated 30 June 1944, Keystone/Hulton Archive/Getty Images, Editorial image #52275633, http://www.gettyimages.ca/detail/news-photo/the-16-year-old-son-of-convicted-murderer-bertie-horace-news-photo/52275633?Language=en-US, accessed 19 December 2013.
30. 'Shot Woman Found in River', *Beds and Herts Saturday Telegraph*, 23 November 1943, 1.
31. Date of burial 26 November 1947, ceremony by Rev. Wearn, buried in prison cemetery. TNA, PCOM 9/1028.
32. TNA, MEPO 3/2263, ASSI 13/87, HO 144/23253.
33. Ivy died in 1955, but Sheila lived until 2020.
34. Estimates vary on the number. In 1935, 120 dead bodies were recovered. Many were suicides from Waterloo Bridge. Superintendent H. Dalton, 'The Thames Police', *Police Journal*, 8, no. 1 (1935), 90–103. Tom Fallon estimated that, on average, one dead body was found in the Thames per week. Tom Fallon, *River Police: The Story of Scotland Yard's Little Ships* (London: Frederick Muller Ltd, 1956), 233.
35. TNA, MEPO 20/3 and 20/4.

7 FOOD STALLS AND CAFÉS

1. TNA, MEPO 3/2288.
2. Stephen Bourne, *Mother Country: Britain's Black Community on the Home Front 1939–1945* (London: History Press, 2010), 11.
3. Caroline Bressey, 'It's Only Political Correctness – Race and Racism in British History', in Caroline Bressey and Claire Dwyer (eds), *New Geographies of Race and Racism* (Aldershot: Ashgate, 2008), 29–39.
4. Fernando Henriques, 'Coloured Men in Civil Defense', *News Letter*, 1 (June 1941), 57–9, quoted in Bourne, *Mother Country*, 70; Fernando Henriques, *Children of Caliban: Miscegenation* (London: Secker and Warburg, 1974).

5. Oliver Ayers, 'Jim Crow and John Bull in London: Transatlantic Encounters with Race and Nation in the Second World War', *Studies in Ethnicity and Nationalism*, 20 (2020), 244–66, quote on 262.

6. E.I. Ekpenyon, *Some Experiences of an African Air Raid Warden* (London: The Sheldon Press, 1943), 10.

7. Henriques, *Children of Caliban*, 3.

8. 'Ground Crew Volunteers', https://www.caribbeanaircrew-ww2.com/.

9. The Canadian military did not keep records of race in the Second World War, but it can be estimated based on census data that there were at least 5,000 available Black volunteers in the Canadian Forces. Simon James Theobald, 'A False Sense of Equality', MA dissertation, University of Ottawa, 43, https://ruor.uottawa.ca/bitstream/10393/27791/1/MR48629.PDF.

10. See C.P. Stacey, *The Canadian Army, 1939–1945: An Official Historical Summary* (Ottawa: King's Printer, 1948) and Sheffield, *The Redcaps*.

11. 'Told to Quit Hotel as a N—: Famous Cricketer', *Daily Mirror*, 20 June 1944, 2.

12. 'Word "N—" Used: Constantine Wins Hotel Suit', *Evening Despatch*, 28 June 1944, 4.

13. Lizzie Seal and Alexa Neale, 'Racializing Mercy: Capital Punishment and Race in Twentieth-Century England and Wales', *Law and History Review*, 38, no. 4 (2020), 883–910, quote on 899.

14. Pureveen was born in Rotterdam, 26 August 1917.

15. TNA, MEPO 20/4 and MEPO 3/2288.

16. Herman Carter Robinson was from Rochester, New York. 'Herman C Robinson', in the New York, US, New York Guard Service Cards, 1906–1918, 1940–1948, ancestry.co.uk. Born 6 March 1920, enlisted 12 February 1944.

17. TNA, MEPO 3/2288.

18. TNA, DPP 2/1349.

19. TNA, MEPO 3/2288.

20. Marke, *In Troubled Waters*, 116.

21. Ernest Marke, *Old Man Trouble* (London: Weidenfeld & Nicolson, 1975), 139.

22. Marke, *In Troubled Waters*, 141.

23. Marke, *In Troubled Waters*, 141.

24. Hakim Adi, *West Africans in Britain, 1900–1960: Nationalism, Pan-Africanism, and Communism* (London: Lawrence & Wishart, 1998), 146.

25. TNA, MEPO 3/2288.

26. Jackson, *Coroner*, 163.

27. TNA, MEPO 3/2288.

28. TNA, DPP 2/1349.

29. 'Death for Coffee Stall Murder', *Daily News*, 15 March 1945, 3.

30. 'Luck once saved "Creeper"', *Daily Mirror*, 15 March 1945, 3.

31. Seal and Neale, 'Racializing Mercy'.

32. Seal and Neale, 'Racializing Mercy'.

33. Susan D. Pennybacker, *From Scottsboro to Munich: Race and Political Culture in 1930s Britain* (Princeton: Princeton University Press, 2009).

34. 'Luck once saved "Creeper"', 3.

35. TNA, MEPO 3/2288.

36. TNA, MEPO 3/2288 with previously closed extract: Subfile 201/44/29.

37. 'High Praise for Club', *Westminster & Pimlico News*, 28 June 1957, 3.

38. 'VE Day', 8 May 1945, International Churchill Society, https://winstonchurchill. org/resources/speeches/1941-1945-war-leader/to-v-e-crowds/.
39. 'Peace on Earth' (1945), https://www.britishpathe.com/asset/67565/.
40. Ayers, 'Jim Crow and John Bull', 245.
41. Ayers, 'Jim Crow and John Bull', 245.
42. Marke, *Old Man Trouble*, 142.
43. Marke, *Old Man Trouble*, 142.
44. Marke, *Old Man Trouble*, 142.
45. Ayers, 'Jim Crow and John Bull', 246.
46. Marke, *Old Man Trouble*, 146.
47. Alan Allport, *Demobbed: Coming Home at the End of the Second World War* (New Haven and London: Yale University Press, 2009), 8.
48. Geoffrey Field, 'Nights Underground in Darkest London: The Blitz, 1940–1941', *International Labor and Working-Class History*, 62 (2002), 11–49.
49. Roy Porter, *London: A Social History* (London: Penguin, 1994), 42.
50. Ian Zweiniger-Bargielowska, 'Bread Rationing in Britain, July 1946–July 1948', *Twentieth Century British History*, 4 (1993), 57–85.
51. Emma Newlands, 'Active Service', in Emma Newlands (ed.), *Civilians into Soldiers: War, the Body and British Army Recruits, 1939–45* (Manchester: Manchester University Press, 2014), 116–53, http://www.jstor.org/stable/j.ctt1mf70t1.11.
52. Allport, *Demobbed*, 28, 48.
53. John C. Spencer, *Crime and the Services* (London: Routledge, 1954), 52.
54. Letter in *The Times*, 27 October 1947, quoted in Spencer, *Crime and the Services*, 52.
55. Ayers, 'Jim Crow and John Bull', 246.
56. Ayers, 'Jim Crow and John Bull', 260.
57. 'Shots through Sweetheart's Letter Ends Last Leave', *Daily Herald*, 27 December 1946, 1.
58. Jérémie Kroubo Dagnini, 'Kingston: A Societal Patchwork', *Études caribéennes* [Online], 39–40 (April–August 2018), published online 15 June 2018, http:// journals.openedition.org/etudescaribeennes/11378, accessed 10 September 2023.
59. TNA, MEPO 3/2749.
60. Martin E. Noble, *Jamaica Airman: A Black Airman in Britain, 1943 and After* (London: New Beacon Books, 1984).
61. TNA, MEPO 3/2739.
62. The average meal at a Lyons outlet in 1946 was one shilling and tenpence. Bryce Evans, 'Eat for Victory: The British Restaurants of WW2', History Extra, 20 January 2023, https://www.historyextra.com/period/second-world-war/british-restaurants-ww2-rationing-canteens/.
63. 'Horseflesh in Café', *Marylebone Mercury*, 28 December 1946, 1. When inspectors came, they found 20 pounds of horse in the refrigerator, with one chicken and two legs of lamb.
64. TNA, MEPO 20/4 and MEPO 3/2739.
65. Lucy Bland, *Britain's 'Brown Babies': The Stories of Children Born to Black GIs and White Women in the Second World War* (Manchester: Manchester University Press, 2019).
66. TNA, MEPO 3/2749.

67. 'She Smashed Plate on Café Killer's Face', *Daily Mirror*, 27 December 1946, 1.
68. 'Shots through Sweetheart's Letter Ends Last Leave', *Daily Herald*, 27 December 1946, 1.
69. TNA, MEPO 3/2749.
70. *Daily News*, 27 December 1946, 1.
71. 'Three Shots', *Daily Herald*, 27 December 1946, 1.
72. 'Shan't be Caught Alive: I'll Shoot it out', *Dundee Evening Telegraph*, 11 January 1947, 8.
73. 'In Gun Battle', *Lincolnshire Echo*, 27 December 1946, 8.
74. '100 Policemen Called Out', *Gloucester Citizen*, 27 December 1946, 1.
75. TNA, MEPO 3/2749.
76. TNA, MEPO 20/3 and 20/4.
77. 'London Shootings', *Belfast Telegraph*, 11 January 1947, 2.
78. TNA, MEPO 3/2737.
79. TNA, MEPO 3/2737.
80. 'Eleven Years for Killing Airman', *Dundee Evening Telegraph*, 13 February 1947, 5.
81. https://www.findagrave.com/memorial/17661882/aloysius-joseph-abbott/photo.
82. 'Ormonde, Almanzora and Windrush', https://beta.nationalarchives.gov.uk/explore-the-collection/stories/ormonde-almanzora-windrush/. Passenger lists for these three ships are at TNA: BT 26/1233, BT 26/1231/41, BT 26/1237.
83. Frank Mort, 'Morality, Majesty, and Murder in 1950s London: Metropolitan Culture and English Modernity', in Gyan Prakash and Kevin M. Kruse (eds), *The Spaces of the Modern City: Imaginaries, Politics, and Everyday Life* (Princeton: Princeton University Press, 2008), 313–35, quote on 335.

8 AFTERMATH

1. Peter Thorley, *Inside 10 Rillington Place: John Christie and Me, the Untold Truth* (London: Mirror Books, 2020), 42.
2. See TNA, HLG 7/336 and 'Return of evacuees to London area and general records on child evacuation' at LMA, LCC/EO/WAR/1/.
3. Stephen Inwood, *A History of London* (London: Basic Books, 1998), 854.
4. 1939 England and Wales Register, England and Wales Civil Registration Birth Index, ancestry.co.uk.
5. 'Prison for Woman Land Worker', *Banbury Advertiser*, 22 October 1941, 4.
6. TNA, MEPO 3/2302.
7. TNA, MEPO 3/2302.
8. TNA, MEPO 3/2302.
9. 'Leave Man on Murder Charge', *Aberdeen Evening Express*, 20 August 1945. 1.
10. TNA, MEPO 3/2302.
11. TNA, MEPO 3/2302.
12. W.A.E. Jones, 'Judge Disagrees with Jury in Court of Weeping', *Daily Herald*, 27 September 1945, 3; 'Stabbed Wife was Expecting Italian's Child', *Birmingham Daily Gazette*, 27 September 1945, 1.
13. 'Acquitted of Murder', *Western Daily Press*, 22 September 1945, 5.
14. 'Killed Unfaithful Wife: Five Years for Soldier: Judge Condemns the Law of the Jungle', *Willesden Citizen, Middlesex Independent and West London Star*, 6 October 1945, 1.

15. TNA, MEPO 20/3.
16. TNA, MEPO 20/3.
17. Thorley, *Inside 10 Rillington Place*, 26.
18. Thorley, *Inside 10 Rillington Place*, 35.
19. Thorley, *Inside 10 Rillington Place*, 42.
20. Thorley, *Inside 10 Rillington Place*, 66.
21. Oates, *John Christie*, 51.
22. Thorley, *Inside 10 Rillington Place*, 62.
23. TNA, MEPO 3/3147.
24. Oates, *John Christie*, 51.
25. TNA, MEPO 3/3147.
26. TNA, CAB 143.
27. Oates, *John Christie*, 54.
28. Oates, *John Christie*, 56.
29. Emma Jones and Neil Pemberton, 'Ten Rillington Place and the Changing Politics of Abortion in Modern Britain', *The Historical Journal*, 57 (2014), 1085–1109, 10.1017/S0018246X14000399.
30. Oates, *John Christie*, 61.
31. Brabin, *Rillington Place 1949: Lord Brabin's Report to Parliament* (1966, reprint 2018), 67.
32. Thorley, *Inside 10 Rillington Place*, 129.
33. TNA, DPP 2/2246.
34. 'Counsel Accuses Witness Giving Evidence in Murder Trial as Killer', *The Daily Mirror*, 13 January 1950, 5; 'Murder Trial Witness Sobs As Death Sentence Is Passed', *The Daily Mirror*, 14 January 1950, 7.
35. TNA, MEPO 3/3147.
36. TNA, MEPO 3/3147; 'Others? I may have', *Daily News*, 24 June 1953, 6.
37. Jones and Pemberton, 'Ten Rillington Place and the Changing Politics of Abortion in Modern Britain'.
38. 'He was the Judge and the Jury', *Sunday Mirror*, 19 July 1953, 6.
39. In 2003, Mary Westlake applied to have Evans' case heard in the Court of Appeal. The judges rejected the request, saying the cost could not be justified, although they accepted that Evans did not murder either his wife or his child. 'Fifty-four Years On, Timothy Evans is Declared Innocent', *Daily Post* (Liverpool), 18 November 2004.
40. Claire Langhamer, '"The Live Dynamic Whole of Feeling and Behaviour": Capital Punishment and the Politics of Emotion', *Journal of British Studies*, 51, no. 2 (2012), 416–41.
41. 'Blackout Crime', *The Daily Herald*, 26 April 1940, 6.
42. Marriage Summary Statistics 2012 (Provisional) and Divorces in England and Wales, 2012. Office for National Statistics, https://www.ons.gov.uk/peoplepopulationandcommunity/birthsdeathsandmarriages/articles/victoryineuropedayhowworldwariichangedtheuk/2015-05-08.
43. Scott, *Your Obedient Servant*, 55.
44. Albert Pierrepoint, *Executioner Pierrepoint* (London: Coronet, 1974), 169; Frank Mort, 'Scandalous Events: Metropolitan Culture and Moral Change in Post-Second World War London', *Representations* (2006) 93, no. 1 (2006), 106–37, quote on 113.

SELECT BIBLIOGRAPHY

HISTORIES

Adey, Peter, David J. Cox and Barry S. Godfrey. *Crime, Regulation and Control during the Blitz: Protecting the Population of Bombed Cities*. London: Bloomsbury Academic, 2016.

Allport, Alan. *Demobbed: Coming Home at the End of the Second World War*. New Haven and London: Yale University Press, 2009.

Anand, Anita. *The Patient Assassin: A True Tale of Massacre, Revenge and the Raj*. London: Simon & Schuster, 2019.

Ayers, Oliver. 'Jim Crow and John Bull in London: Transatlantic Encounters with Race and Nation in the Second World War', *Studies in Ethnicity and Nationalism*, 20 (2020), 244–66.

Bell, Amy Helen. *London was Ours*. London: I.B. Tauris, 2002.

Bland, Lucy. *Britain's 'Brown Babies': The Stories of Children Born to Black GIs and White Women in the Second World War*. Manchester: Manchester University Press, 2019.

Bourne, Stephen. *Mother Country: Britain's Black Community on the Home Front 1939–1945*. London: History Press, 2010.

Burney, Ian and Neil Pemberton. 'Bruised Witness: Bernard Spilsbury and the Performance of Early Twentieth-Century English Forensic Pathology'. *Medical History*, 55, no. 1 (2011), 41–60.

Burney, Ian and Neil Pemberton. *Murder and the Making of the English CSI*. Baltimore: Johns Hopkins University Press, 2016.

Calder, Angus. *The Myth of the Blitz*. London: Pimlico, 1992.

Calder, Angus. *The People's War*. London: Jonathan Cape, 1969.

Carr, Gilly and Rachel Pistol (eds). *British Internment and the Internment of Britons: Second World War Camps, History and Heritage*. London: Bloomsbury, 2023.

Collingham, Lizzie. *The Taste of World War Two and the Battle for Food*. London: Penguin, 2013.

Emsley, Clive. *Hard Men: The English and Violence since 1750*. London: Hambledon, 2005.

Emsley, Clive. *The Great British Bobby*. London: Quercus, 2009.

Feigel, Lara. *The Love-charm of Bombs: Restless Lives in the Second World War*. London: Bloomsbury, 2013.

Field, Geoffrey. *Blood, Sweat, and Toil: Remaking the British Working Class, 1939–1945*. Oxford: Oxford University Press, 2012.

Fielding, Steve. *The Hangman's Record, Vol 3: 1930–1964*. London: Chancery House, 2005.

Gardiner, Juliet. *'Over Here': The GIs in Wartime Britain*. London: Collins & Brown, 1992.

Gardiner, Juliet. *Wartime: Britain 1939–1945*. London: Headline, 2004.

Gillman, Peter and Leni. *'Collar the Lot!': How Britain Interned and Expelled its Wartime Refugees*. London: Quartet Books, 1980.

Glass, Charles. *The Deserters: A Hidden History of World War II*. New York: Penguin, 2013.

Grant, Thomas. *Court Number One: The Trials and Scandals that Shocked Modern Britain*. London: John Murray, 2019.

Grayzel, Susan. *At Home and Under Fire: Air Raids and Culture from the Great War to the Blitz*. Cambridge: Cambridge University Press, 2011.

Harrisson, Thomas. *Living through the Blitz*. London: Penguin, 1990.

Houlbrook, Matt. *Queer London: Perils and Pleasures in the Sexual Metropolis, 1918–1957*. Chicago: Chicago University Press, 2005.

Hylton, Stuart. *Their Darkest Hour: The Hidden History of the Home Front 1939–1945*. Surrey: Sutton, 2001.

Inwood, Stephen. *A History of London*. London: Basic Books, 1998.

Jones, Emma and Neil Pemberton. 'Ten Rillington Place and the Changing Politics of Abortion in Modern Britain', *The Historical Journal*, 57 (2014), 1085–109.

Kilday, Anne-Marie. *A History of Infanticide in Britain, c. 1600 to the Present*. Basingstoke: Palgrave Macmillan, 2013.

Kirby, Dick. *London's Gangs at War*. Barnsley: Pen & Sword, 2017.

Laite, Julia. *Common Prostitutes and Ordinary Citizens: Commercial Sex in London 1885–1960*. Basingstoke: Palgrave Macmillan, 2013.

Langhamer, Claire. ' "The Live Dynamic Whole of Feeling and Behaviour": Capital Punishment and the Politics of Emotion', *Journal of British Studies*, 51, no. 2 (2012), 416–41.

Mackay, Robert. *Half the Battle: Civilian Morale in Britain during the Second World War*. Manchester: Manchester University Press, 2003.

Mort, Frank. *Capital Affairs: The Making of the Permissive Society*. New Haven and London: Yale University Press, 2010.

Mort, Frank. 'Scandalous Events: Metropolitan Culture and Moral Change in Post-Second World War London', *Representations*, 93, no. 1 (2006), 106–37.

Morton, James. *Gangland: London's Underworld*. London: Warner, 1992.

Moss, Eloise. *Night Raiders: Burglary and the Making of Modern Urban Life in London, 1860–1968*. Oxford: Oxford University Press, 2019.

Neale, Alexa. *Photographing Crime Scenes in Twentieth-Century London: Microhistories of Domestic Murder*. London: Bloomsbury, 2020.

Noakes, Lucy. *Dying for the Nation: Death, Grief and Bereavement in Second World War Britain*. Manchester: Manchester University Press, 2020.

Nott, James. *Going to the Palais: A Social and Cultural History of Dancing and Dance Halls in Britain, 1918–1960*. Oxford: Oxford University Press, 2015.

Oates, Jonathan. *John Christie of 10 Rillington Place*. Barnsley: Wharncliffe True Crime, 2017.

Porter, Roy. *London: A Social History*. London: Penguin, 1994.

Read, Simon. *Dark City: Crime in Wartime London*. Hersham: Ian Allen, 2010.

Reynolds, David. *Rich Relations: The American Occupation of Britain, 1942–1945*. London: HarperCollins, 1995.

Roberts, Mary Louise. 'The Leroy Henry Case: Sexual Violence and Allied Relations in Great Britain, 1944', *Journal of the History of Sexuality*, 26, no. 3 (2017), 402–23.

Roodhouse, Mark. *Black Market Britain, 1939–1955*. Oxford: Oxford University Press, 2013.

Rose, Sonya O. *Which People's War? National Identity and Citizenship in Britain, 1939–1945*. Oxford: Oxford University Press, 2003.

Seal, Lizzie and Alexa Neale. 'Racializing Mercy: Capital Punishment and Race in Twentieth-Century England and Wales', *Law and History Review*, 38, no. 4 (2020), 883–910.

Sharpe, James. *A Fiery and Furious People*. London: Random House, 2016.

Shore, Heather. *London's Criminal Underworlds, 1720–1930*. London: Palgrave Macmillan, 2015.

Smithies, Edward. *Crime in Wartime*. London: George Allen & Unwin, 1982.

Summers, Julie. *Dressed for War: The Story of Audrey Withers, Vogue Editor Extraordinaire from the Blitz to the Swinging Sixties*. London: Simon & Schuster, 2020.

Sweet, Matthew. *The West End Front: The Wartime Secrets of London's Grand Hotels*. London: Faber & Faber, 2012.

Thomas, Donald. *An Underworld at War: Spivs, Deserters, Racketeers and Civilians in the Second World War*. London: John Murray, 2003.

Vickers, Emma. *Queen and Country: Same-Sex Desire in the British Armed Forces*. Manchester: Manchester University Press, 2013.

Walkowitz, Judith. *Nights Out: Life in Cosmopolitan London*. New Haven and London: Yale University Press, 2012.

Ward, Laurence (ed.). *The London County Council Bomb Damage Maps 1939–1945*. London: Penguin, 2016.

Wasson, Sara. *Urban Gothic of the Second World War: Dark London*. Basingstoke: Palgrave Macmillan, 2010.

Webster, Wendy. *Mixing It: Diversity in World War Two Britain*. Oxford: Oxford University Press, 2018.

White, Jerry. *The Battle of London 1939–45: Endurance, Heroism and Frailty under Fire*. London: The Bodley Head, 2021.

Ziegler, Philip. *London at War*. London: Sinclair-Stevenson, 1995.

MEMOIRS AND BIOGRAPHIES

Anderson, Verily. *Spam Tomorrow*. London: Dean Street Press, 2019.

Arbib, Robert S. *Here We Are Together: The Notebook of an American Soldier in Britain*. London: Longman Green & Co., 1946.

SELECT BIBLIOGRAPHY

Beardmore, George. *Civilians at War: Journals 1938–1946*. Oxford: Oxford University Press, 1986.

Bell, Reginald. *The Bull's Eye: A Tale of the London Target*. London: Cassell, 1943.

Browne, Douglas and E.B. Tullet. *Bernard Spilsbury: His Life and Cases*. London: George G. Harrap, 1952.

Caswell, J.D. *Only Five Were Hanged*. London: Corgi, 1964.

Cockett, Olivia and Robert Malcolmson (eds). *Love and War in London: A Woman's Diary 1939–1942*. Waterloo: Wilfred Laurier University Press, 2005.

Crisp, Quentin. *The Naked Civil Servant*. London: Jonathan Cape, 1968.

Daley, Harry. *This Small Cloud: A Personal Memoir*. London: Weidenfeld & Nicolson, 1987.

Ekpenyon, E.I. *Some Experiences of an African Air Raid Warden*. London: The Sheldon Press, 1943.

Fabian, Robert. *Fabian of the Yard*. London: Naldrett Press, 1950.

Faviell, Frances. *A Chelsea Concerto*. London: Cassell, 1959.

Fraser, Frankie. *Mad Frank: Memoirs of a Life of Crime*. London: Little, Brown, 1994.

Graves, Charles. *Londoner's Life*. London: Hutchinson, 1942.

Graves, Charles. *Off the Record*. London: Hutchinson, 1942.

Hill, Billy. *Boss of Britain's Underworld*. London: Naldrett Press, 1955.

Hogson, Vere. *Few Eggs and No Oranges: A Diary Showing How Unimportant People in London and Birmingham Lived through the War Years 1940–45*. Bath: Persephone Books, 1999.

Hughes, Marian. *No Cake, No Jam: Hardship and Happiness in Wartime London*. Leicester: Ulverston, 1994.

Jackson, Robert. *Coroner: The Biography of Sir Bentley Purchase*. London: Harrap, 1963.

Learie, Constantine. *Colour Bar*. London: Stanley Paul & Co., 1954.

Lefebure, Molly. *Evidence for the Crown: Experiences of a Pathologist's Secretary*. London: W. Heinemann, 1955.

Levinson, Maurice. *The Trouble with Yesterday*. London: Peter Davies, 1946.

Marke, Ernest. *In Troubled Waters: Memoirs of My Seventy Years in England*. London: Karia, 1986.

Marke, Ernest. *Old Man Trouble*. London: Weidenfeld & Nicolson, 1975.

Model, Douglas. *Memories of a Wartime Childhood in London*. Cheltenham: The History Press, 2022.

Morris, Mary. *A Very Private Diary: A Nurse in Wartime*. London: Lume Press, 2020.

Nicolson, Harold. *The War Years Diaries and Letters: 1939–45*. London: Collins, 1967.

Nixon, Barbara. *Raiders Overhead: A Diary of the London Blitz*. London: Scolar Press, 1980.

Noble, Martin E. *Jamaica Airman: A Black Airman in Britain, 1943 and After*. London: New Beacon Books, 1984.

O'Connor, Sean. *Handsome Brute: The True Story of a Ladykiller*. London: Simon & Schuster, 2013.

Panter-Downes, Mollie. *London War Notes, 1939–1945*. Bath: Persephone Books, 2015.

Perry, Colin. *Boy in the Blitz: The 1940 Diary of Colin Perry*. Stroud: Amberley, 2011.

Pierrepoint, Albert. *Executioner Pierrepoint*. London: Coronet, 1974.

Piper, Ron. *Take Him Away*. Brighton: Queenspark Books, 1993.

Reynolds, Quentin. *A London Diary*. New York: Random House, 1941.

Scott, Sir Harold. *Scotland Yard*. London: Andre Deutsch, 1954.

Scott, Sir Harold. *Your Obedient Servant*. London: Andre Deutsch, 1959.

Simpson, Keith. *Forty Years of Murder*. London: W.H. Allen, 1978.

Sparks, Ruby. *Burglar to the Nobility*. London: Arthur Baker, 1961.

Thorley, Peter. *Inside 10 Rillington Place: John Christie and Me, the Untold Truth*. London: Mirror Books, 2020.

Thorp, Arthur. *Calling Scotland Yard*. London: Allan Wingate, 1954.

Tipper, Kathleen. *A Woman in Wartime London: The Diary of Kathleen Tipper 1941–1945* (ed. Patricia Malcolmson and Robert Malcolmson). London: London Record Society, 2006.

Weymouth, Anthony. *Plague Year*. London: Harrap, 1942.

Wheal, Donald. *World's End: A Memoir of a Blitz Childhood*. London: Century, 2005.

Wilmott, Phyllis. *Coming of Age in Wartime*. London: Peter Owens, 1985.

INDEX

Page numbers in *italics* indicate a figure.